IMAGES
of America

WAUKEGAN
ILLINOIS

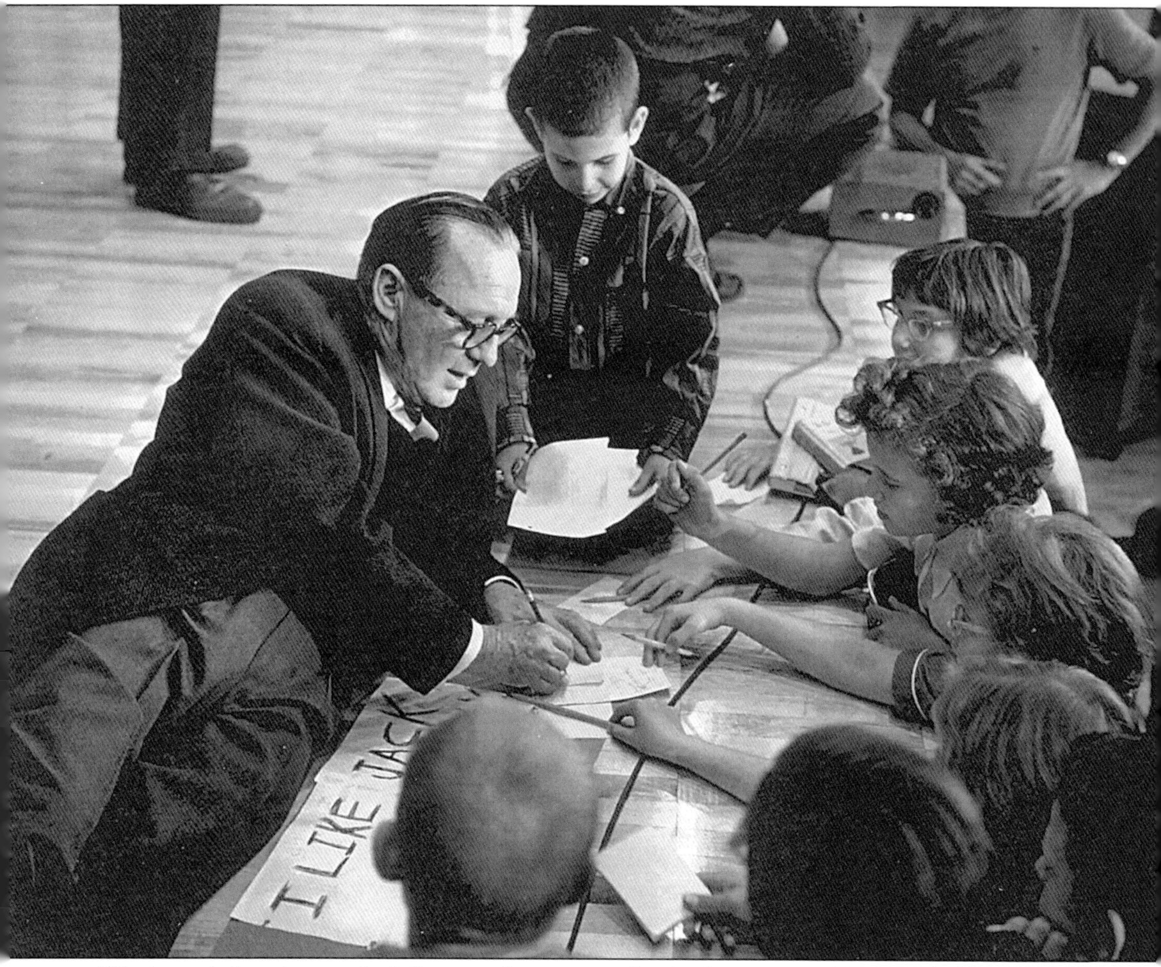

Waukegan's favorite son, Jack Benny, often returned to his hometown. He attended fund-raising events, participated in concerts and parades, and just visited with many life-long friends. Here, in 1961, he mingled with students at the school named after him.

IMAGES
of America

WAUKEGAN
ILLINOIS

The Waukegan Historical Society

ARCADIA
PUBLISHING

ISBN 978-0-7385-0836-8

Published by Arcadia Publishing
Charleston, South Carolina

Printed in the United States of America

Library of Congress Catalog Card Number: 00108017

For all general information contact Arcadia Publishing at:
Telephone 843-853-2070
Fax 843-853-0044
E-mail sales@arcadiapublishing.com
For customer service and orders:
Toll-Free 1-888-313-2665

Visit us on the Internet at www.arcadiapublishing.com

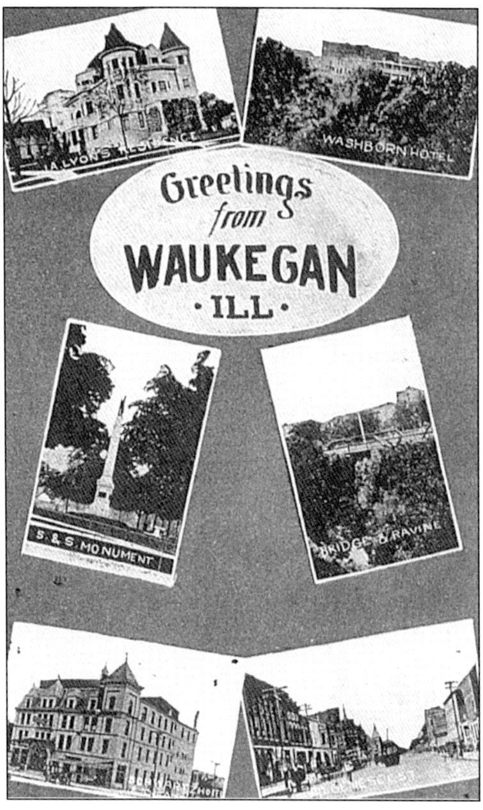

Hello! Waukegan, its people and places, welcomes you to wander through the community. Pictures from throughout the city will allow you to see what once was and what still is. Hopefully memories will be stirred and you can reminisce fondly.

Contents

ACKNOWLEDGMENTS

The archives of the Waukegan Historical Society, from which these photos were selected, are composed of those items which interested citizens once donated. Without those donations the archives would not exist and this publication would not have been possible. We wish to thank all those individuals.

We also wish to thank W.B. Reprographics, which provided invaluable help in preparing these images for inclusion in the book.

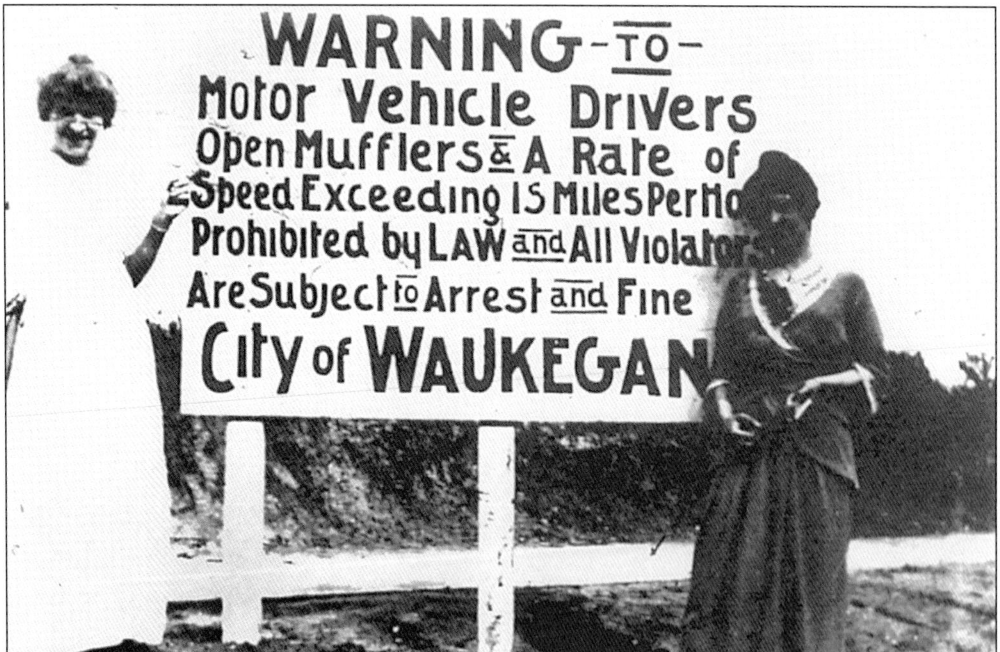

However, as these ladies of long ago remind us, don't speed through the book. Take your time and savor what you see, and remember.

INTRODUCTION

Why should there be a photo history of Waukegan? Isn't it just like numerous other cities across the country? No, it isn't. Throughout its history, Waukegan has had its own personality, created by people, businesses, and natural wonders. It is this uniqueness that we hope to capture in this book.

That is also the reason why the pictures selected are only from Waukegan. Obviously the city has never existed in a vacuum. Interaction with adjoining communities, the rural portions of Lake County, and nearby institutions such as Great Lakes Naval Training Center, are all part of daily life in the city. However, because Waukegan covers such a large area, we have focused on it alone.

No individual volume could do justice to everyone or everything that has made this city great. There is just too much history in the area. Another limitation is that all images were selected from the collection of the Waukegan Historical Society. Even if a person or place was deserving of inclusion, it could only be so honored if an appropriate photograph were available. While very extensive, the archives do not cover every aspect of the city's past.

Founded originally as a trading post named Little Fort, the area was home at one time or another to several Native American tribes. Illinois, Miami, Sac and Fox, and Pottawatomie all lived here. The last Native Americans left the area in the early 1830s, about the time Lake County separated from McHenry County. The county seat was originally at Burlington (Libertyville) but was moved via referendum to Little Fort. A courthouse, post office, schools, and churches followed as the population rose and the area was settled.

In 1849 the populace tired of their town being viewed as "Little," so they voted to change the name to Waukegan—an approximate Pottawatomie translation of Little Fort. Population continued to grow as a fire department was established, a railroad came to town, and the bank opened.

Growth stagnated after the Civil War. Agriculture still was dominant in the county, but Waukegan had little to attract new population. A significant change occurred when the E J & E Railroad moved its terminus to Waukegan. Now transportation for supplies and finished products was available and heavy industry could locate here. In a short period at the end of the 19th century, the U.S. Sugar Refinery, Washburn and Moen, Chicago Safe and Lock Company, the U.S. Starch Company, and several other companies built giant industrial complexes along the lakefront. Lake Michigan was needed for transportation, for water used in the manufacturing processes, and, unfortunately, for the deposit of industrial waste.

To run all these mills required manpower, and lots of it. The call went out to Europe advertising jobs and a future in this wonderful area called Waukegan. Locals wrote to family members still in the old country and told them of the marvelous opportunities. Skilled craftsmen were raised by the factories as they were needed, but basic human labor was necessary, and the people came to the jobs.

And did they come. People came from all over, with particular emphasis on Scandinavia and the countries of Eastern Europe. Waukegan's population, which had been declining, doubled between 1890 and 1900, and virtually doubled again by 1910. Often the men came first to get the jobs and establish homes, and then sent passage money for their wives and children.

Typically the new arrivals settled alongside those previously arrived from the same city, area, or nation. With them they brought their language, customs, foods, and religion. Those enclaves stayed to themselves as small communities within the city. Restaurants, stores, and social clubs rose to fulfill the needs of the different ethnic populations.

Initially the communities resisted interaction or intrusion. Concerns originally fostered in the homelands continued here. Gradually, however, those walls came down. Jobs and schools forced interaction which carried over to social situations. Marriages often forged bonds between different groups. The celebrations of one section were enjoyed by many others and were reciprocated. Contributions from all these ethnic groups, as well as from people within the United States bringing regional variations, created the tapestry which became Waukegan.

Progress continued as the population rose. New schools, hospitals, and homes dotted the landscape. The city's borders expanded to include more. But the progress came with a cost. Familiar structures fell victim to time and wear. Buildings were razed to make way for new ones. Roads and houses cut into formerly open space.

Similar changes continue today. Many wish for a return to "the good old days". While we cannot provide that, we can provide a glimpse into our collective past. The following photos were selected to give the viewer a chance to see scenes again as they once were, and to visit familiar spots throughout the city. May all your memories be fond.

One

Lakefront

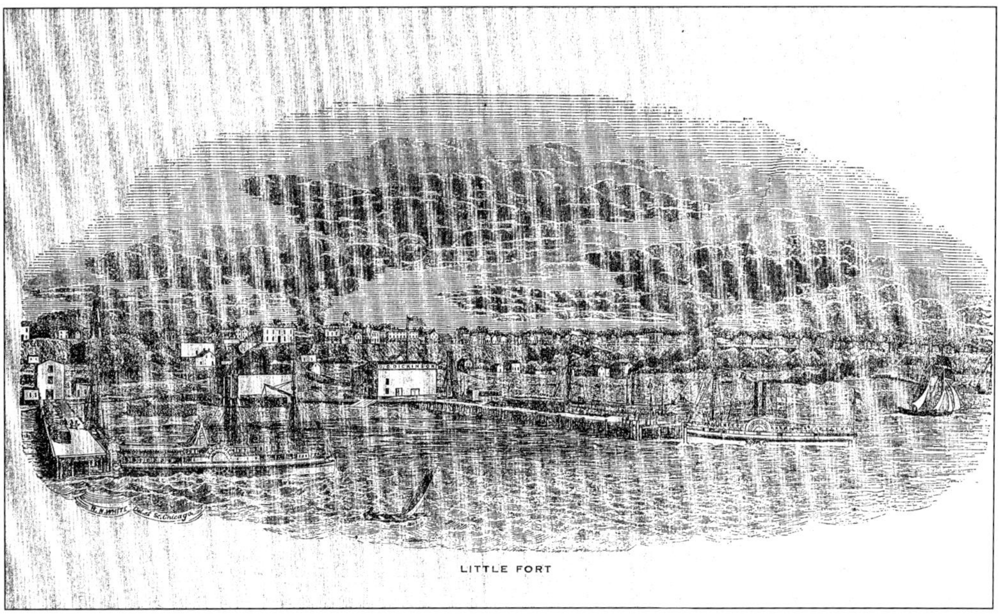

Little Fort began as a trading post, probably as early as the late 1600s. Not much changed from those initial log cabins for many years. Thomas Jenkins opened a store in 1836, and a school and post office followed in the early 1840s. When the county seat moved here from Libertyville, growth accelerated through 1849 when the citizens voted to change its name to Waukegan.

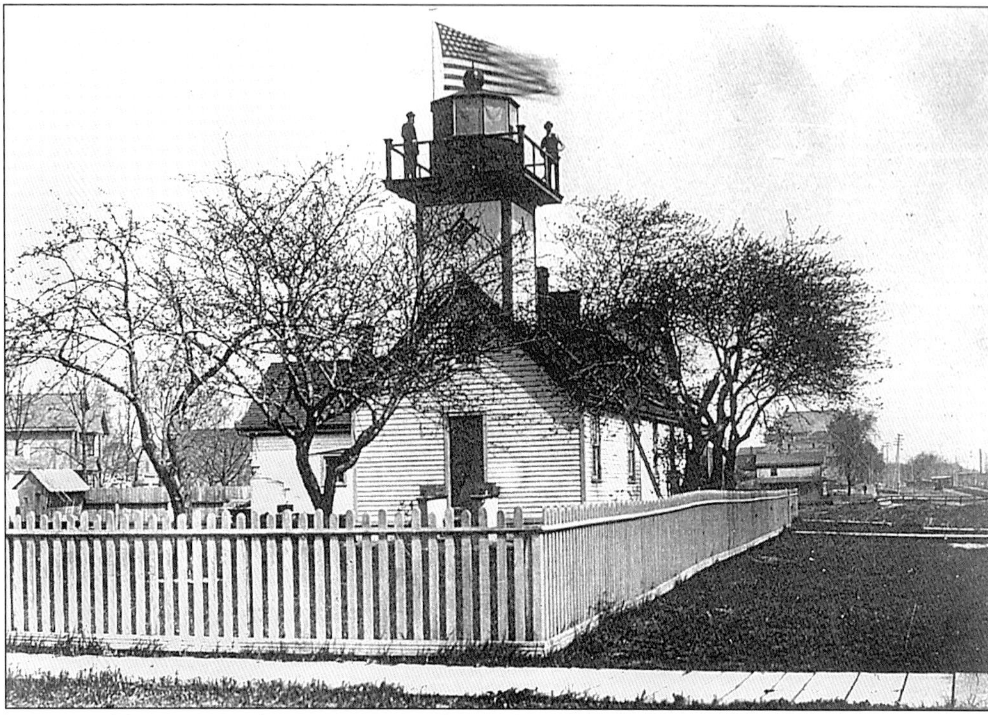

Because of the amount of commerce on Lake Michigan, the U.S. Government built a lighthouse at Little Fort in March 1847. Four-thousand dollars allowed the construction of a 35-foot brick tower on south State Street (Sheridan Road). By 1860 a much-needed new lighthouse was erected 50 feet north of the original house, but still on the same lot at State and Lake Streets.

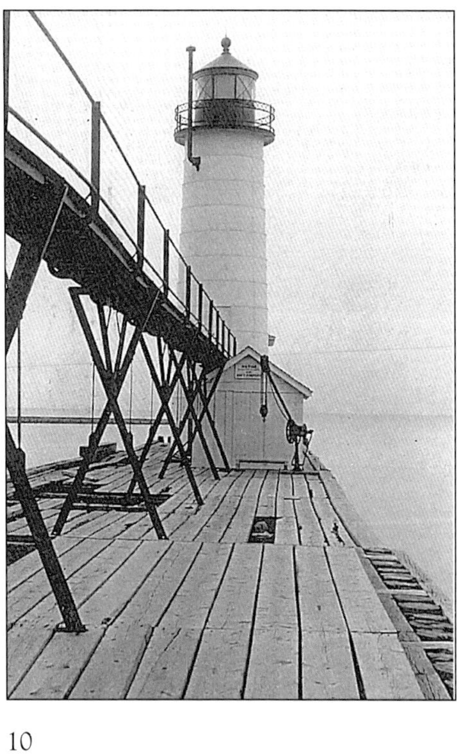

January 1, 1899, saw the completion of a new light at the end of the pier. The former lighthouse property was sold to the city. The new lighthouse was 36 feet above the water and included a foghorn to warn ships on the lake. The catwalk kept maintenance crews dry.

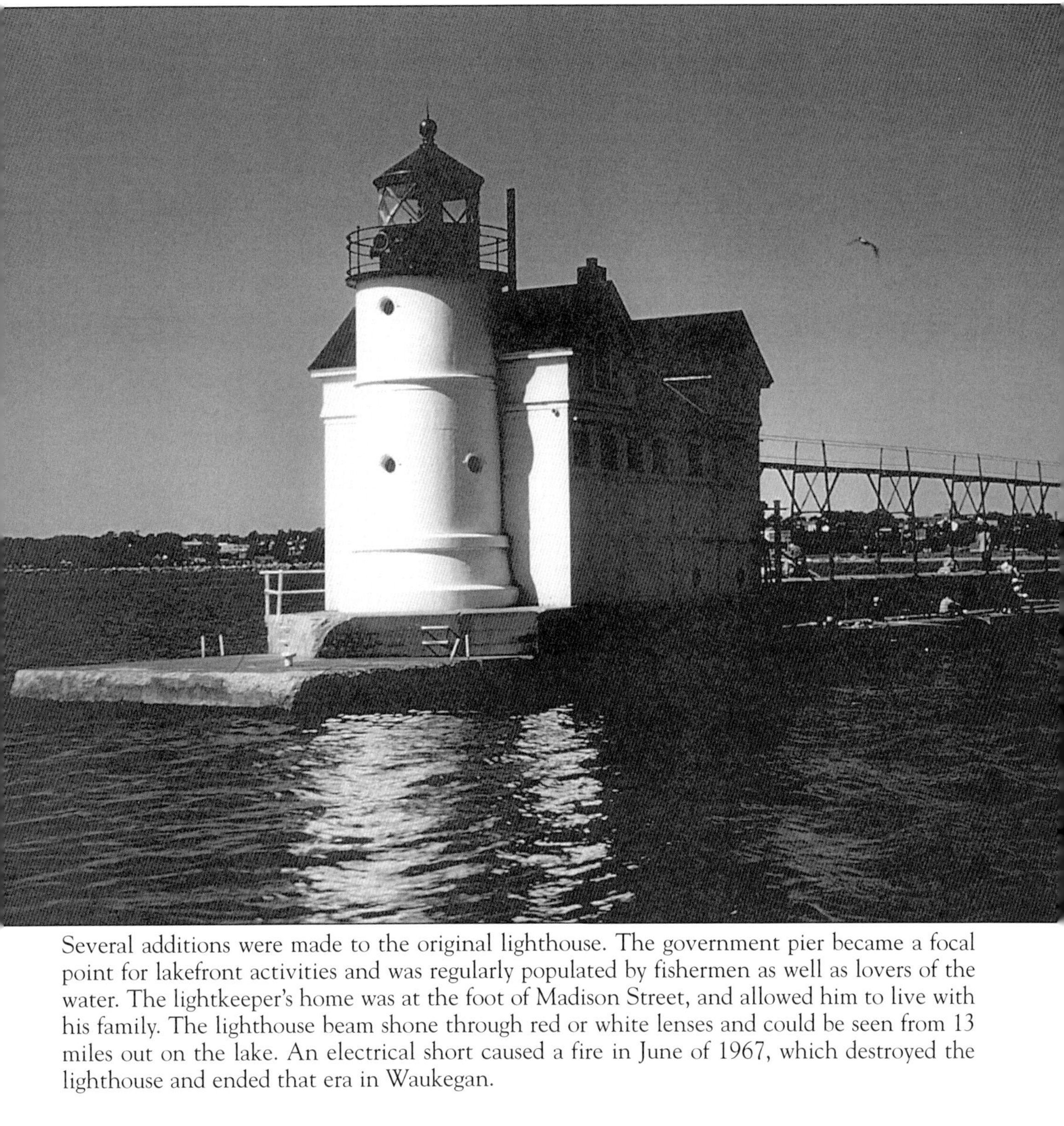

Several additions were made to the original lighthouse. The government pier became a focal point for lakefront activities and was regularly populated by fishermen as well as lovers of the water. The lightkeeper's home was at the foot of Madison Street, and allowed him to live with his family. The lighthouse beam shone through red or white lenses and could be seen from 13 miles out on the lake. An electrical short caused a fire in June of 1967, which destroyed the lighthouse and ended that era in Waukegan.

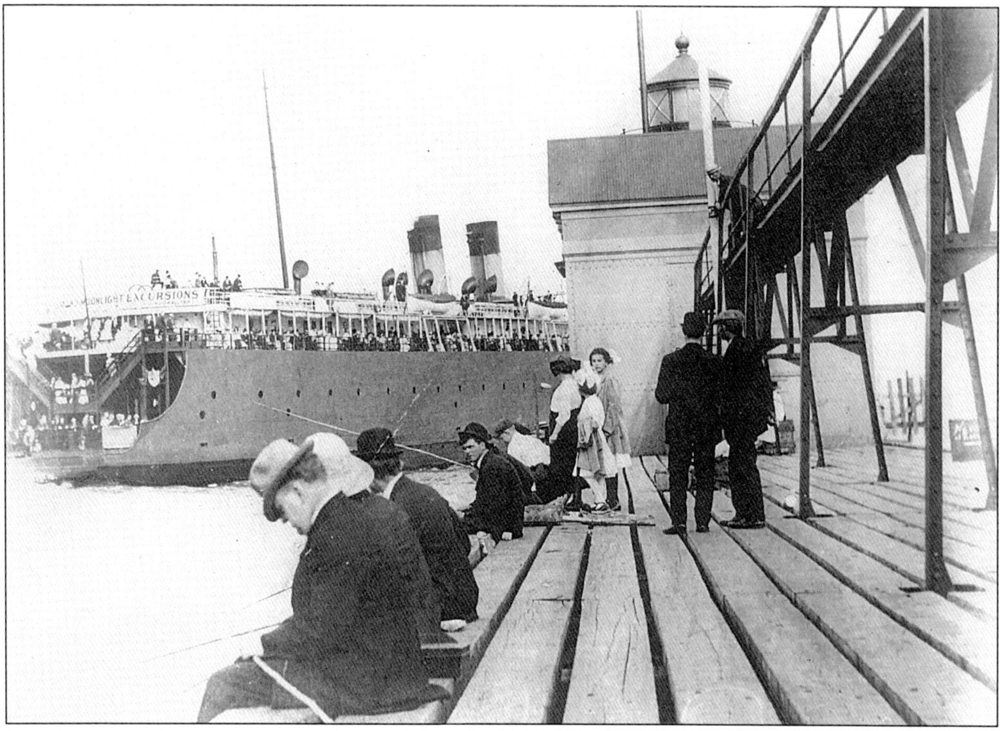

People were a shipping commodity in the early 1900s. Daily sailing excursions to Chicago could be made for 35¢. This Pere Marquette ship left the harbor on this trip in 1906 and continued in similar service until it was lost in a lake storm in September 1910.

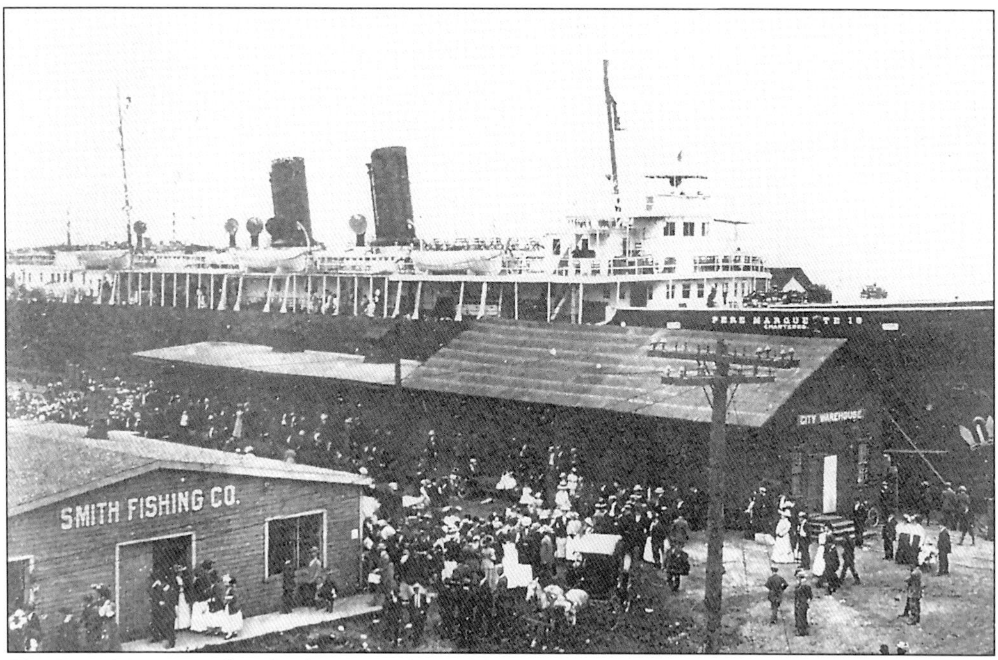

The Pere Marquette line had any number of ships and offered several excursions. The number of people on the dock can attest to the popularity.

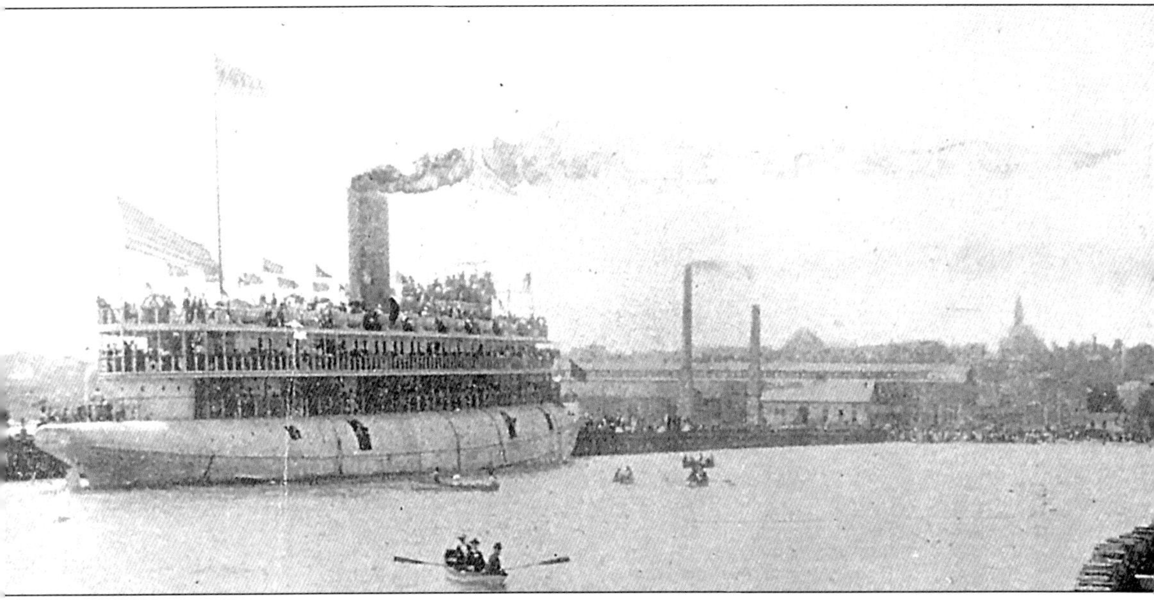

There were a number of lines catering to the passenger ferry business. The Goodrich Line built the *Christopher Columbus*, or *Whaleback*, in 1893 for visitors of the World Fair in Chicago. Later it was the only vessel of its experimental type to be used in regular lake service as it ran between Chicago, Waukegan, and Milwaukee.

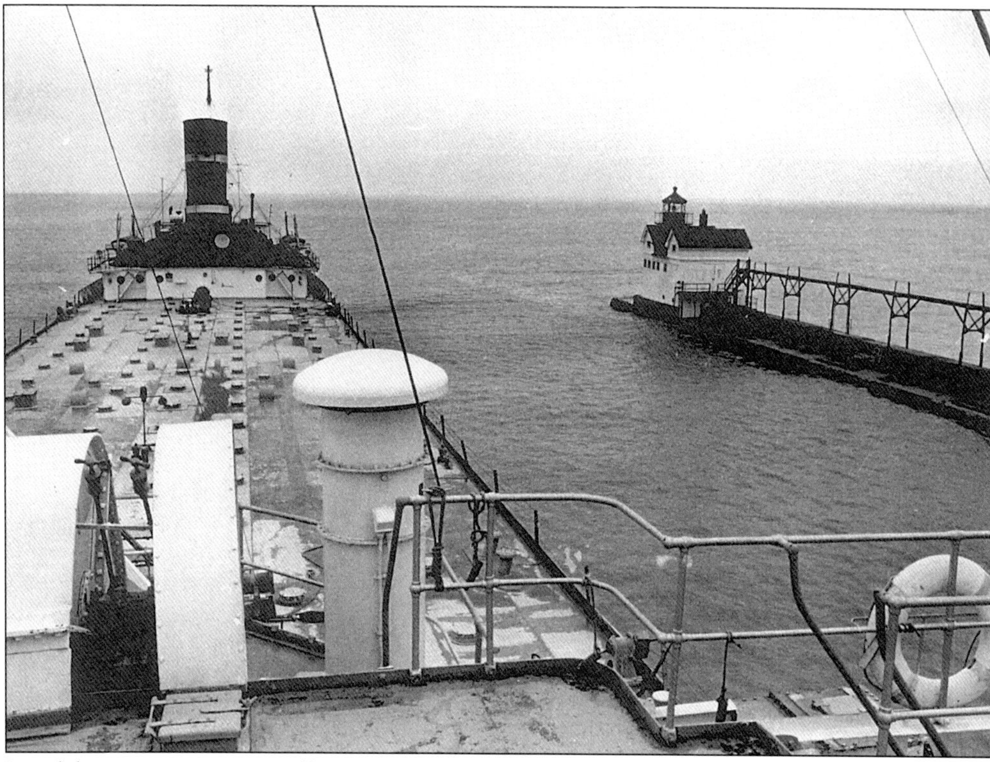

Interlake commerce, especially of raw materials, became very important in later years. In 1908 the primary products received were coal, coke, iron, steel, salt, stone, and general merchandise.

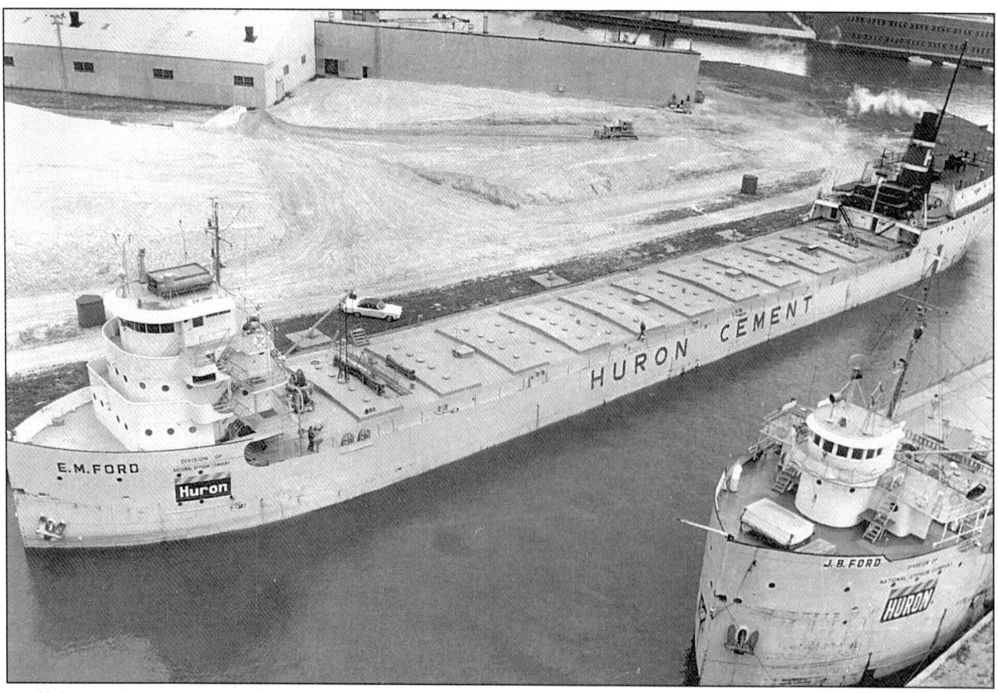

Still later those materials changed to products like cement and gypsum.

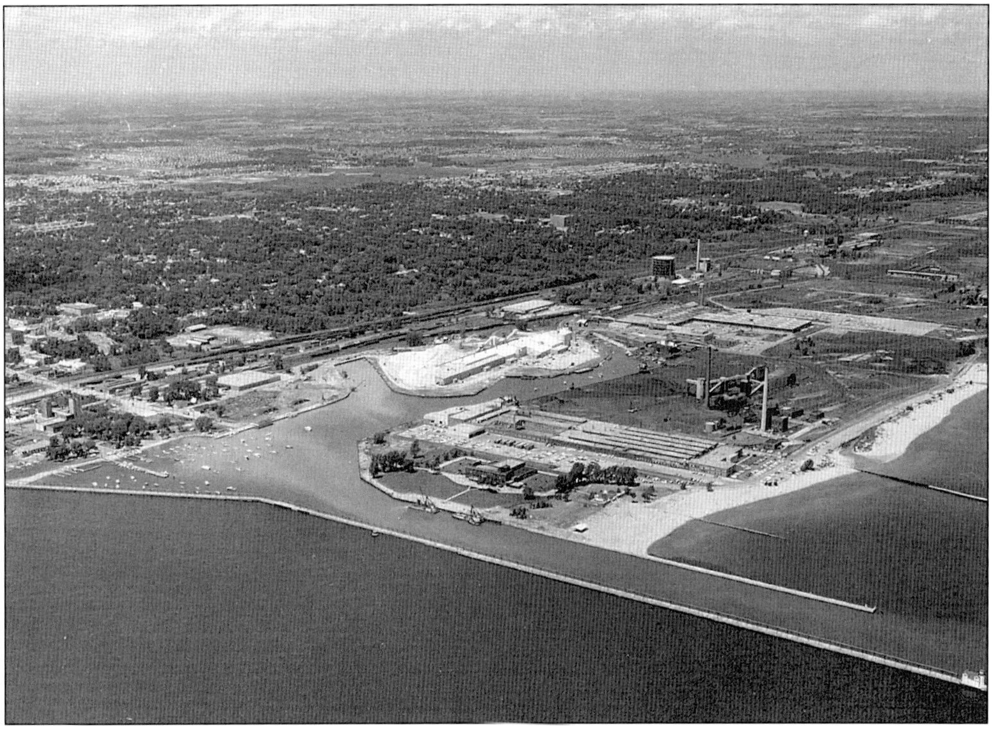

The lakefront was a major site for industry in the area. From this angle one can see North Shore Gas Co., Griess-Pfleger Tannery, and Pacific Steel Boiler.

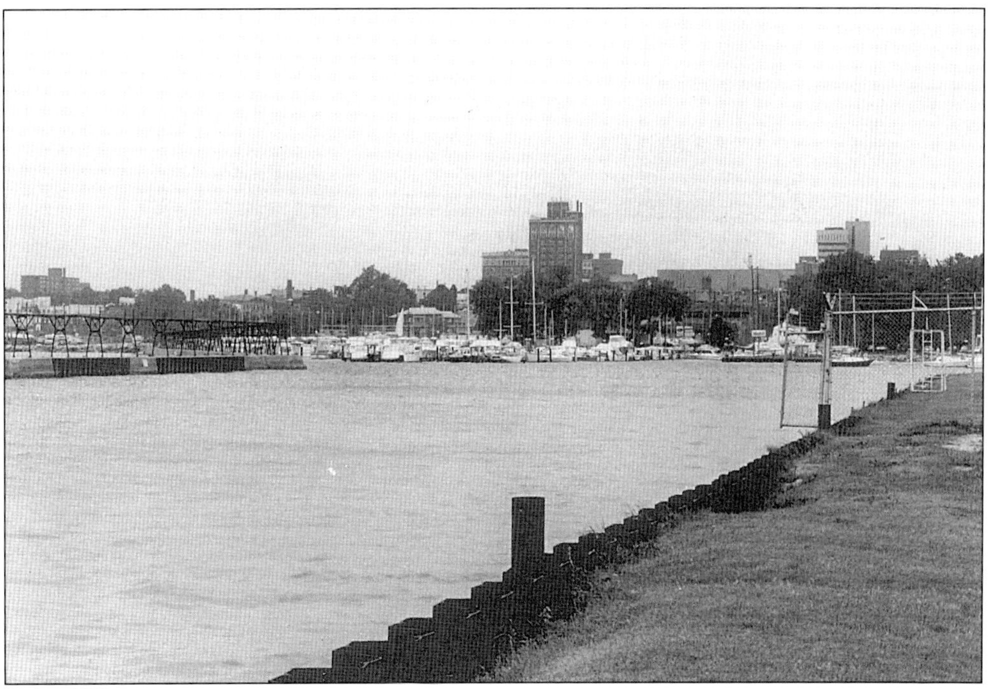

However, the industrial segments of the harbor area do not detract from other, more pleasurable pastimes.

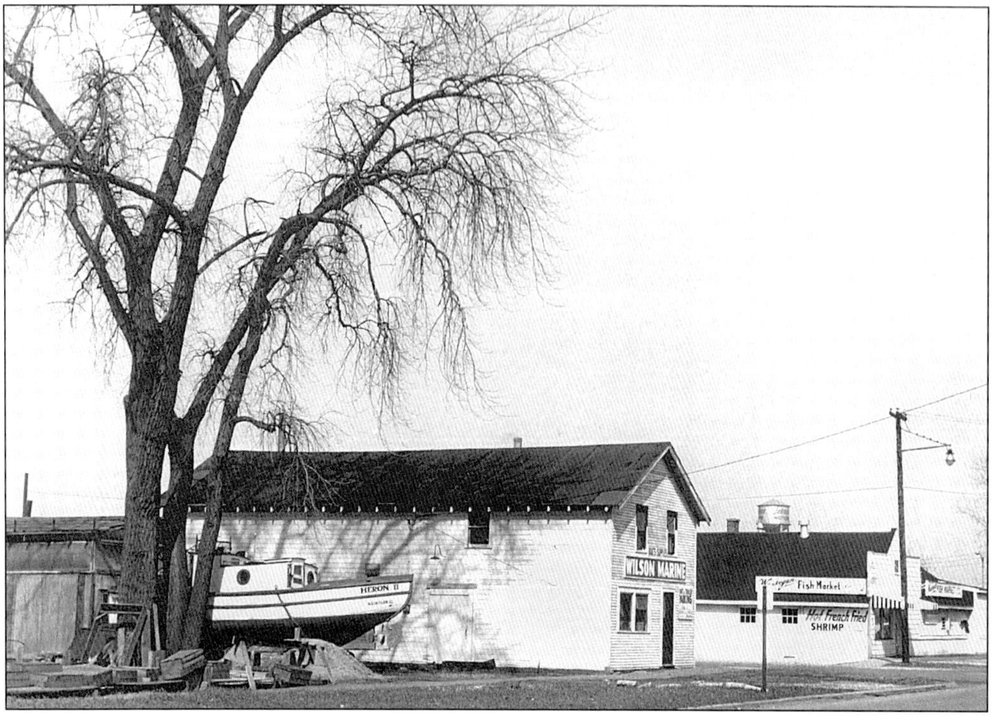

Lake Michigan gave small business opportunities as well.

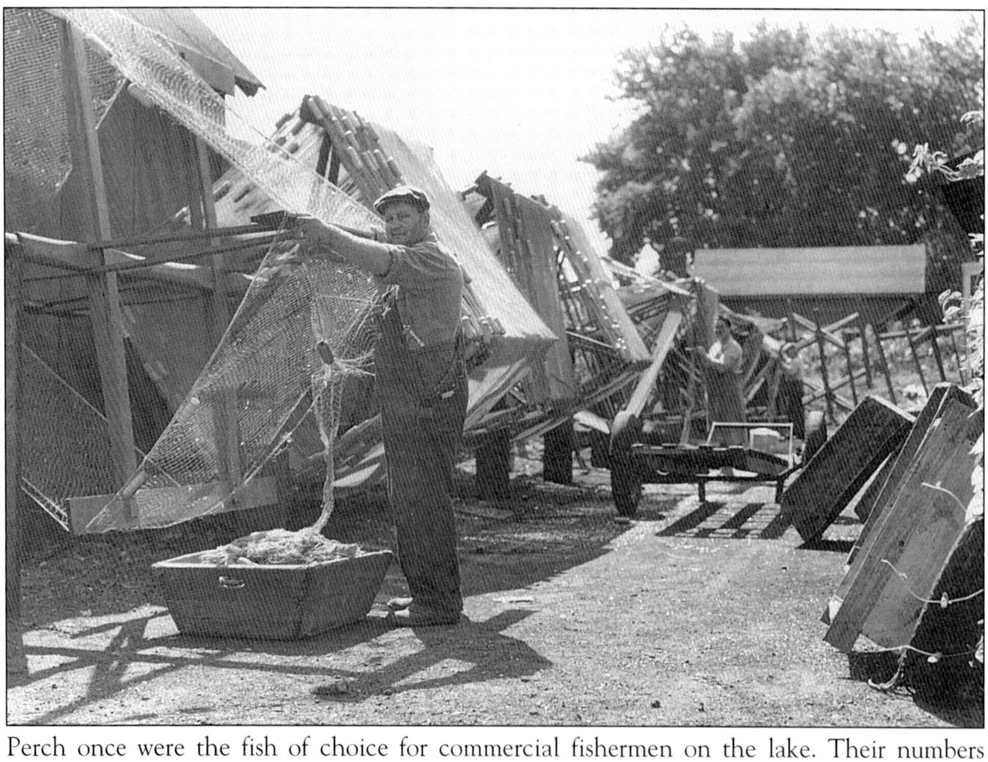
Perch once were the fish of choice for commercial fishermen on the lake. Their numbers declined over time.

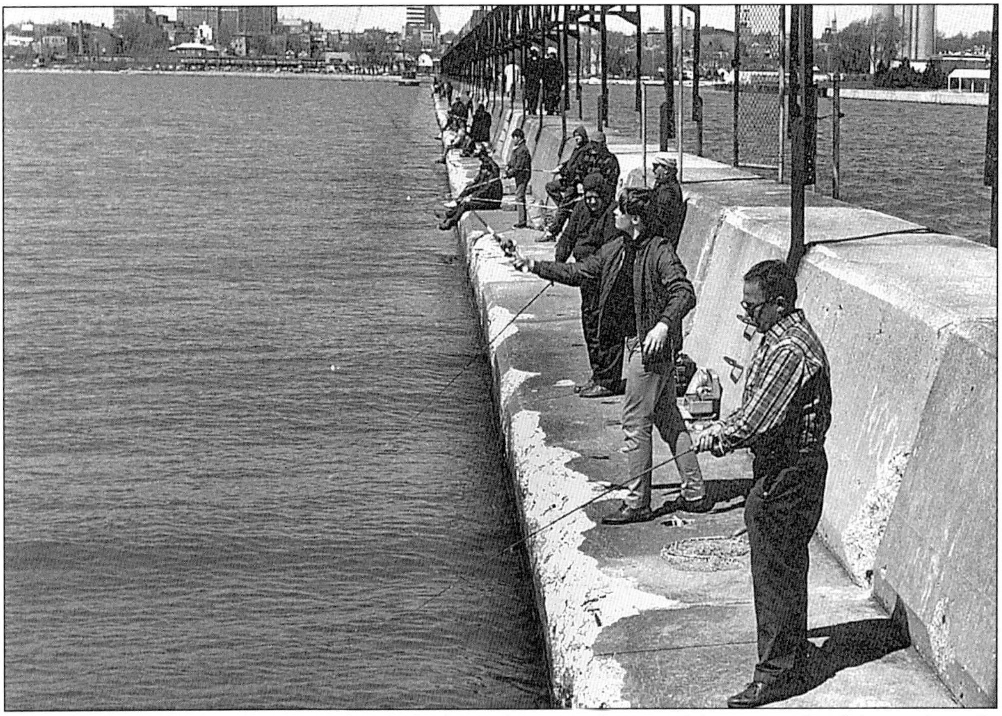

The growth in popularity of coho and chinook revived sport fishing on the lake and made Waukegan the salmon fishing capital of the Midwest.

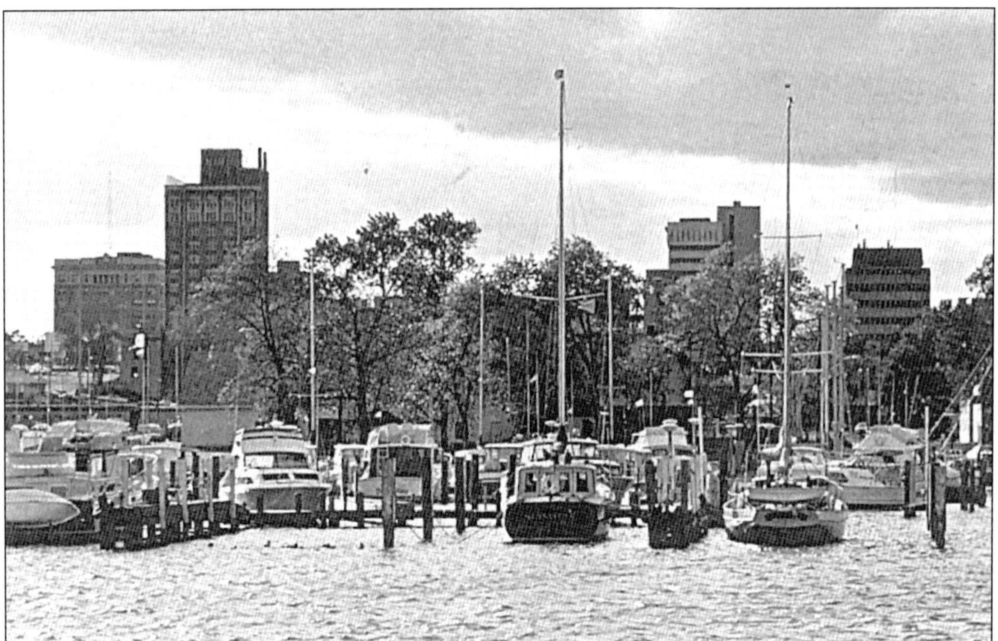

Private boating has also been popular among many people.

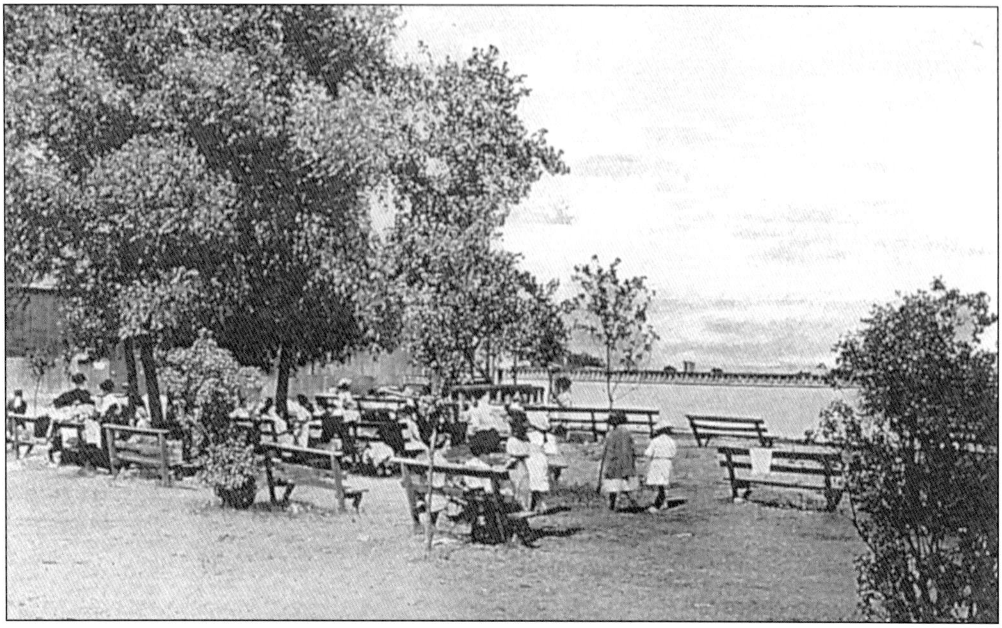

Many residents wanted simply to enjoy the proximity of the lake. A cooling breeze coming across the water was welcome on hot summer days, and no one had to get wet.

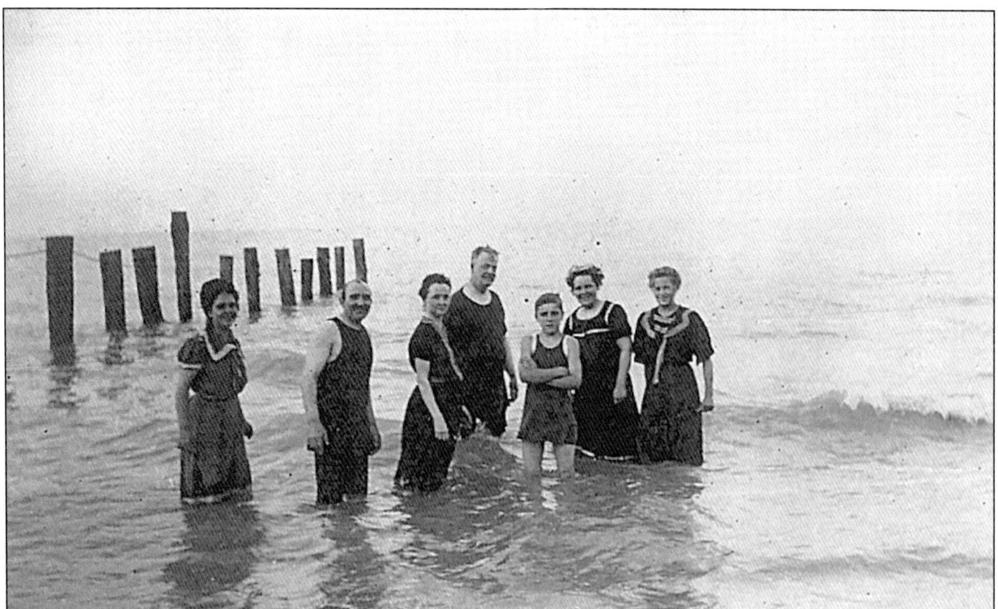

But getting wet was what others sought. However, maybe only from the knees down satisfied these waders.

Two

DOWNTOWN

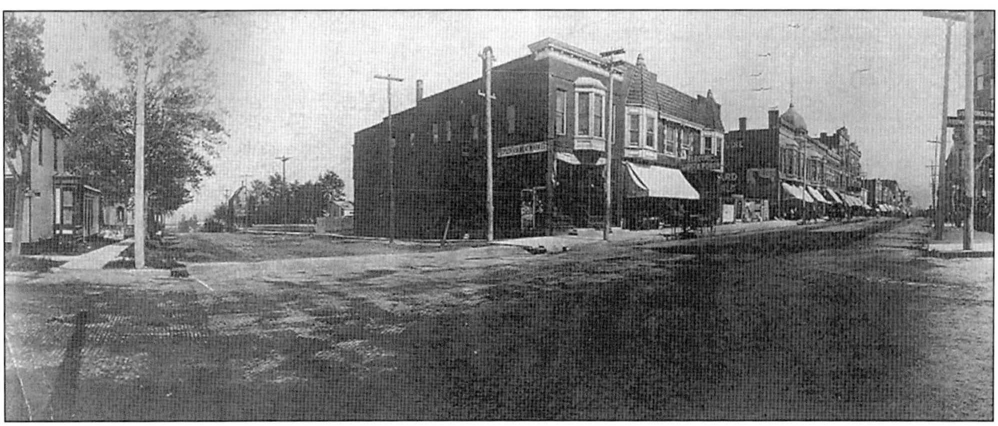

Looking south on Genesee from the northwest corner at Clayton, one can see the downtown in the late 1890s. The business at the far right is J. Lanyon & Son hardware. The area on the far left of the picture would be the future home of the YMCA and later the Genesee Theatre.

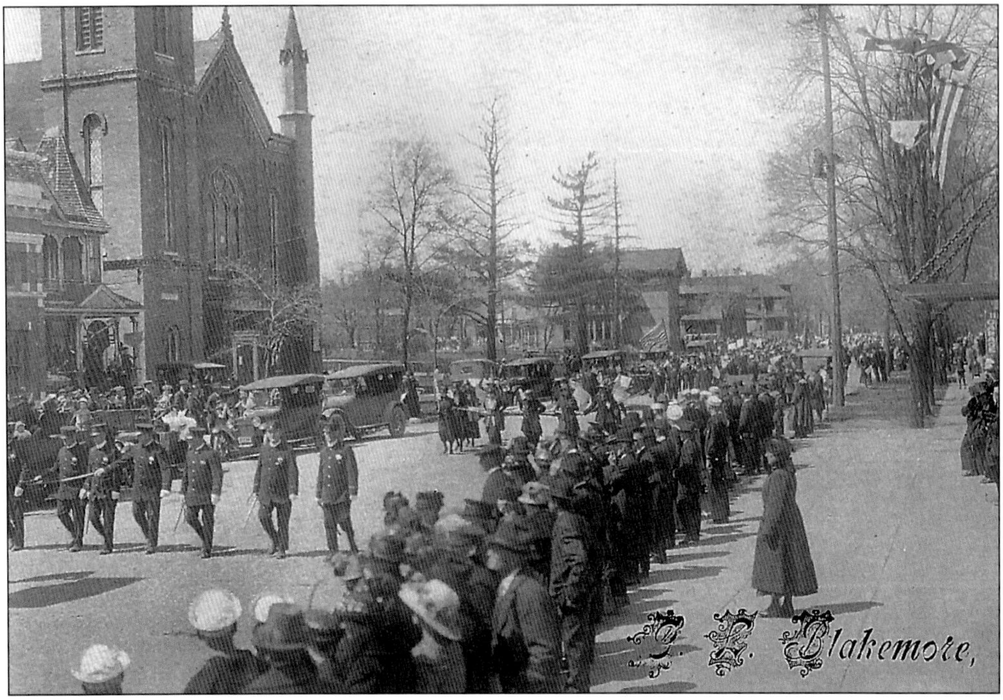

A World War I welcome-back parade moves south along north Genesee Street. The First Baptist Church can be seen in the left background.

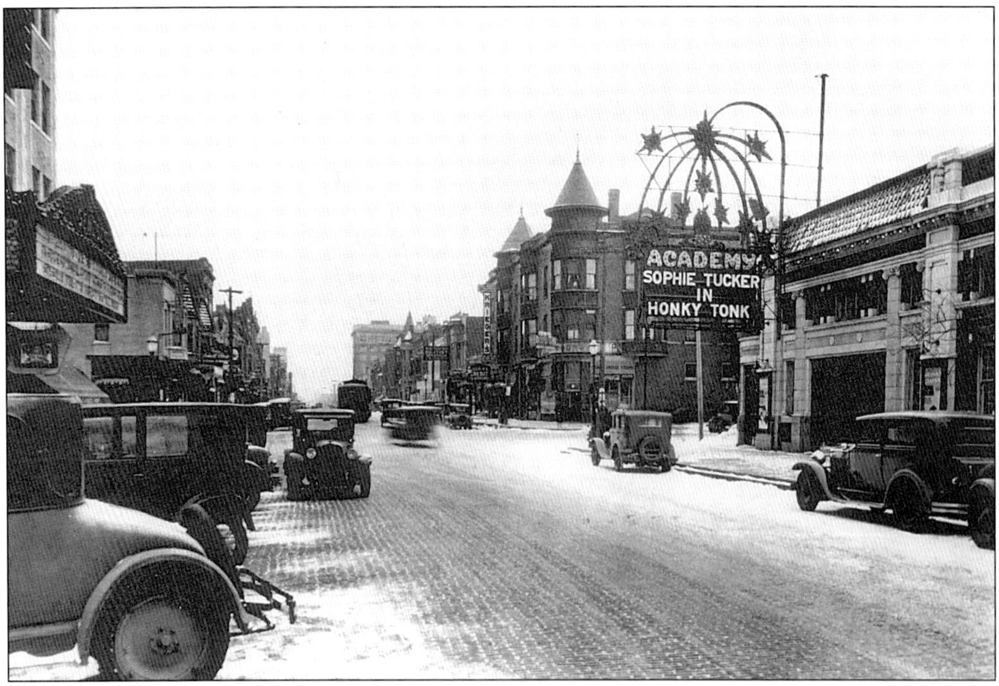

Looking south from roughly the same location, but about ten years later, one again can see the downtown area. Two major theatres, the Genesee on the left and the Academy on the right, are in full swing.

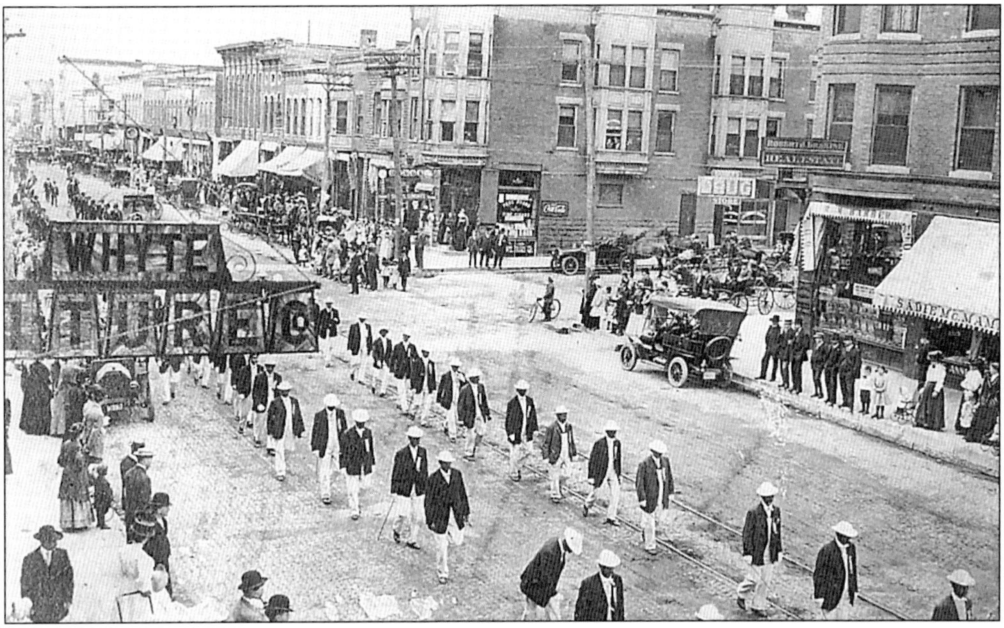

Parades were a popular pastime along Genesee Street. This one looks across Genesee to the intersection with Madison. The picture, from the early 1900s, shows Whyte Furniture and Robert Erskine Real Estate, among other businesses.

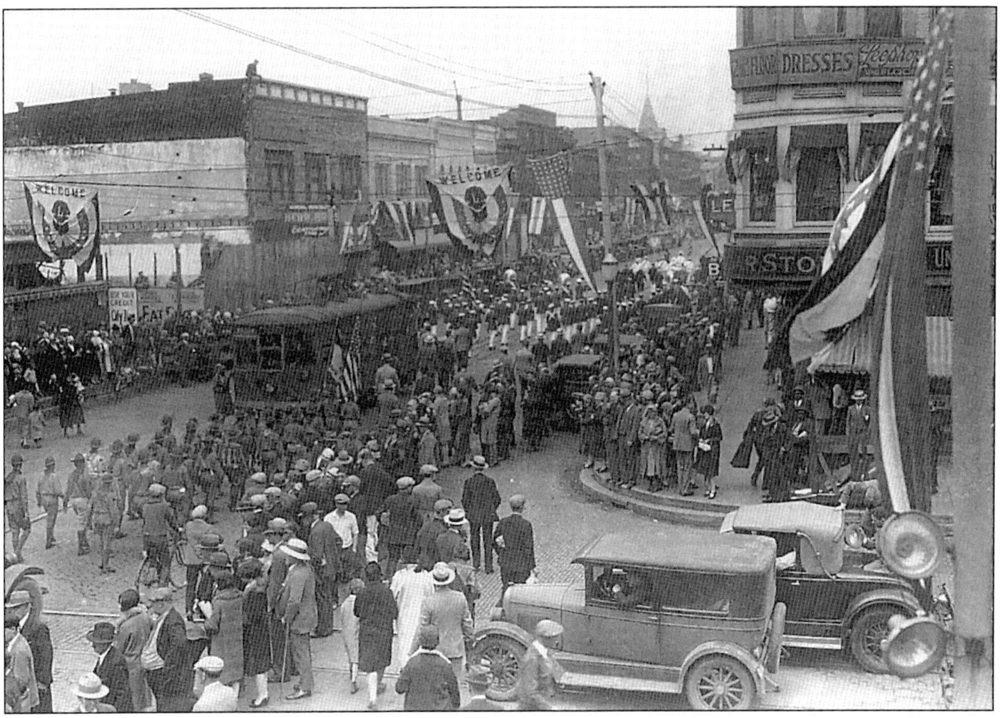

Another parade, with a streetcar in the middle, moves north on Genesee from Washington. This picture, from the late 1920s, shows Herr Bros. men's furnishings across the street. The Lee Shop and United Cigar are on the right side.

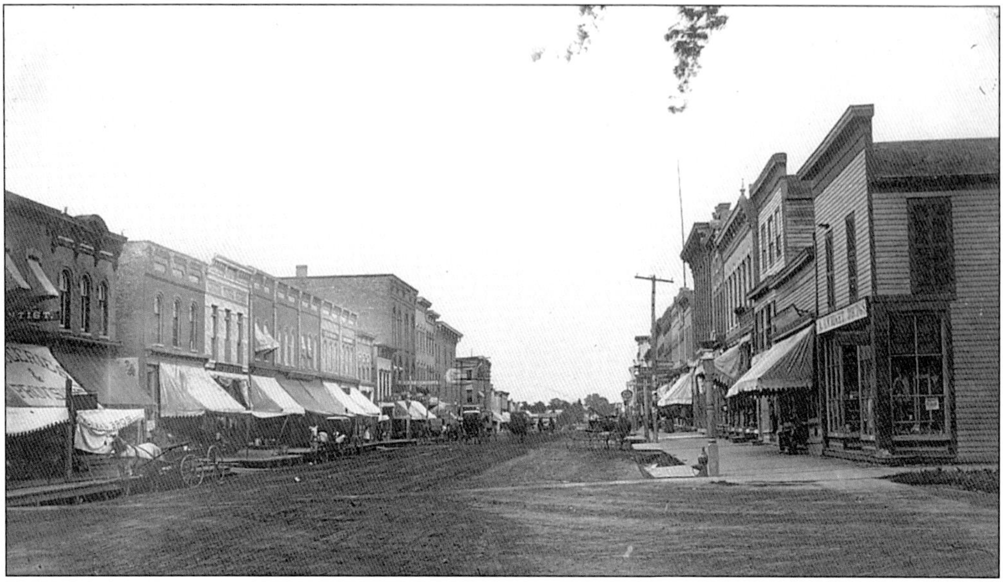

Looking south from Madison in the early 1890s, one can see the A.O. Wright Drug Store on the right and Martin Abbott's grocery across the street. Going down Genesee, signs are visible for G.B. Watrous hardware, Yeoman's jewelry store, and Dietmeyer's saloon.

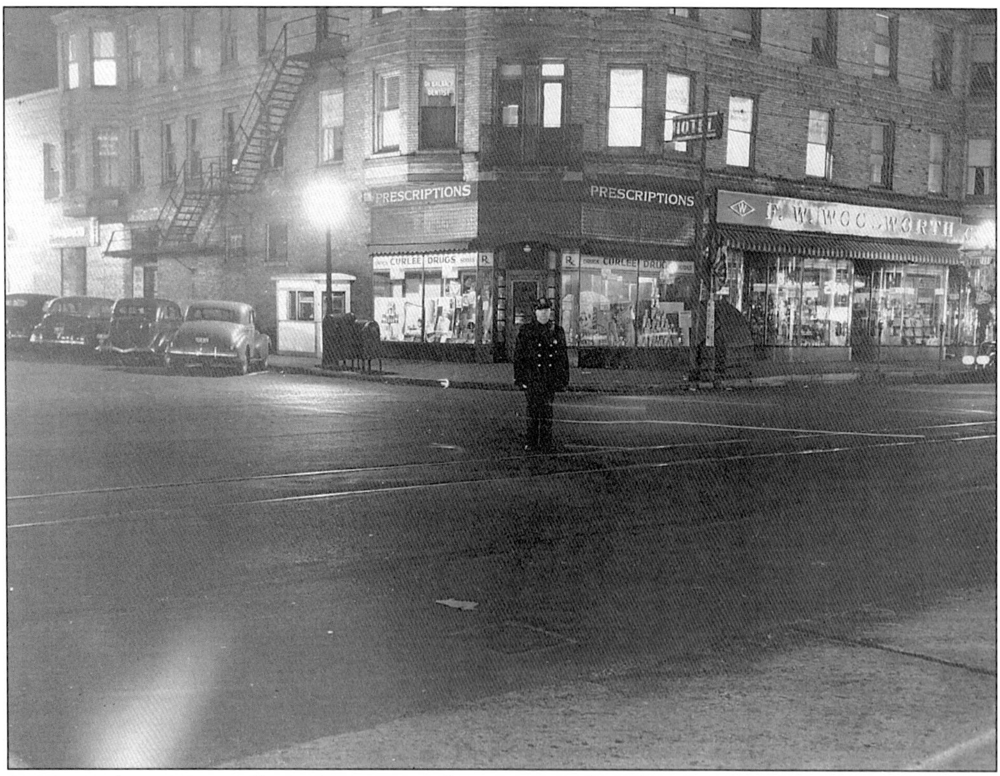

In November 1944, traffic at the corner of Genesee and Madison was controlled by the police. The offices of Dr. George Balbach, dentist, were in the Hotel Madison. Curlee Drugs and F.W. Woolworth were popular retail stops along the street.

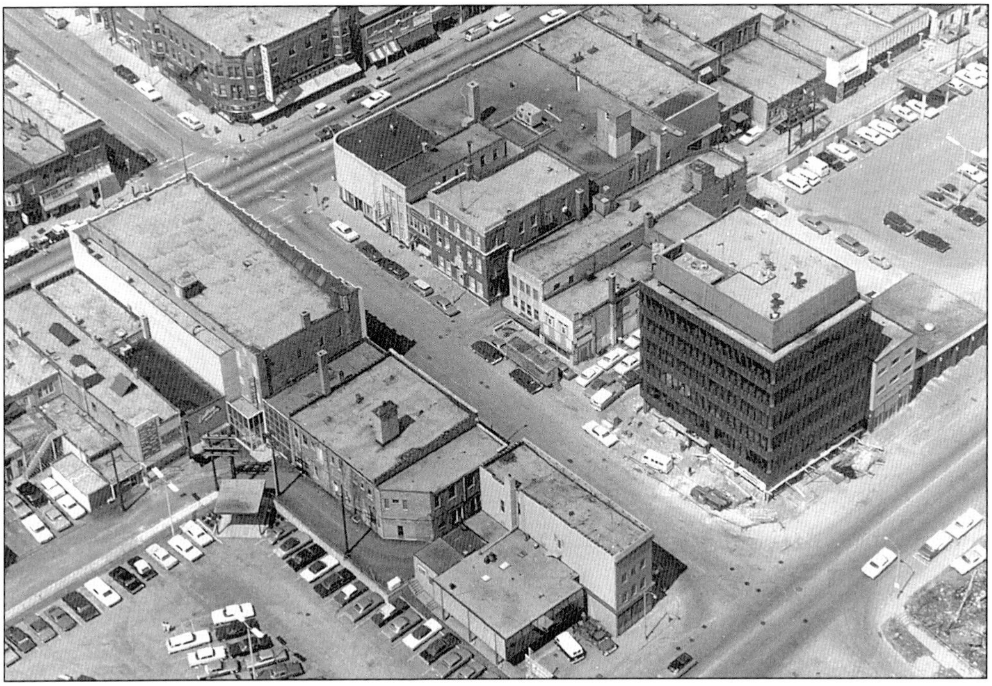

The intersection looks different many years later. Genesee continues as a main thoroughfare and Madison has not yet been closed off. The former police and fire station still stands and the *News-Sun* building is nearing completion.

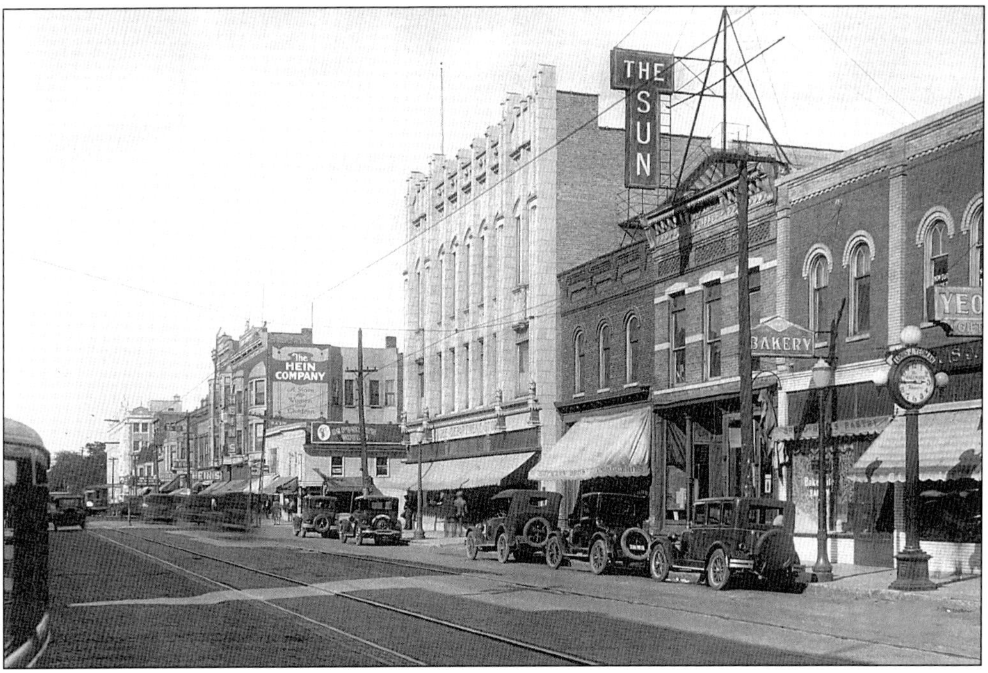

In 1927 the east side of Genesee, just north of Washington, featured Louis J Yeoman, jeweler, Bake-Rite Bakery, the Waukegan *Daily Sun*, Hoffman Bros. grocery, and the Globe Department. Store. The next block featured The Hein Co. and, eventually, the Elite Theatre.

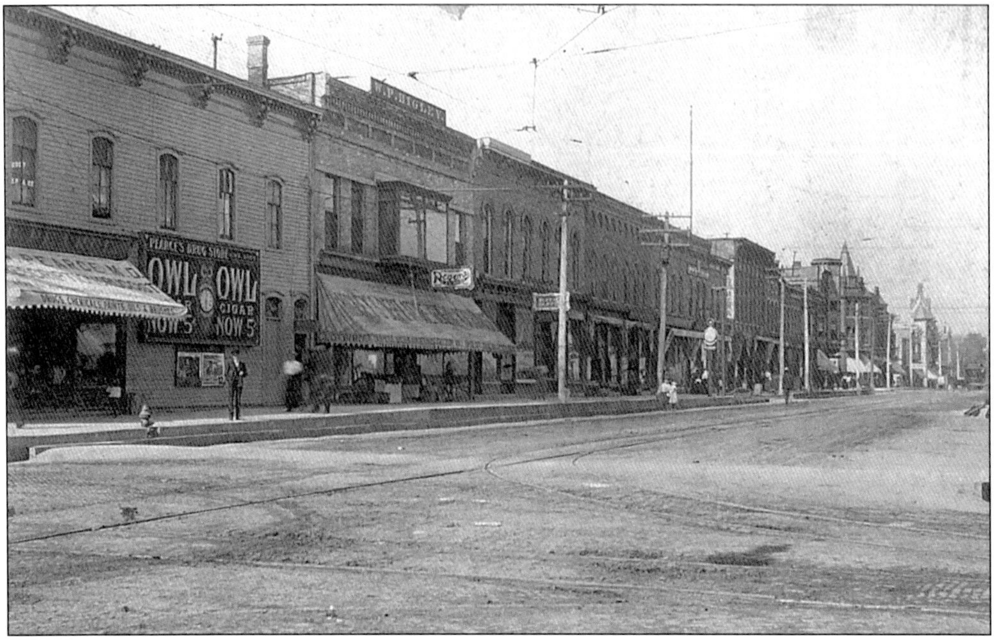

Across Genesee Street, about 1905, one could see Pearce Drugs, Higley's Department Store, and the Buffalo Buffet among the store fronts.

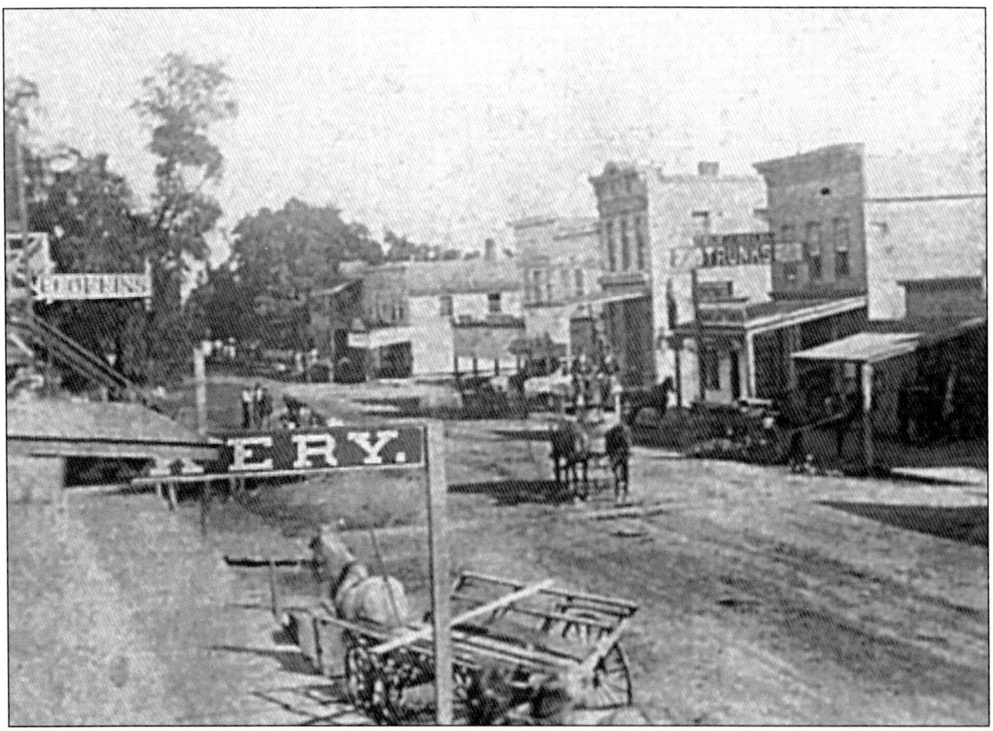

The same street, but around 1870, gives a very different look. A bakery in the foreground and a coffin maker down the street dominate the west side. On the east side was D.T. Hall, specializing in trunks.

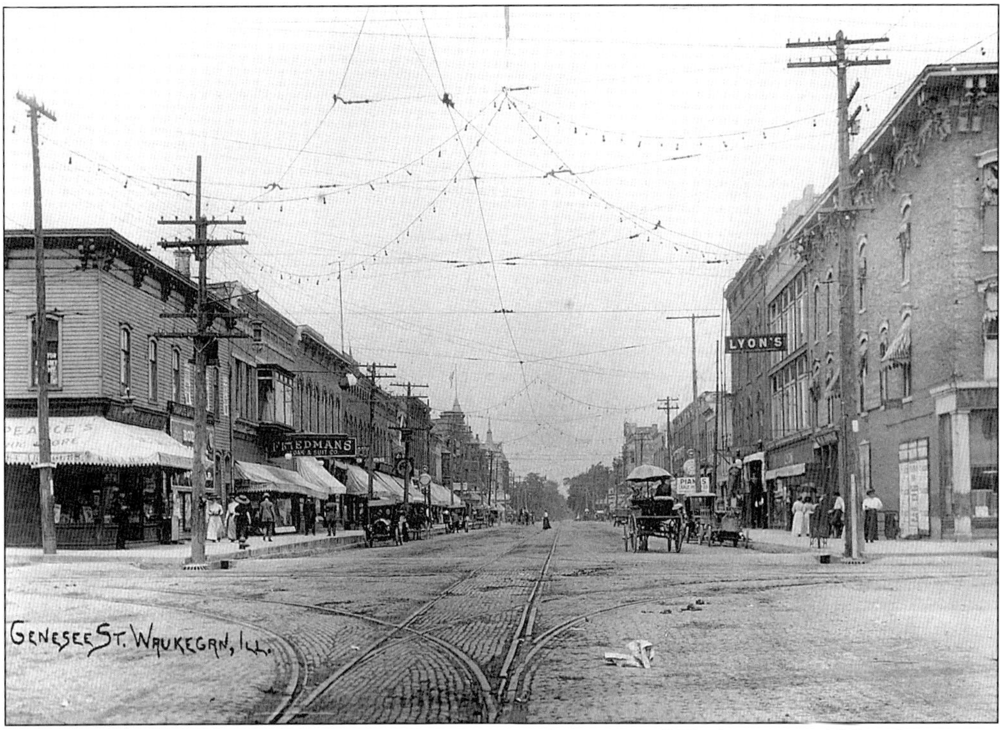

Looking north from downtown's major intersection, Genesee and Washington, old familiar names are seen. The Pearce, Yeoman, and Lyon stores all show in this picture of the early 1900s.

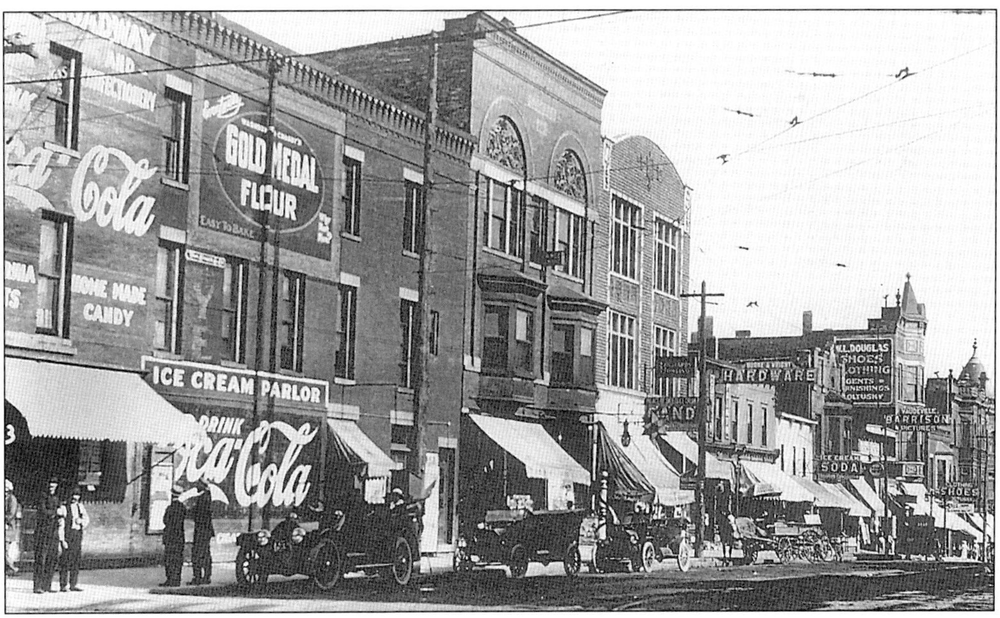

Around 1915 the east side of Genesee between Washington and Water held several familiar stops. Nathan Fisher's candy shop and Burke & Wright hardware provided for customer needs, while the Barrison Theatre gave vaudeville shows and moving pictures to the public.

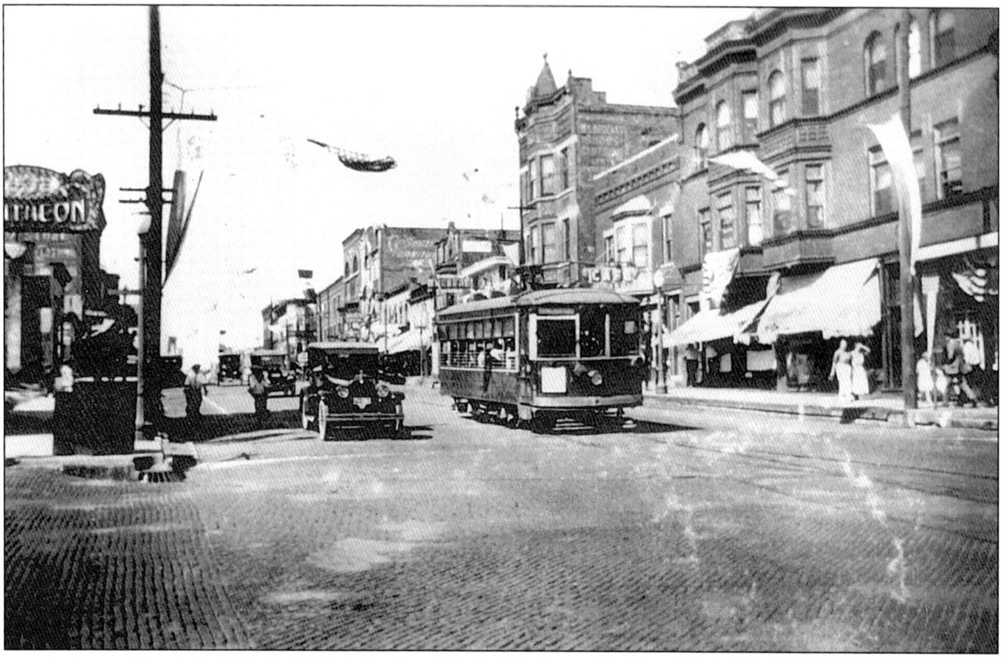

Looking at the same block some years later, but this time from Water Street, one can see the Pantheon Ice Cream Parlor on the left side and Tony's Cafe on the right. The theatre is still visible, but by now has had a name change to the Rialto.

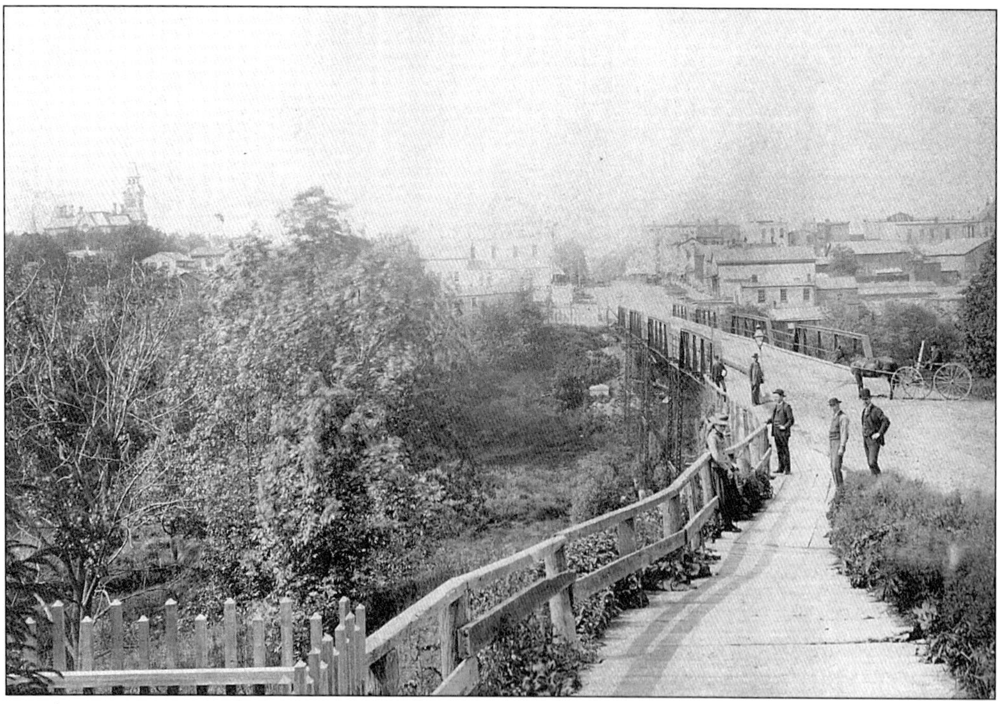

Waukegan's ravines were quite an impediment to traffic through town in the early days. A wooden bridge solved the problem on Genesee Street when it was erected around 1850. It was eventually replaced by this iron and steel bridge.

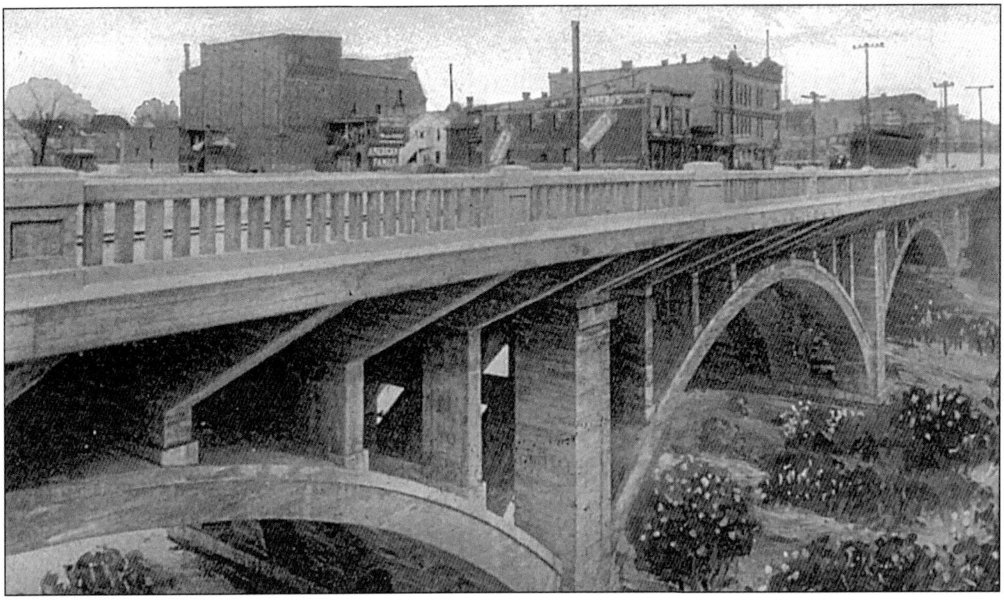

The metal bridge was not entirely safe in its later days. Streetcar passengers had to dismount, walk across the bridge and reboard the streetcar. A new, modern concrete structure was erected in 1913.

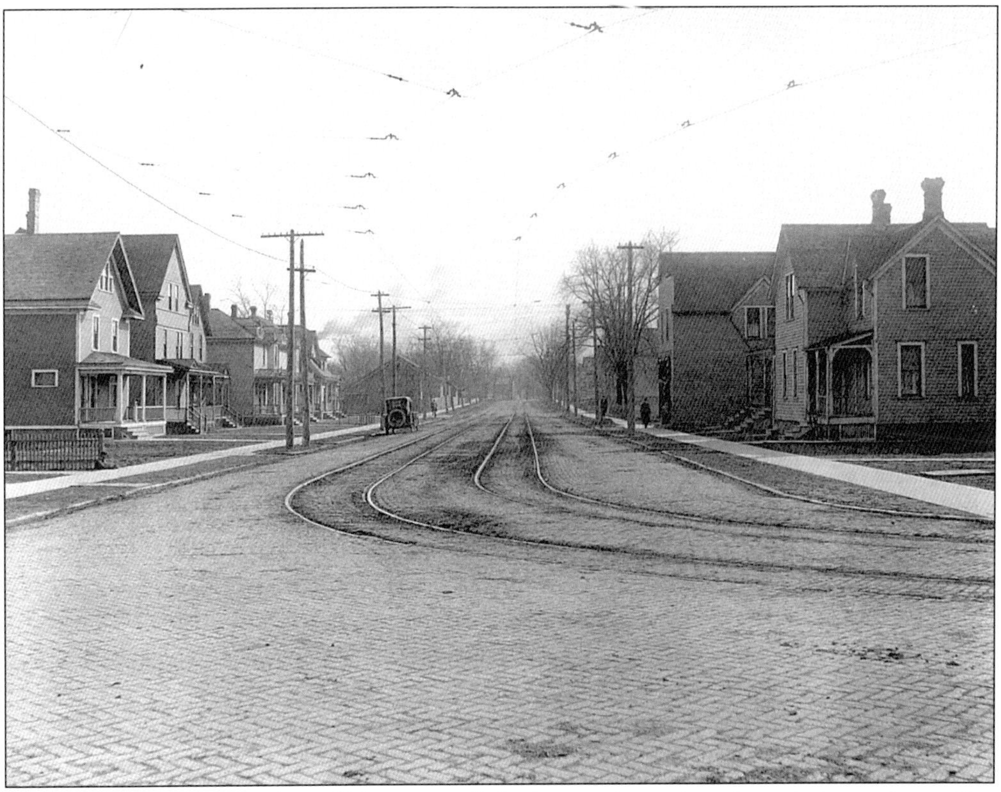

Genesee Street made a large "S" turn at Belvidere and continued south from there. The streetcar tracks made the same turn and followed down the middle of the street.

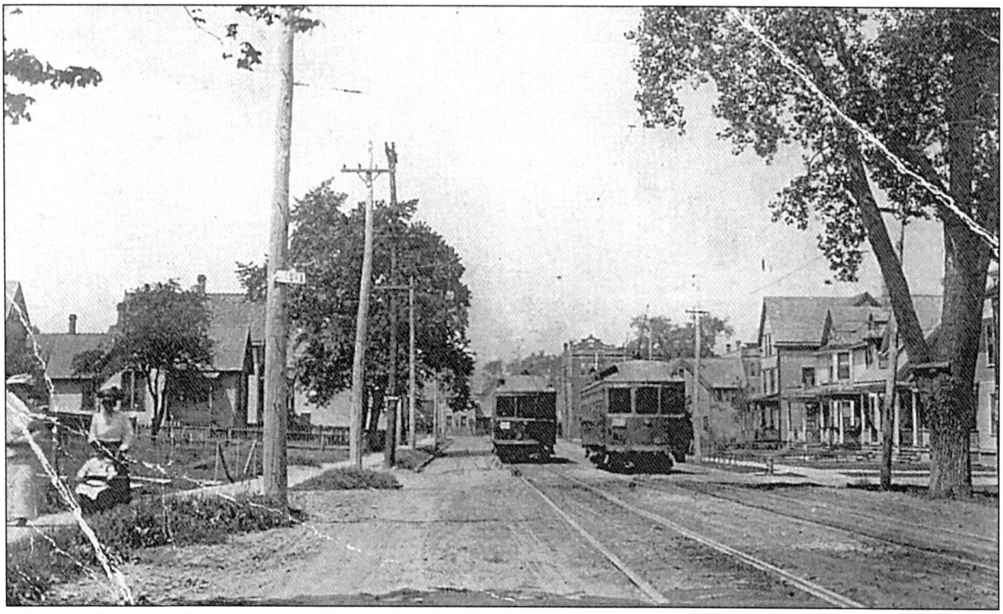

The southern end of Genesee, beyond Belvidere, was called Marion until about 1920. Then the name was dropped and South Genesee simply continued to the city limits.

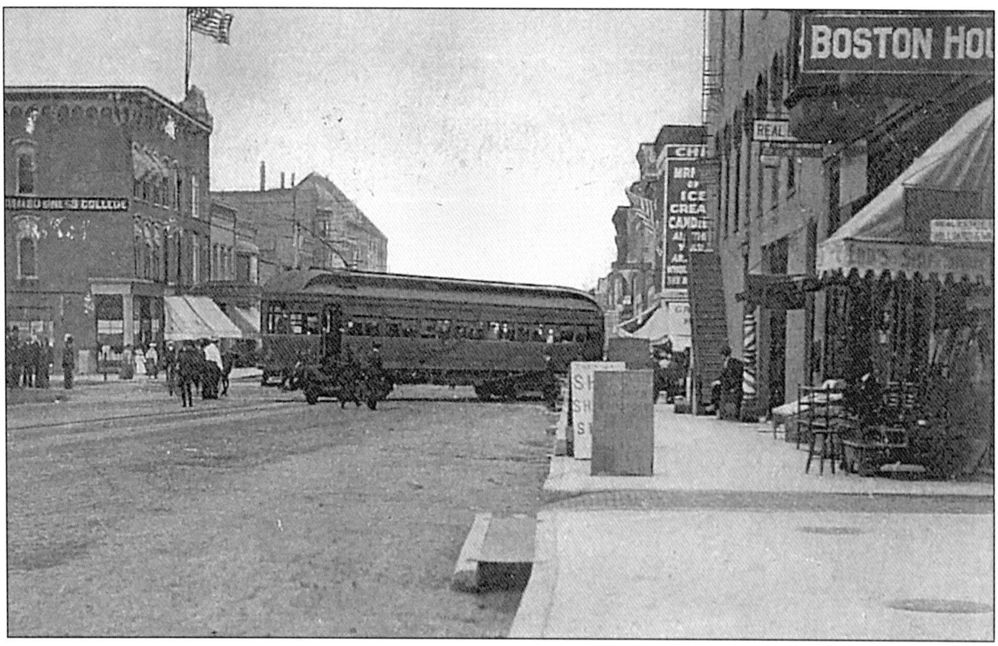

As the north bound streetcar turned west from Genesee onto Washington, the passengers could catch a glimpse of the Waukegan Business College before passing the Boston House Restaurant on the other side.

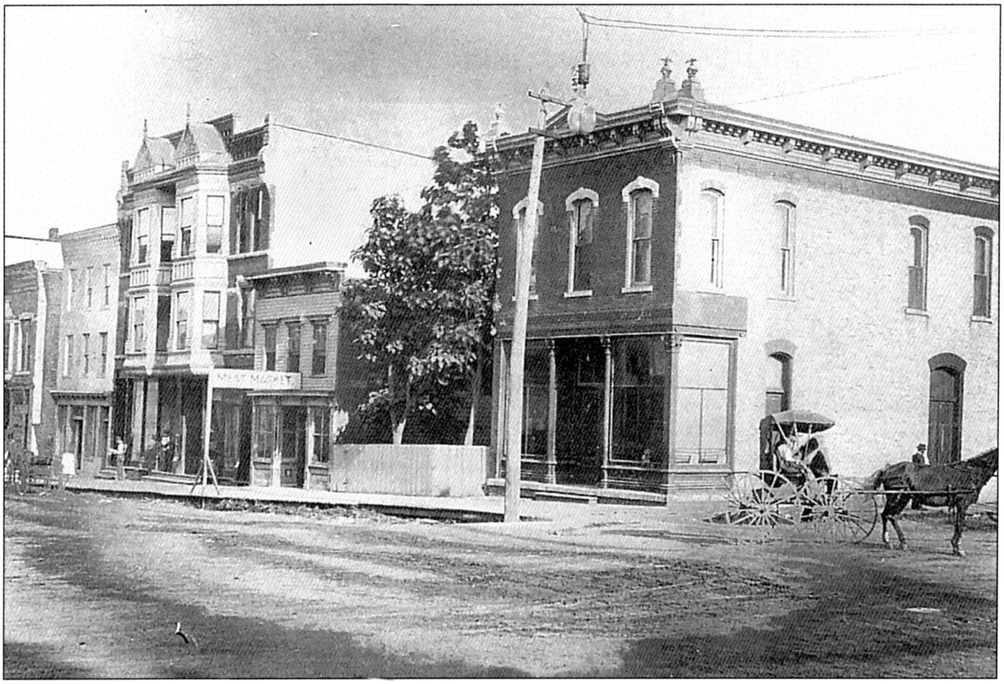

At the southeast corner of County and Washington Streets, one could see a meat market among the interesting architecture on the buildings of the era.

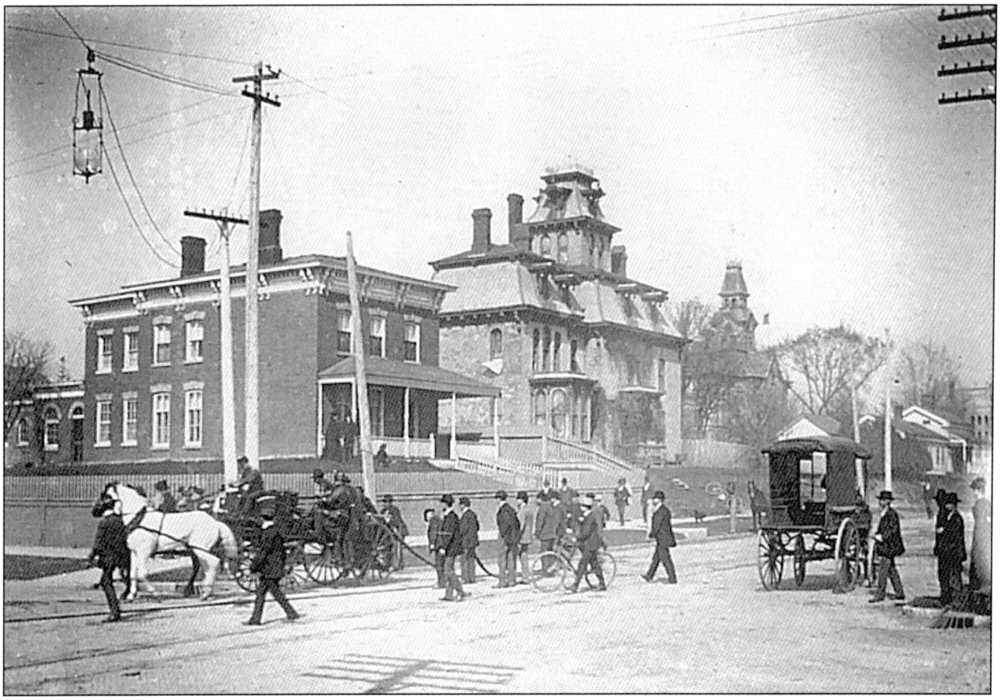

The Fire Department turns off Washington in pursuit of its duties. They had just passed the Fox Hotel (in the center of the picture.). The Lake County Courthouse can be seen in the background.

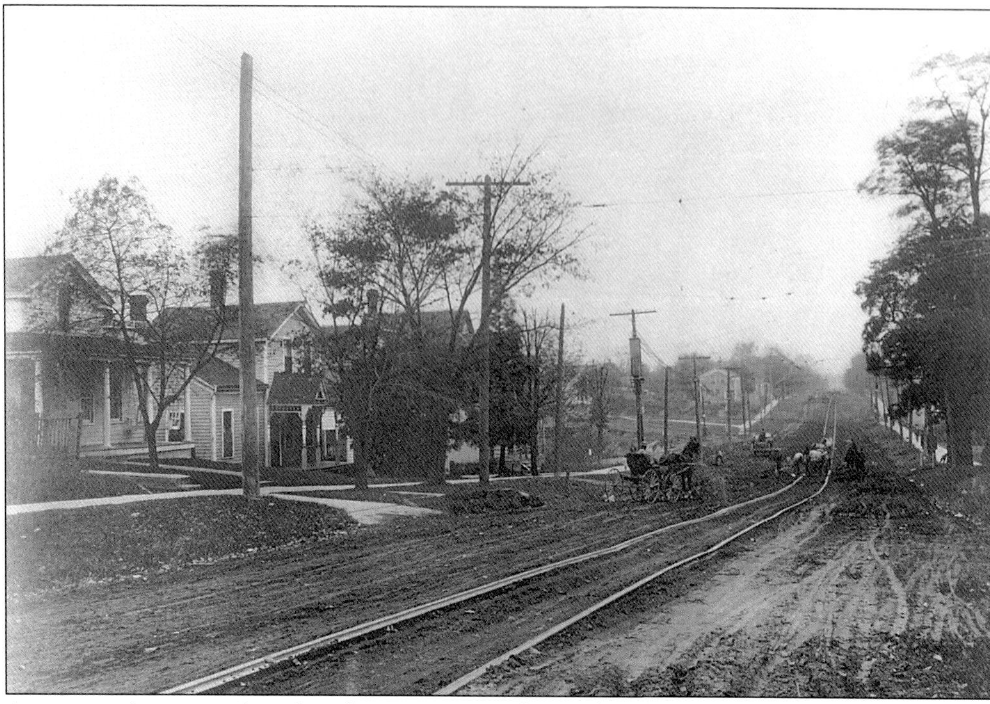

As we travel our paved roads today, it is easy to forget that they weren't always that way. Dirt faced the horse and buggy when the tracks were laid on Washington Street.

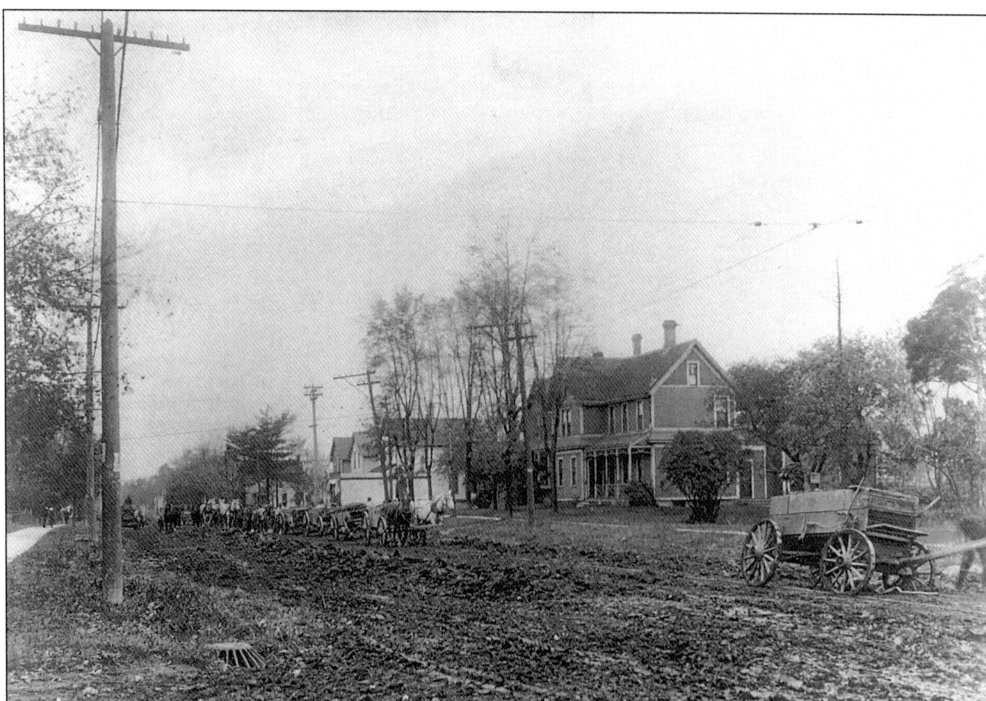

The dirt roads turned to mud whenever the rains came. That made it difficult for the wagons, and especially for the horses.

Three

BUSINESS

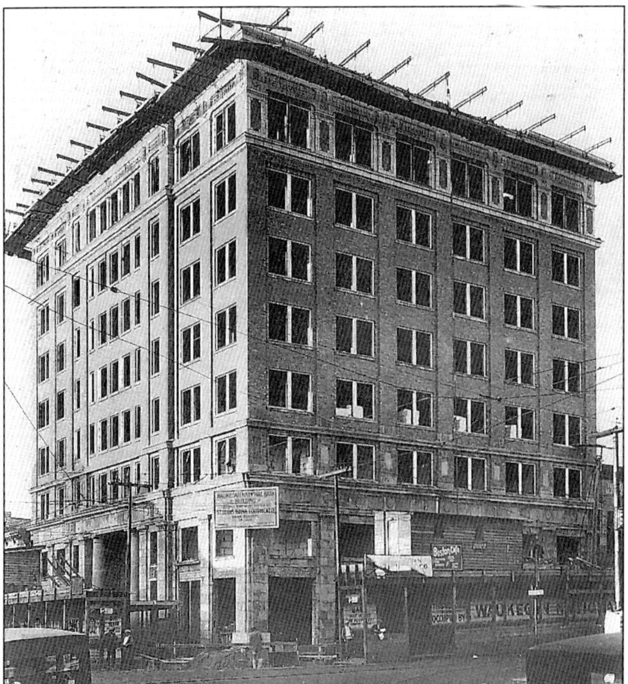

October 1924 saw the Waukegan National Bank Building nearing completion. The former three-story building had been demolished earlier in the year. The new bank opened on March 7, 1925, but eventually fell victim to the Depression and closed in 1931. Citizens National Bank occupied the premises from 1937 until it moved across Washington Street.

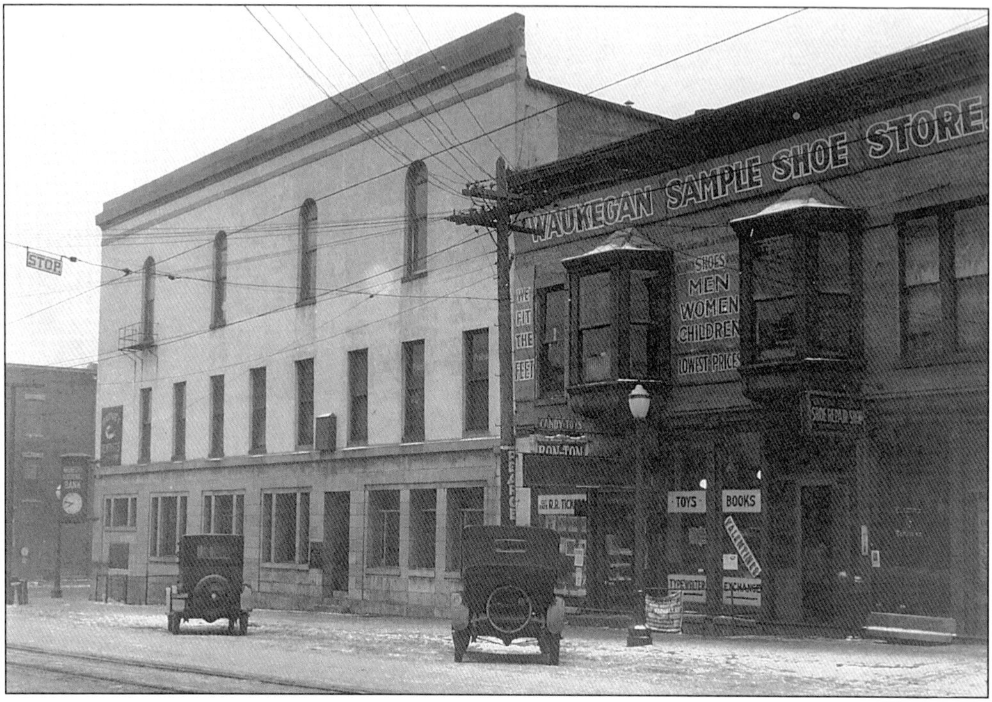

The Washington Street side of the old bank building adjoined the Waukegan Sample Shoe Store. The demolition and construction did not affect the shoe store, which continued in business.

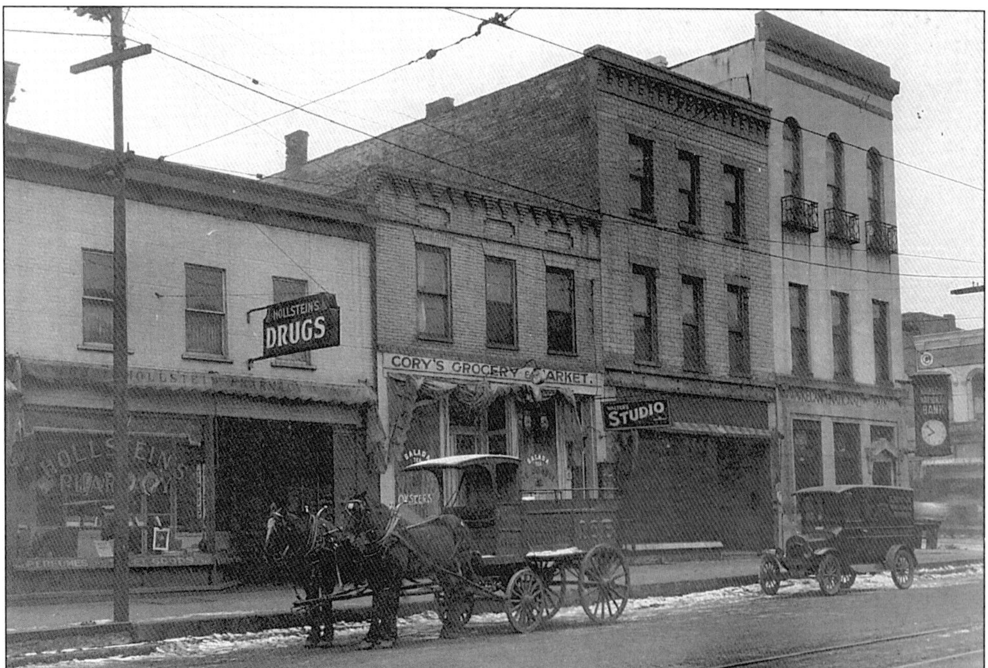

Buildings on the Genesee Street side were impacted by the bank construction, The buildings that had housed Whyte Furniture Co., Walters Studio, and Cory Grocery fell to the wreckers. The new bank building would occupy all that space.

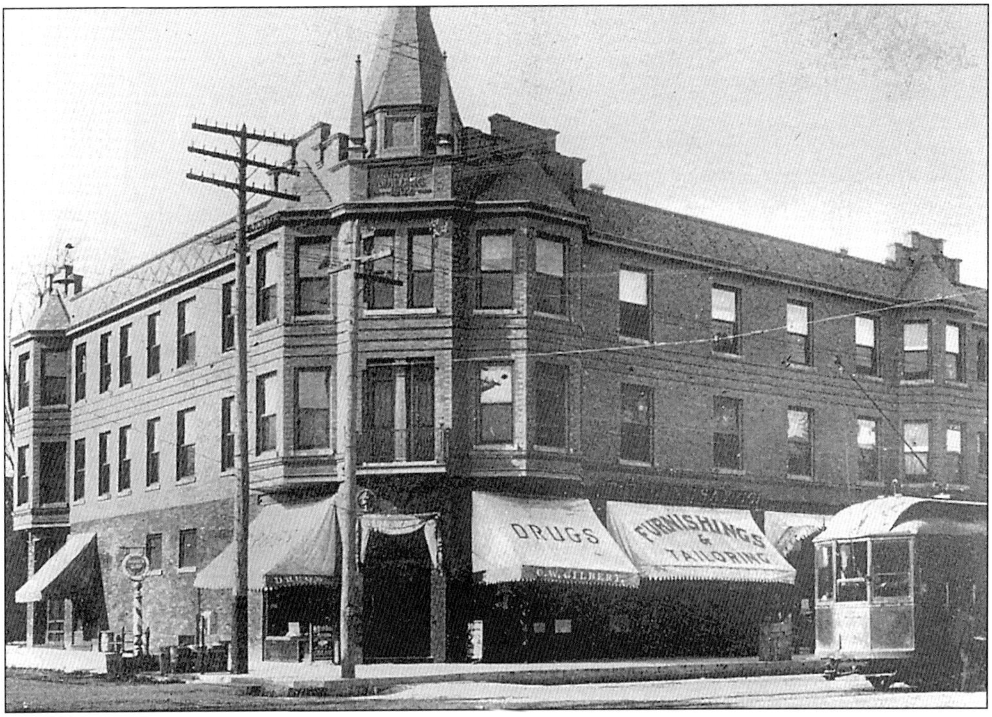

The year 1903 saw the opening of the Murray Building at the northwest corner of Madison and Genesee. At that time space was occupied by Tompkins' barber shop, Gilbert's Drug Store, and Lindsay's clothiers.

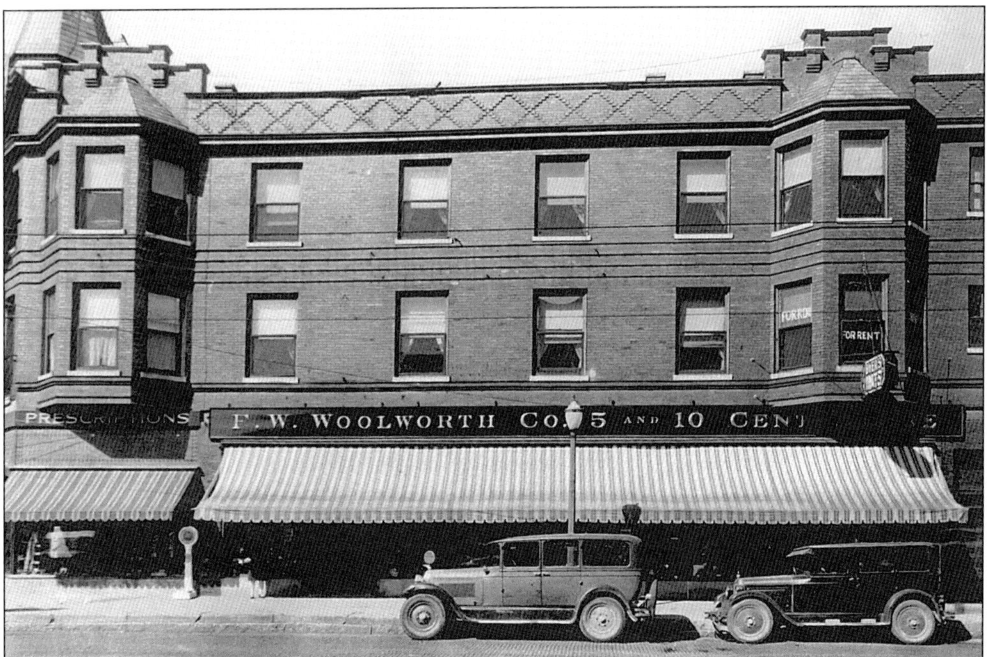

By the late 1920s, the pharmacy was Curlee's. F.W. Woolworth had brought a variety store to the block, and part of the Murray Block was occupied by Byers Millinery.

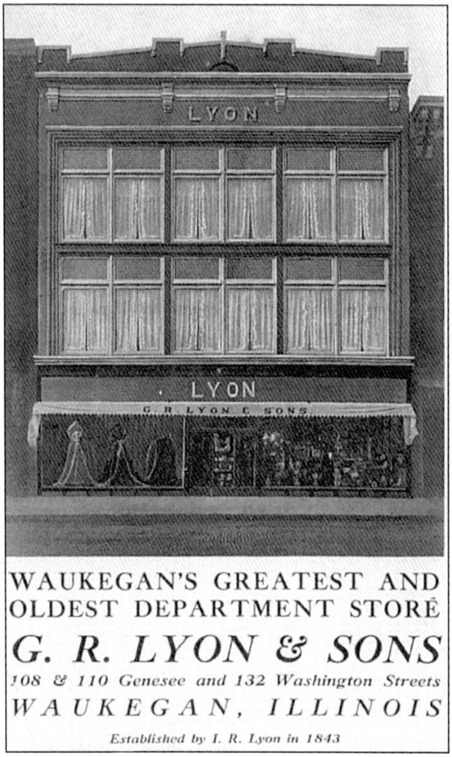

Isaac R Lyon arrived in Little Fort in 1843 and opened a general merchandise store. At his death in 1883, the business passed to his son, George R. The building wrapped around another building on the northeast corner of Genesee and Washington, and the store had entrances on both streets.

About 1910 the workers inside G.R. Lyon & Sons were ready to provide the customers with all their needs.

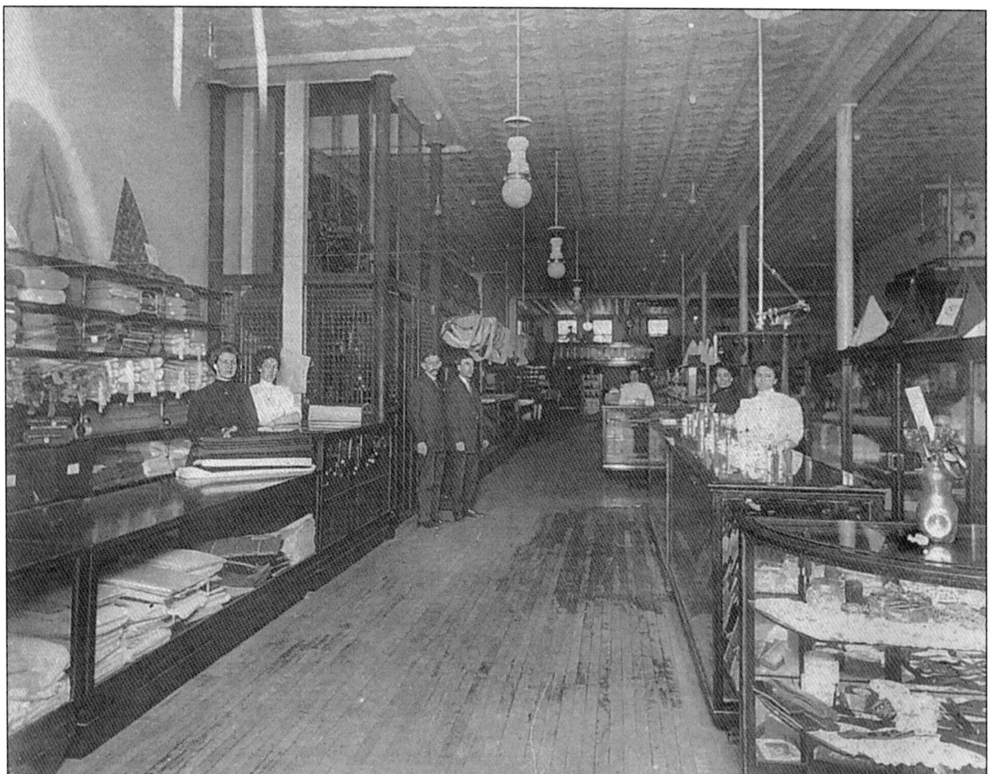

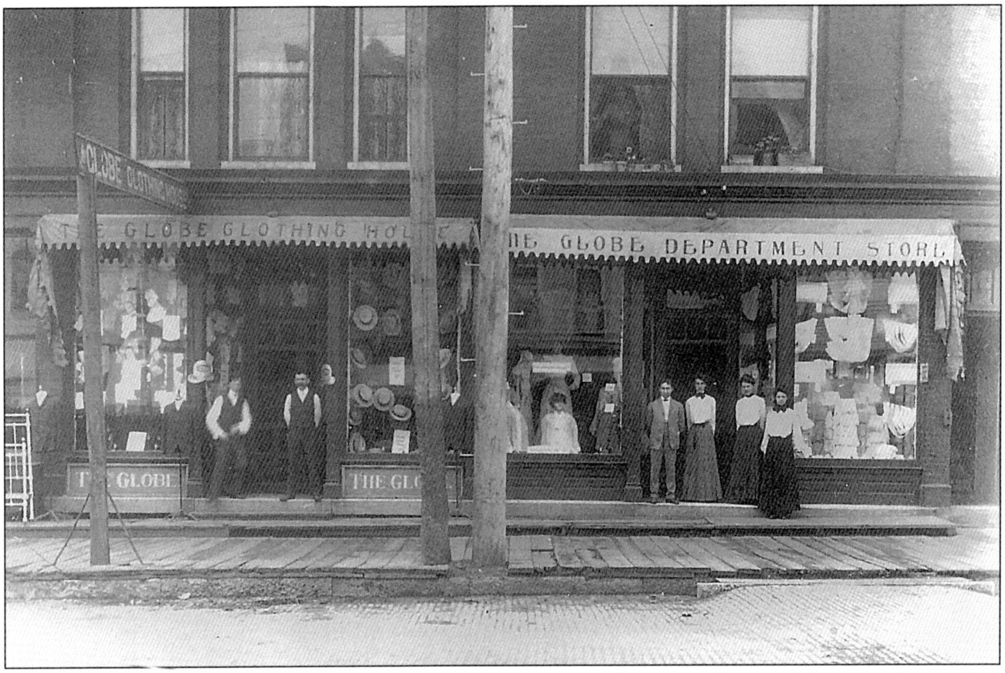

Globe Department Store was another early business in the city. Charles Morrison began his store on Washington Street in 1899, and moved to the corner of Madison and Genesee in 1906 where this picture was taken.

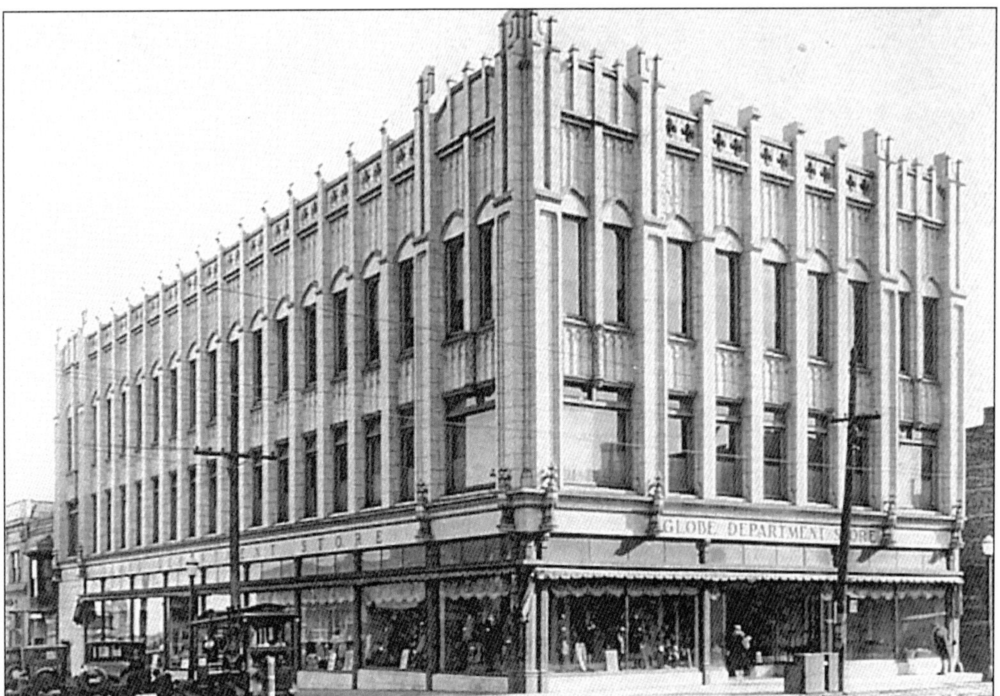

A new, larger and more modern building was built at the same location in 1925. It served the area's customers through many years and several remodelings until the store finally closed in 1979.

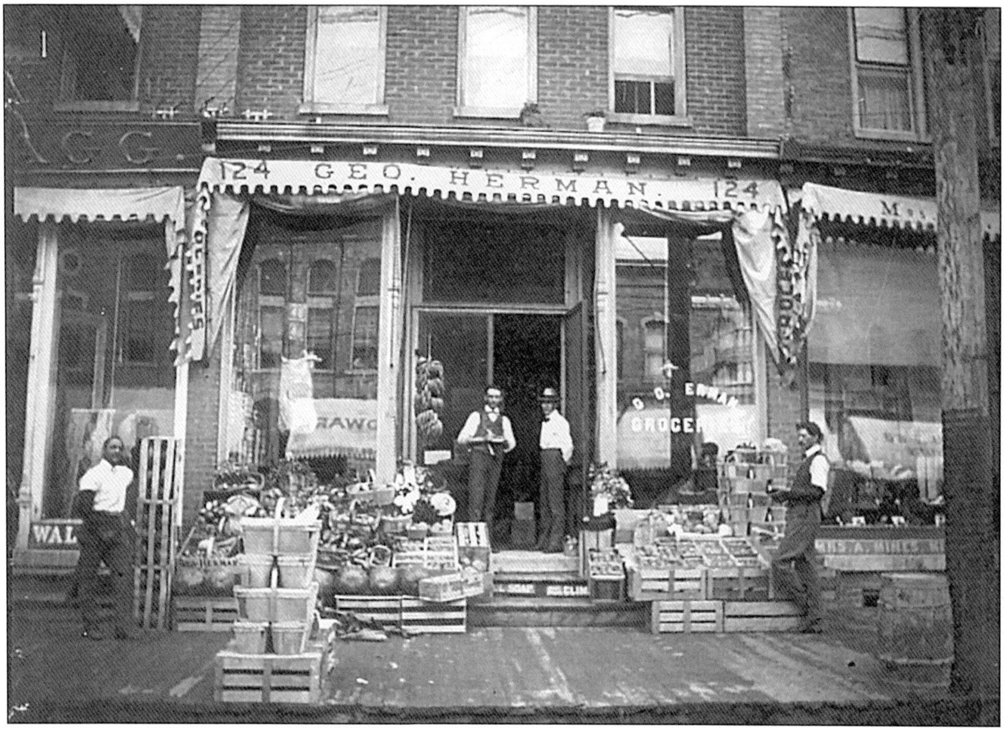

George Herman came to Waukegan in the 1860s and worked as a fisherman. Eventually he opened a grocery, initially called Herman Brothers, and later known as George Herman's Sons The Grocers. He moved several times and was at this location between 1895 and 1904.

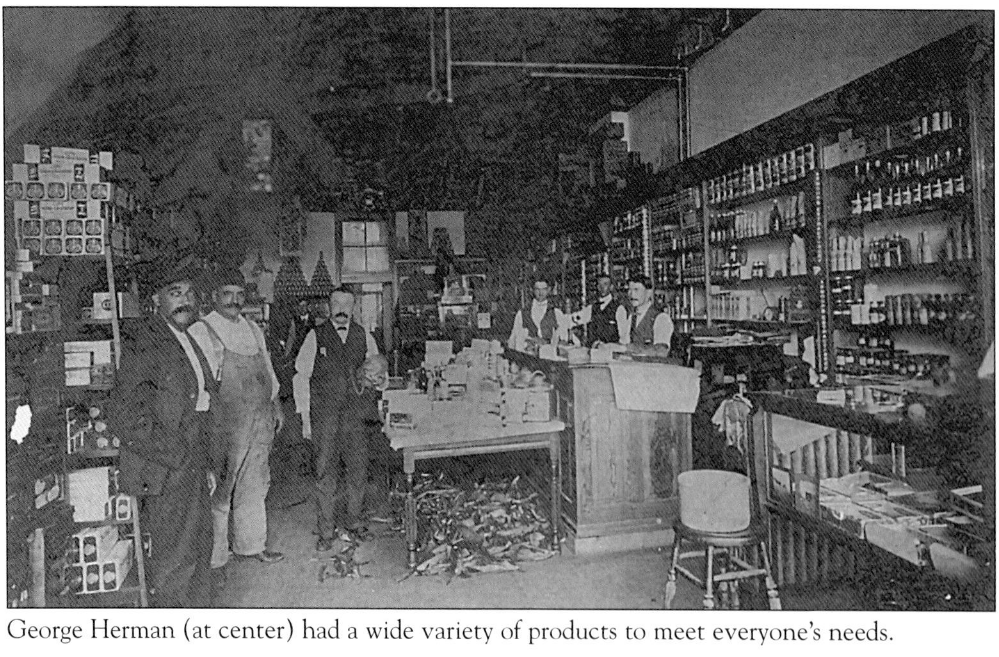

George Herman (at center) had a wide variety of products to meet everyone's needs.

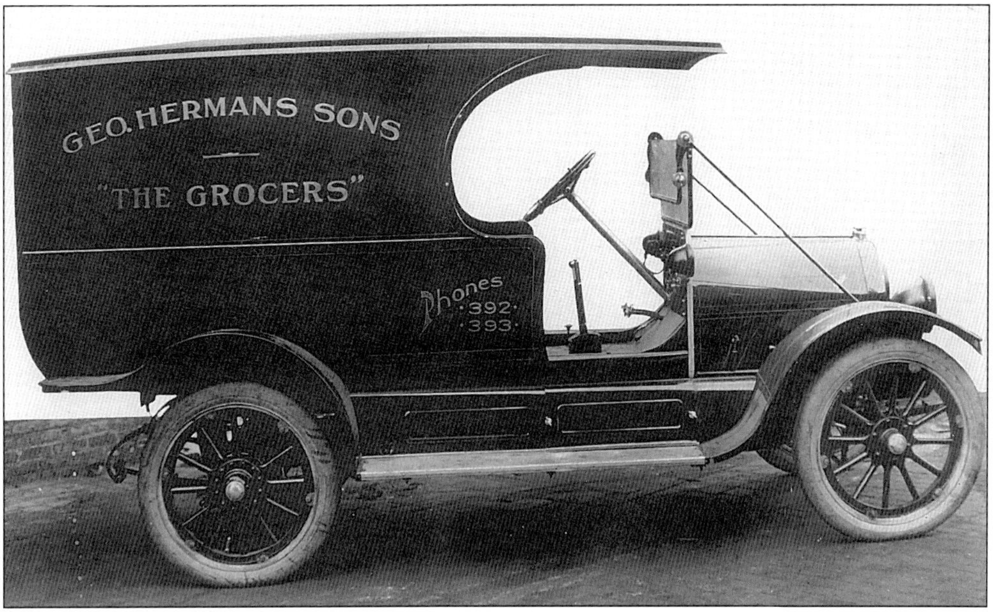

In later years George Herman offered the most modern method of delivering groceries. By now he was located at 233 N. Genesee, which became 134 N. Genesee when street numbers were changed in 1922.

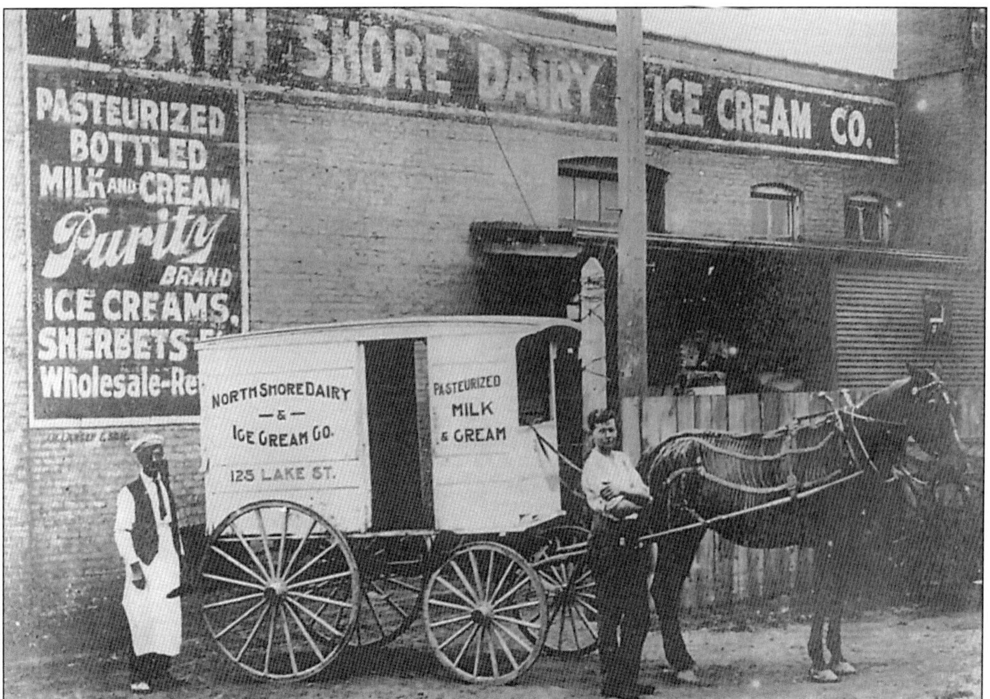

The North Shore Dairy and Ice Cream Co. originated with Alfred Johnson about 1881. Subsequent changes in ownership brought the dairy to the Brumund family, which operated it until 1951. Alvin L. Brumund was one of the founders of the Waukegan Historical Society. Here, Daisy is set to pull the wagon along its delivery route.

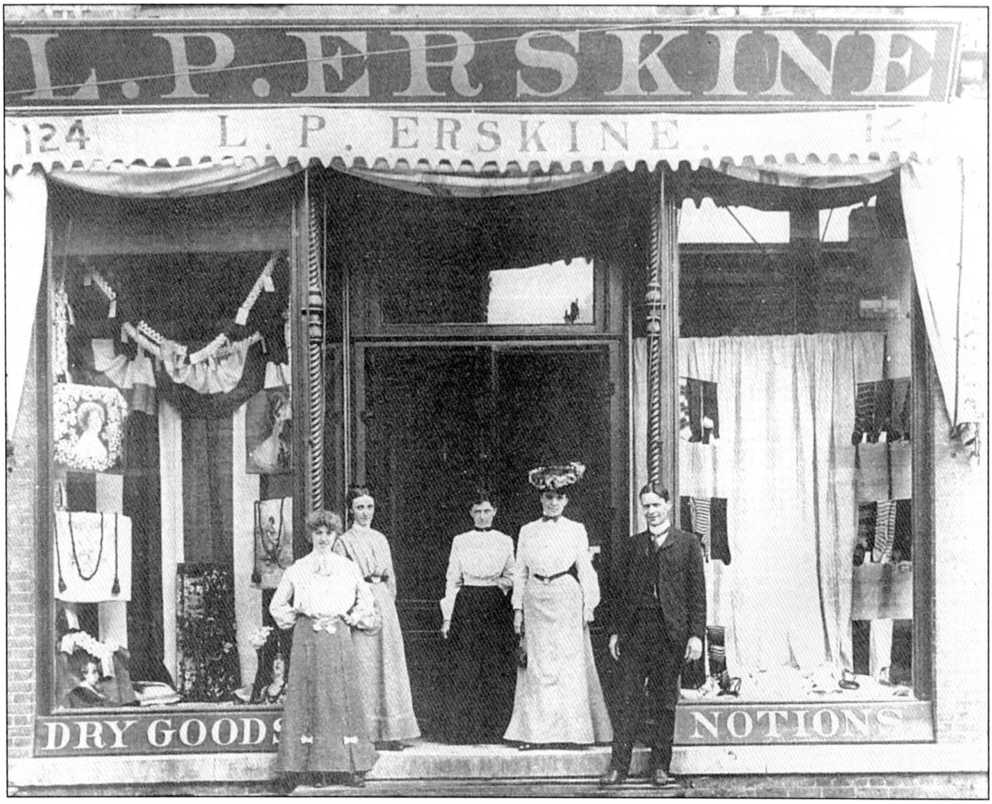

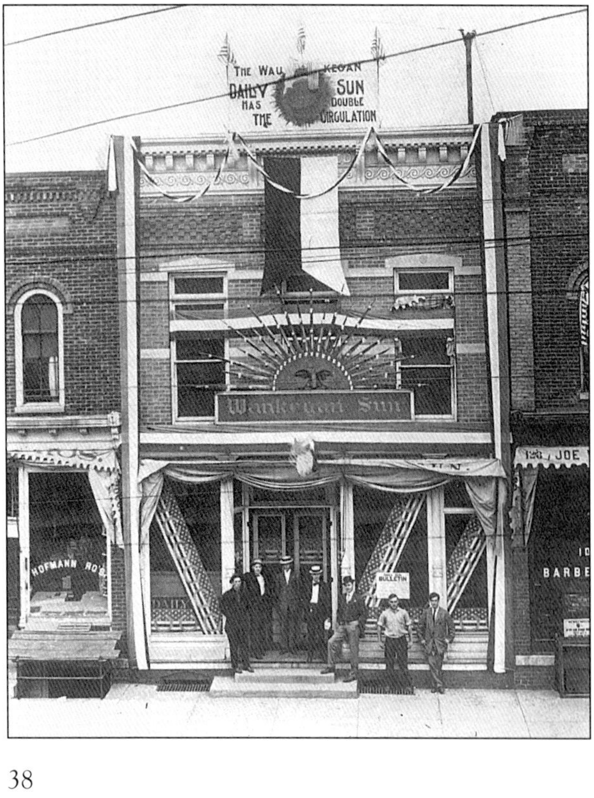

Customers could find the finest in dry goods, notions, and ladies' furnishing goods at the store owned by Lewis P. Erskine. This North Genesee Street establishment opened in 1905.

The *Waukegan Sun* was first published by Arthur K. Stearns in 1897. Later, sales brought the paper to the Just family who merged the paper with the *News* in 1930. At the time of this picture, the *Sun* was located on the east side of Genesee between Madison and Washington.

James Yeoman was born in England in 1813. He came to Little Fort in 1846 and began farming. After selling the farm, he began business as a tailor, an undertaker, and a dealer in furniture. He retired from that business in 1881. His family remained in business in Waukegan for many years, primarily as jewelers.

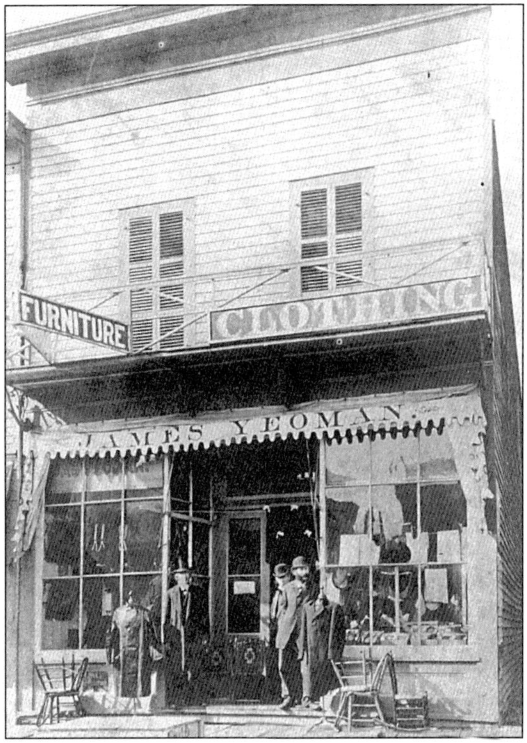

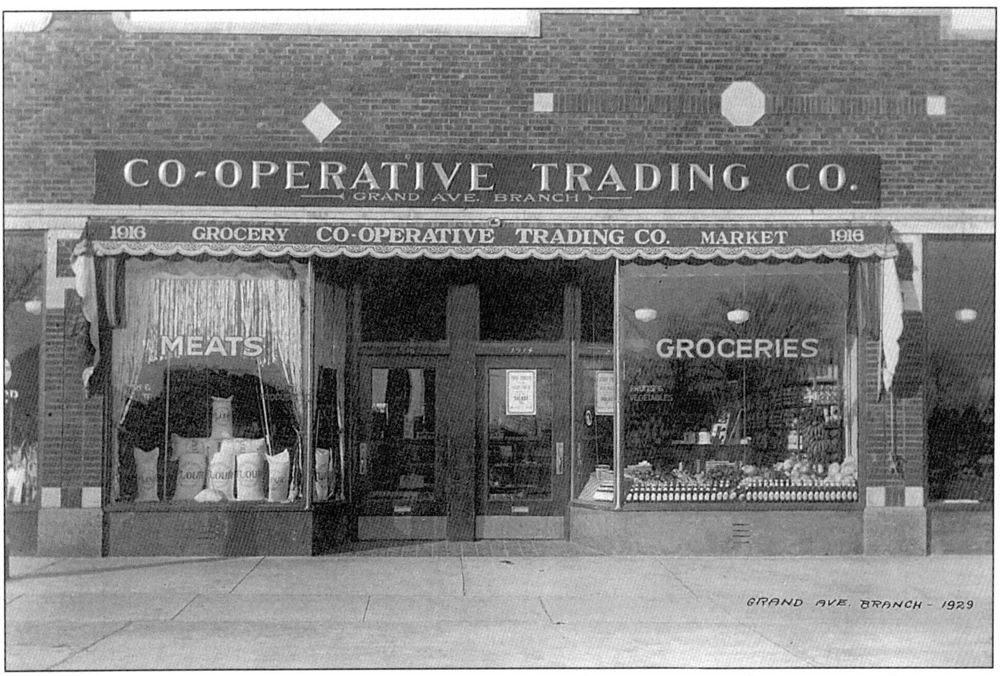

Co-operative Trading Co. began as a dairy on McAlister Avenue about 1911. The Co-op expanded to a full-line grocery and meat store, and had as many as five locations within the city, including this one on Grand Avenue which opened in 1929. The number of outlets reduced over time until the Co-op closed in the late 1960s.

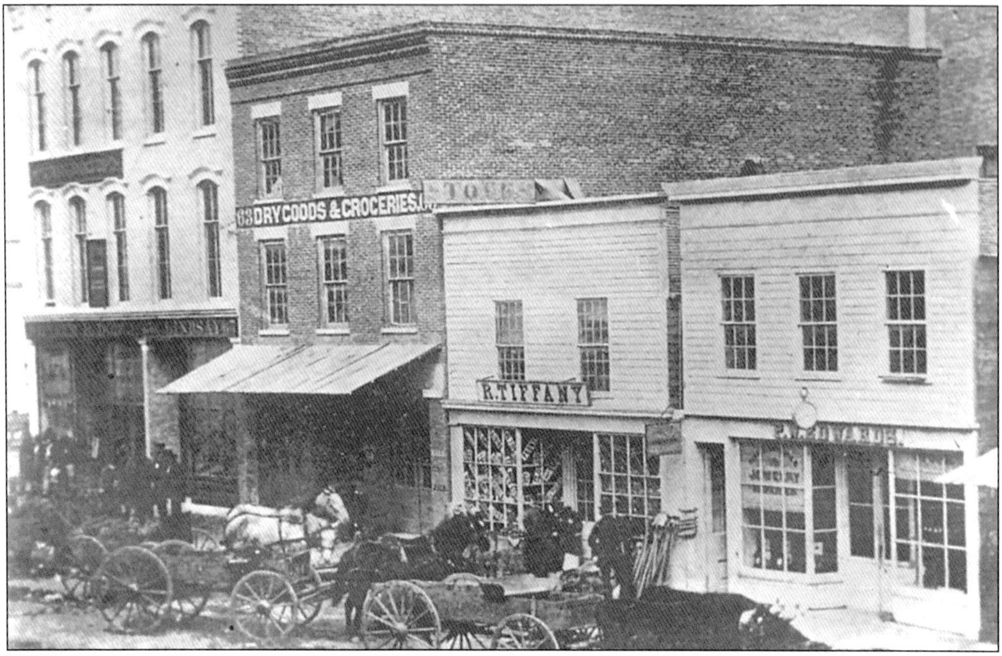

Around 1870, the north side of Washington, just east of Genesee, had several stores. Among the stores lining the block were William B. Dodge and Lindsay, clothiers; I.R. Lyon, dry goods; R. Tiffany, hardware; and P.W. Edwards, jewelry repairs.

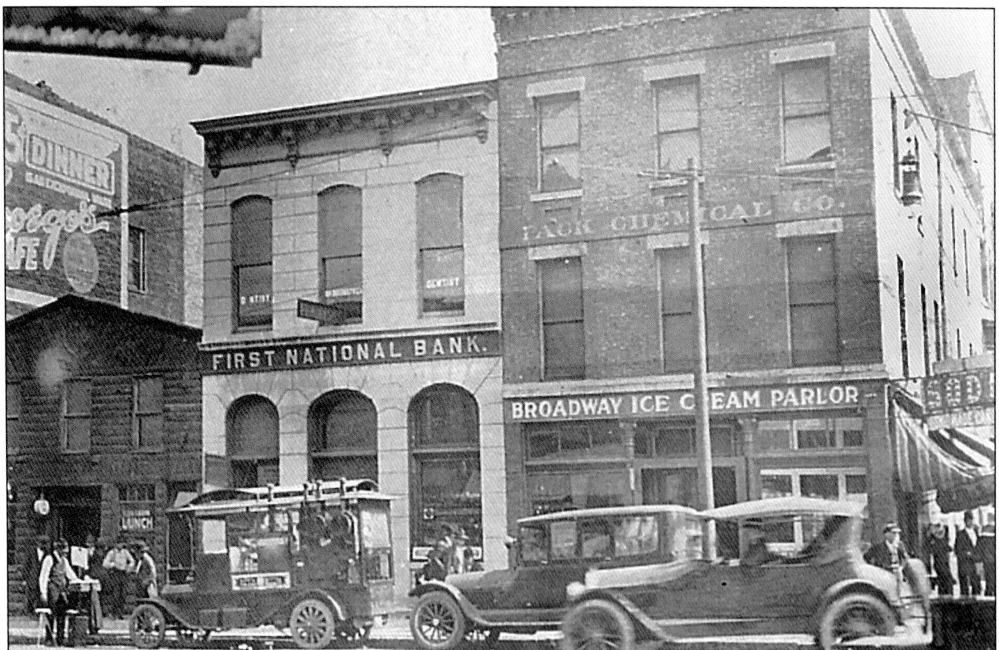

Immediately south of Washington, on the east side of Genesee, was the First National Bank. It was the successor of a private bank and began operating under a national charter in April 1865. The name stayed the same until a modern day switch to the Bank of Northern Illinois. Here the bank and Broadway Ice Cream Parlor can be seen in 1917.

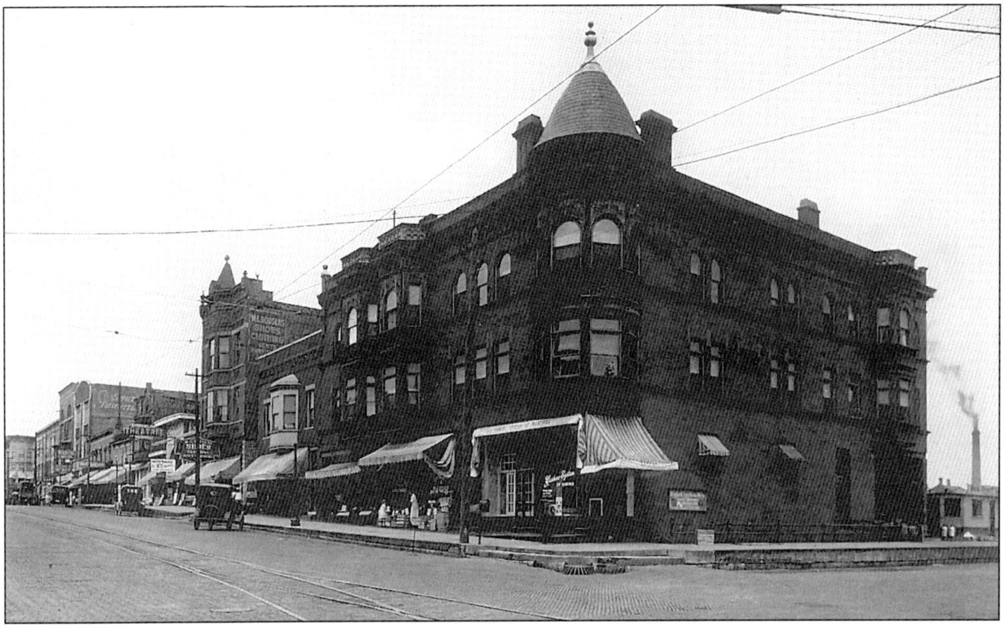

At the northeast corner of Genesee and Water stands the Sauter Building. At this time, about 1922, it was the home of Lindberg's Men's Furnishings, the Wizelman Bros. grocery, Standard Sheet Metal Works, and the Yankee Bakery.

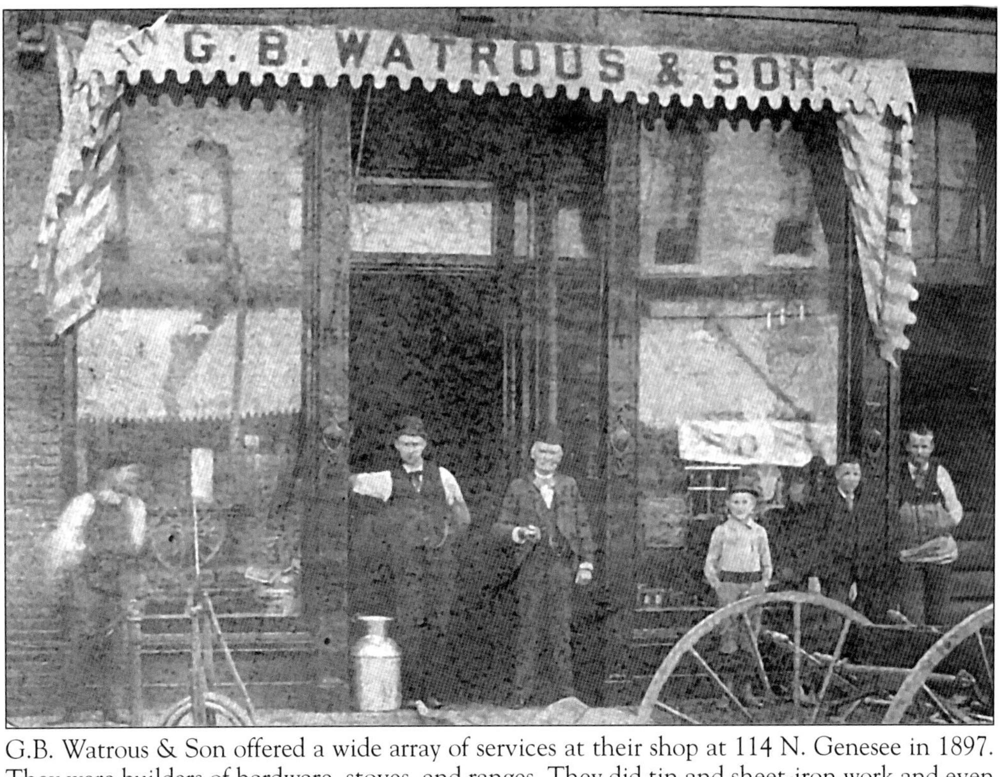

G.B. Watrous & Son offered a wide array of services at their shop at 114 N. Genesee in 1897. They were builders of hardware, stoves, and ranges. They did tin and sheet-iron work and even manufactured bicycles, as well as repairing them.

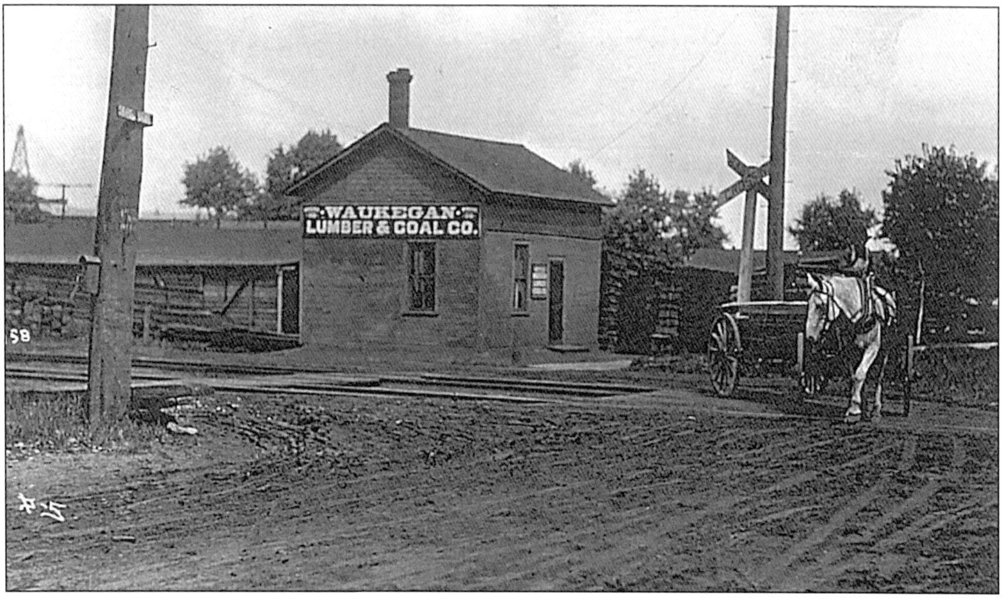

From their location at Sand and Clayton, the Waukegan Lumber and Coal Co. was ready to deliver building and fuel needs to all their customers. They began operation about 1913.

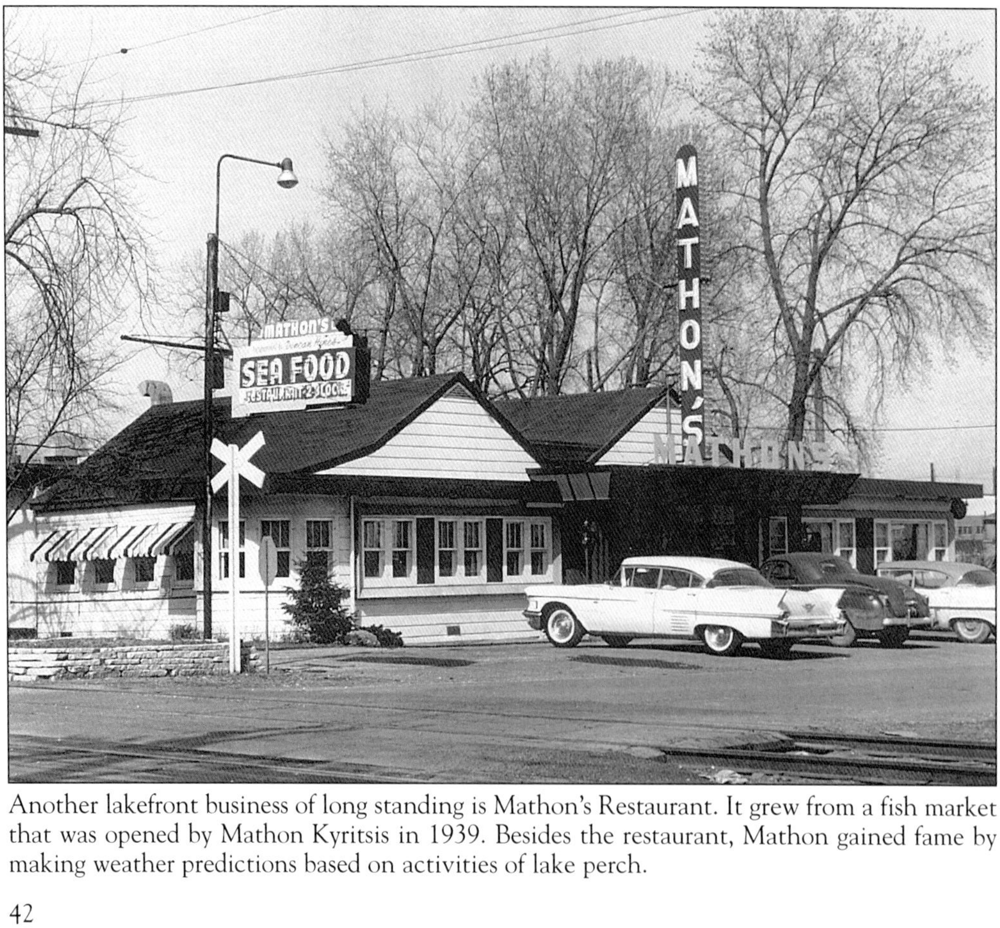

Another lakefront business of long standing is Mathon's Restaurant. It grew from a fish market that was opened by Mathon Kyritsis in 1939. Besides the restaurant, Mathon gained fame by making weather predictions based on activities of lake perch.

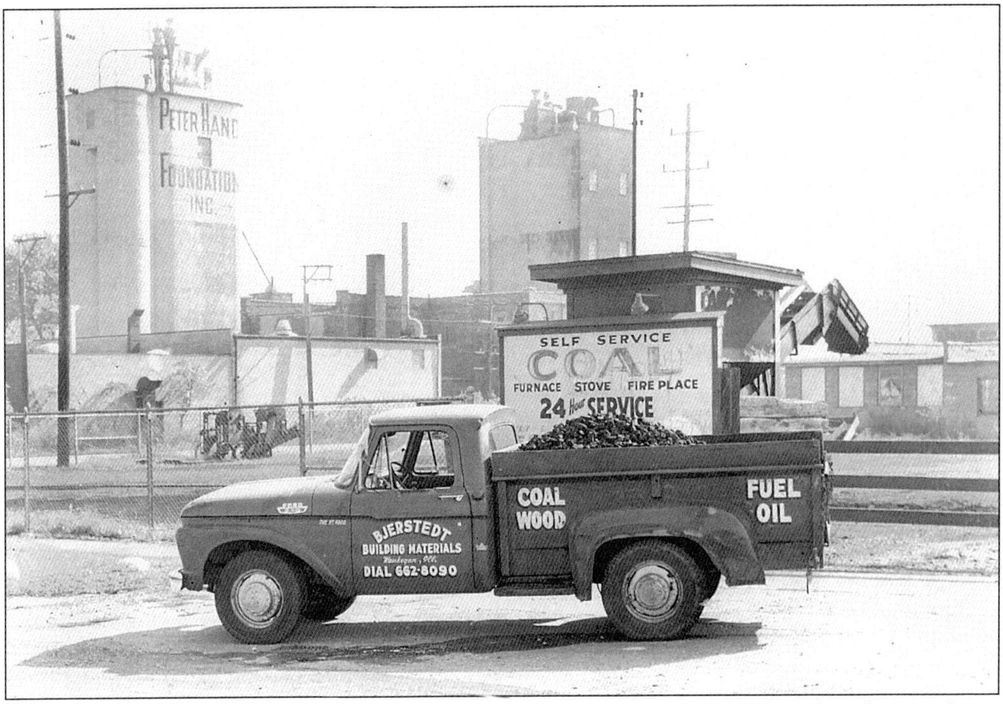

Coal was the primary home heating fuel for many years until replaced by oil and natural gas. Over that time span several companies provided coal to Waukegan customers. This photo shows what is claimed to be the last coal delivery made by Bjerstedt & Son Coal Co.

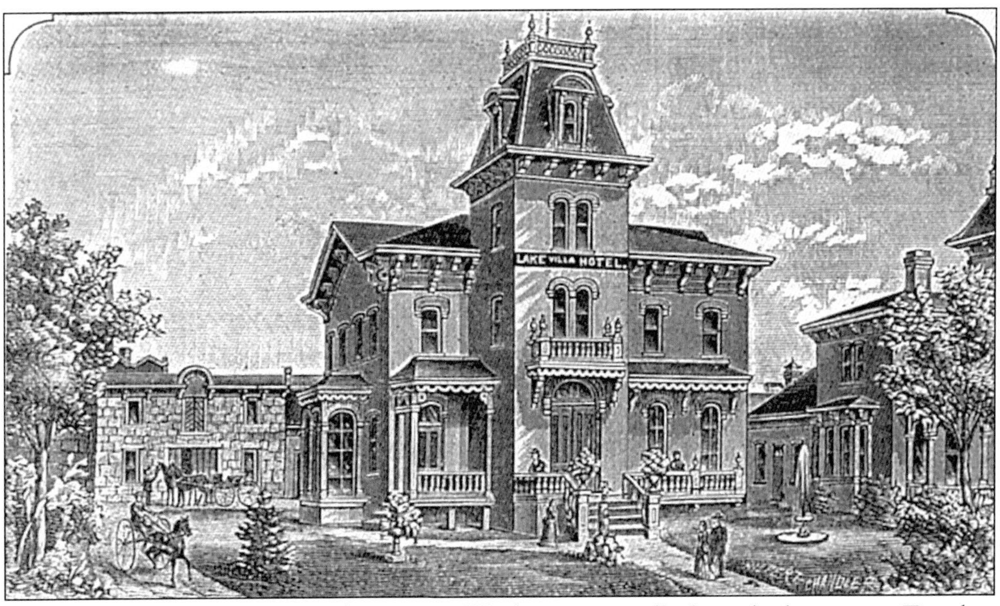

Hotels have been an important business in Waukegan, virtually from the beginning. Travelers between Chicago and Milwaukee, as well as farmers from western Lake County, often would spend the night. Others used the hotel as their primary residence. Among the early hotels was the Lake Villa on State Street (Sheridan Road). It offered unequalled accommodations and a livery, as well as medical and vapor baths.

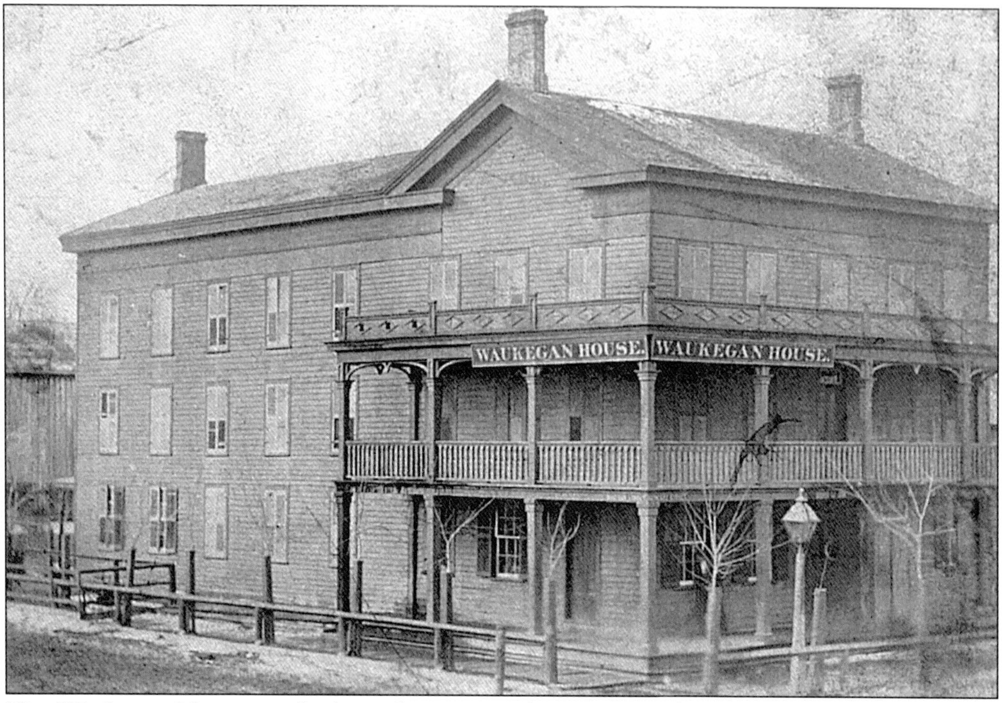

The Waukegan House was built at the corner of Genesee and Madison in 1846. The hotel featured a horse-drawn bus that met trains at the railroad station. Elm trees eventually surrounded the building and provided ample shade. The building was demolished in 1902 to allow for construction of the Murray Block.

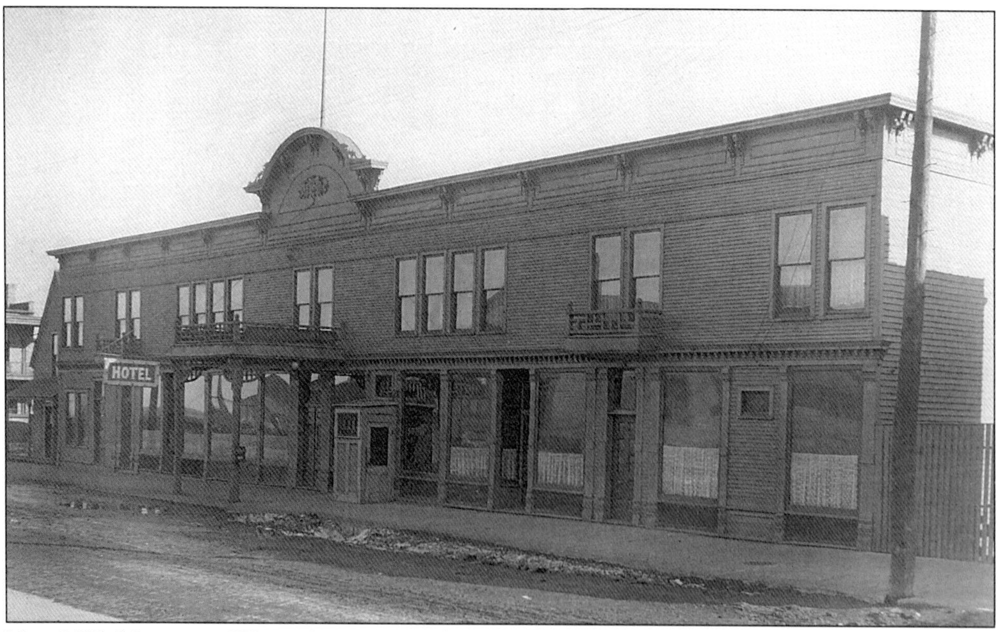

Hotel Washburn, on Water Street east of Genesee, opened in 1892. It was noted for lodging traveling salesmen. In 1913 it cost $2 a day, with an additional 50¢ if the patron wanted a room with bath. It was demolished in 1924.

The Fox Hotel, at 420 Washington, was originally the residence of Charles Fox. Built in the late 1840s, it was a Waukegan landmark until destroyed by fire on January 23, 1929.

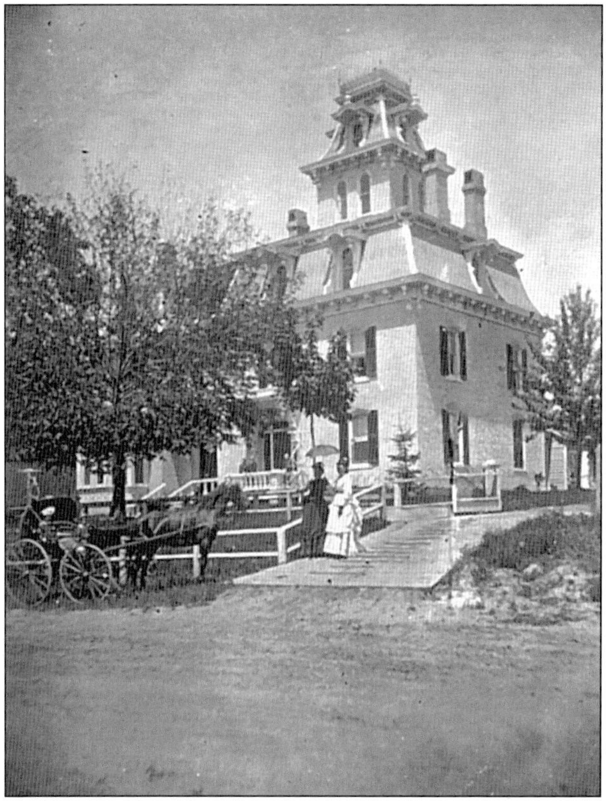

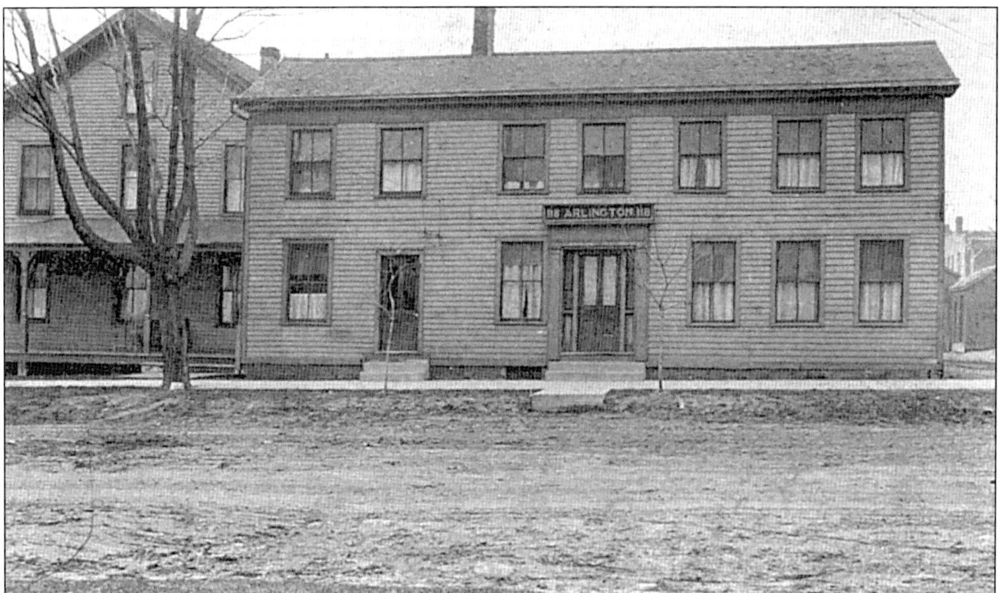

On County, between Washington and Water, a hotel opened in 1845 called the Farmers Rest. The name was soon changed to the City Hotel, and eventually to the Arlington in 1900. Prior to its demolition in 1947 it had served for 20 years as the ticket office and waiting room for the North Shore Line.

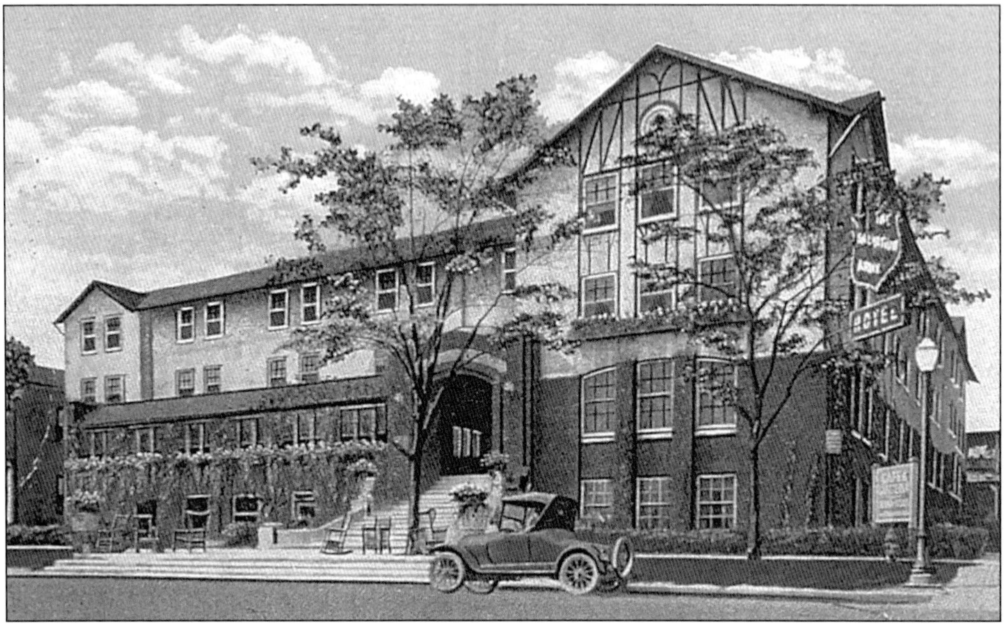

Built as the Salvation Army Hotel in 1921 and changed to the Clayton Hotel later that decade, this building was located at Clayton and Sheridan. It included 113 residential units, one of which was the site of the wedding of Jack Benny and Mary Livingstone. Finally determined to be unsafe, the hotel was demolished in 1963.

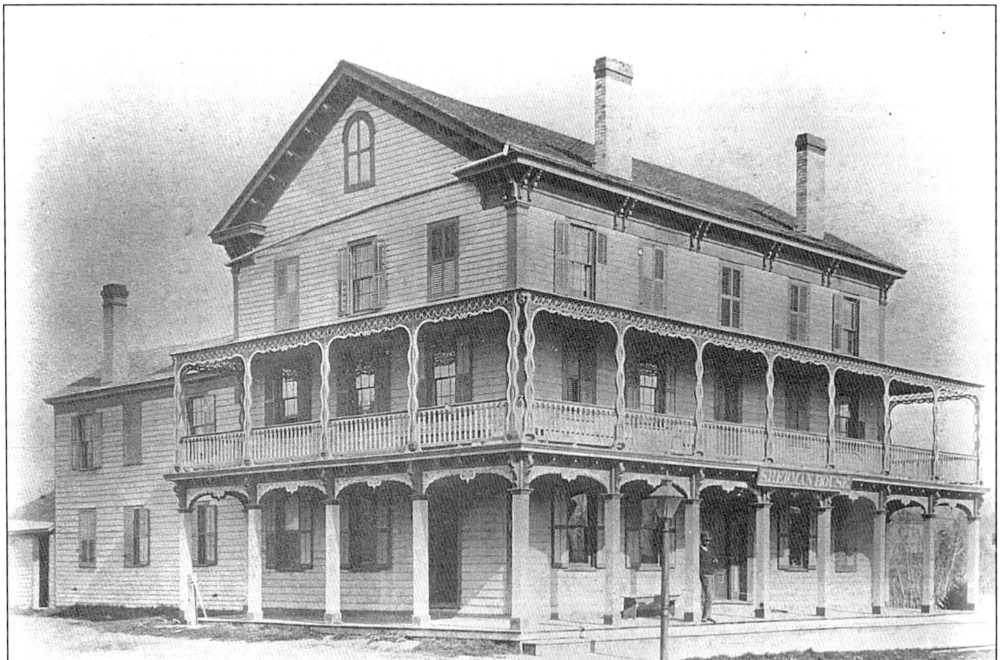

The Sherman Hotel, at Genesee and Lake, was built in 1852. It was the focal point for area farmers who sold their produce and livestock in front of the hotel, and then spent the night within. It was razed in the early 1920s.

Four

Industry

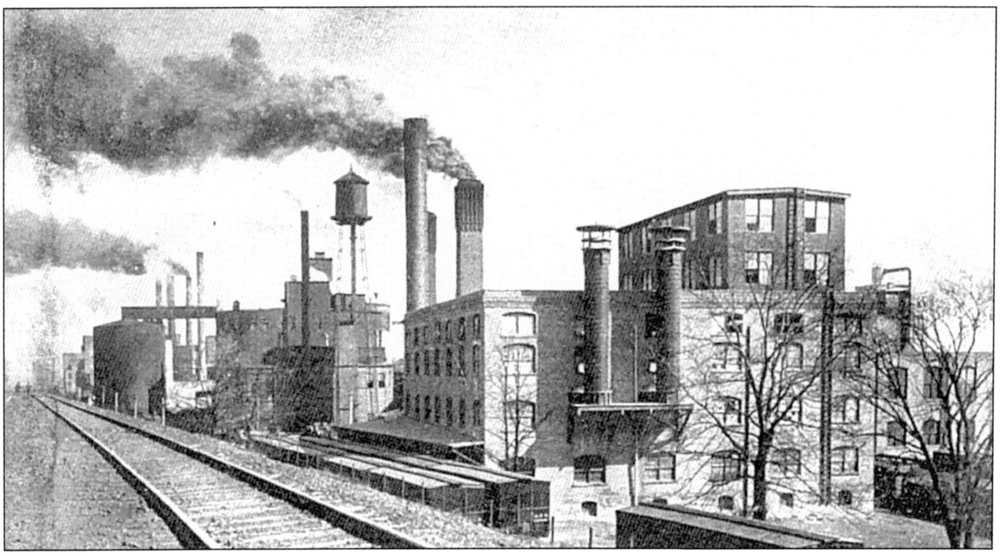

Through various names and a variety of owners, the sugar refinery operated sporadically from 1890 to 1913 at the south end of Market Street. Several explosions and fires marked the plant's existence over the years, but the one in November 1912 was the most notable. That occurrence, which killed 14 men, remains the worst industrial accident in Lake County history.

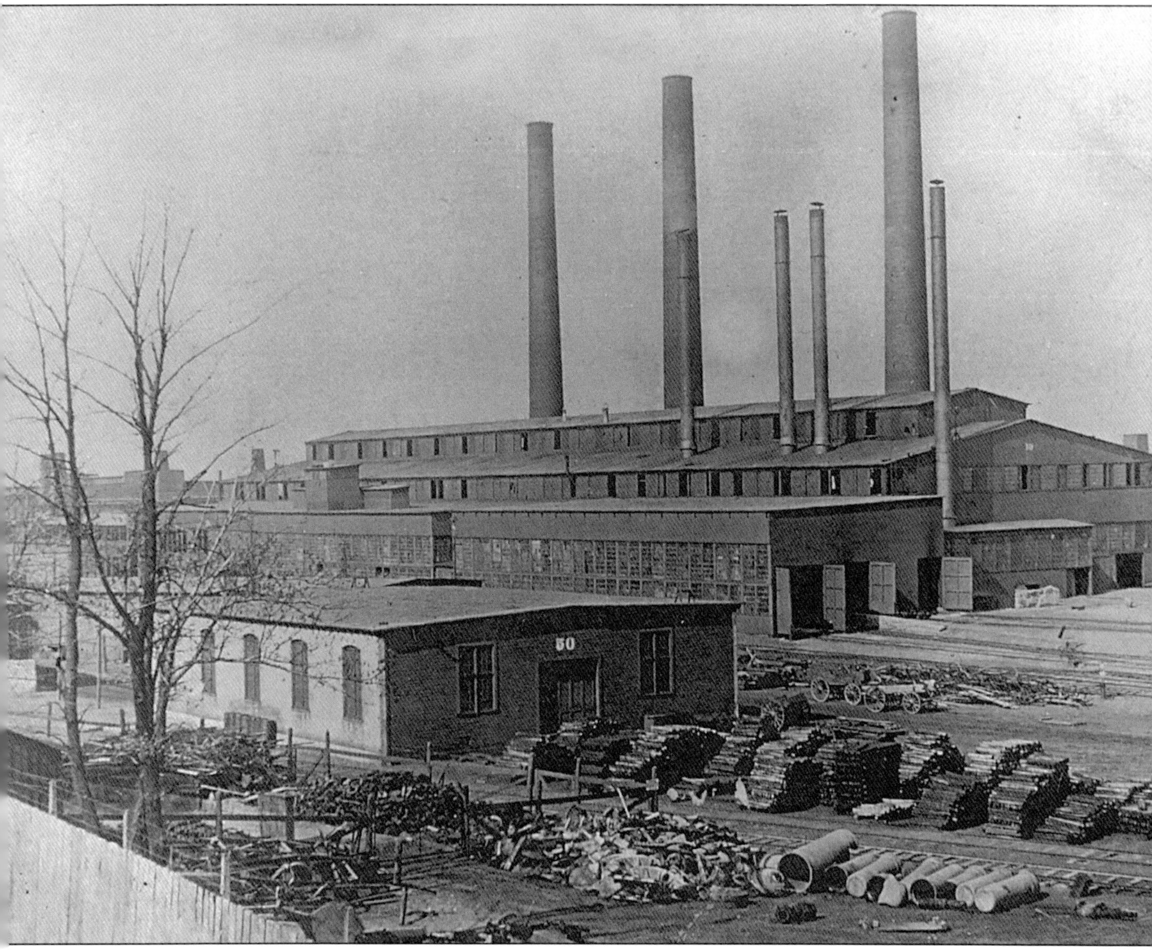

Washburn and Moen manufacturing of Worcester, Massachussetts, built a mill here in 1891. That mill was acquired by American Steel and Wire Company in 1899. Later it became part of the United States Steel Corporation and continued to operate into the 1970s, when it closed.

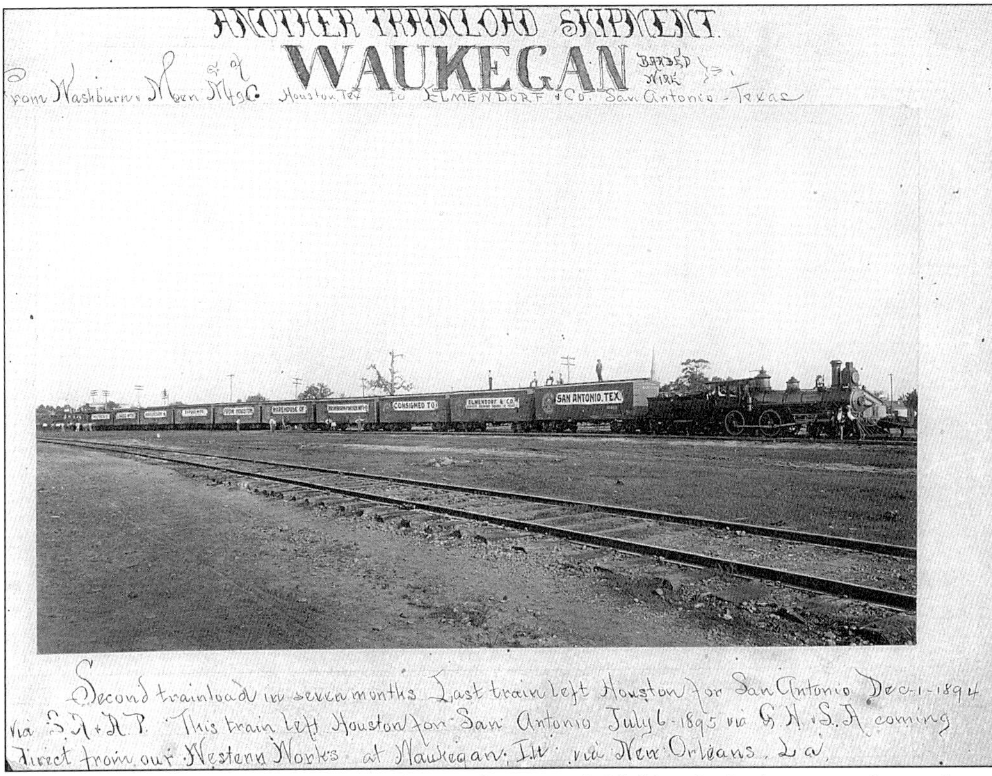

Washburn and Moen was a principal manufacturer of Glidden barbed wire, and introduced Waukegan barbed wire in 1892. That wire was used throughout the country, and demand for the product even necessitated entire trains, such as this one bound for San Antonio.

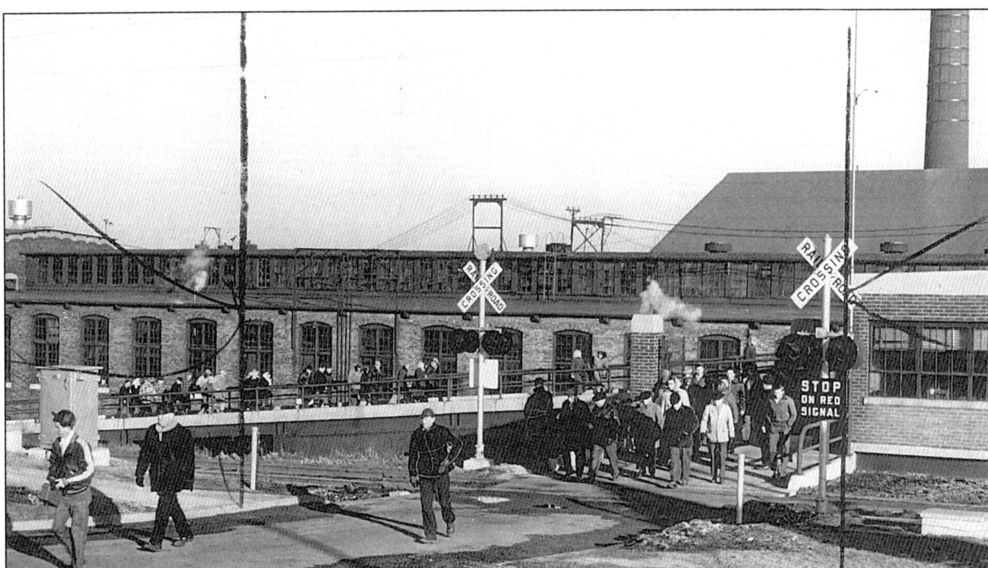

The Wire Mill employed thousands over the years and was instrumental in large population growth, specifically from Eastern European countries. Along with other lakefront manufacturers, the mill helped Waukegan become the ethnically diverse place it is.

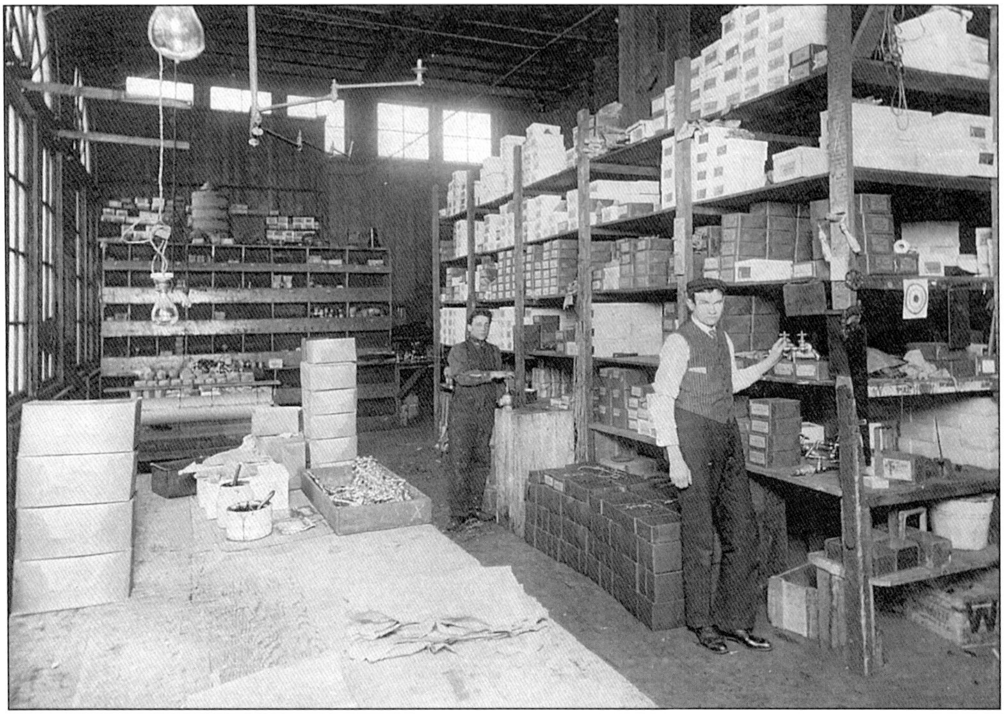

The Thomas Brass and Iron Co. arrived about 1895 and set up business at the lakefront between Washington and Madison Streets. Faucets were one of the items manufactured. The plant burned to the ground in July 1910.

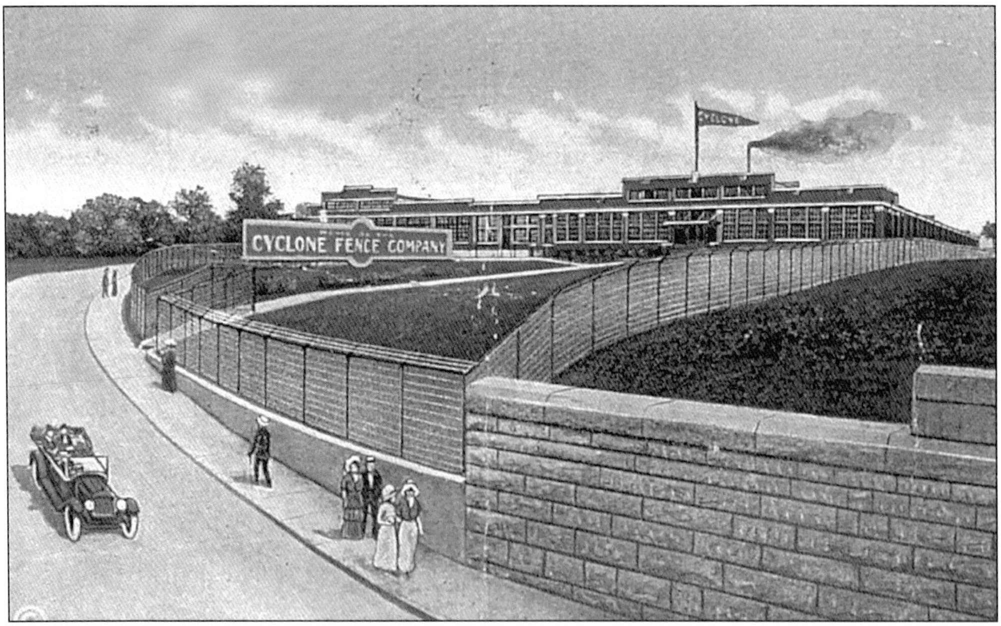

Originally known as the Cyclone Woven Wire Fence Co., this company began operating locally before 1900. As The Cyclone Fence Co., it became the world's largest manufacturer of ornamental fencing and gates. As early as 1911, over 125 men were employed by the company.

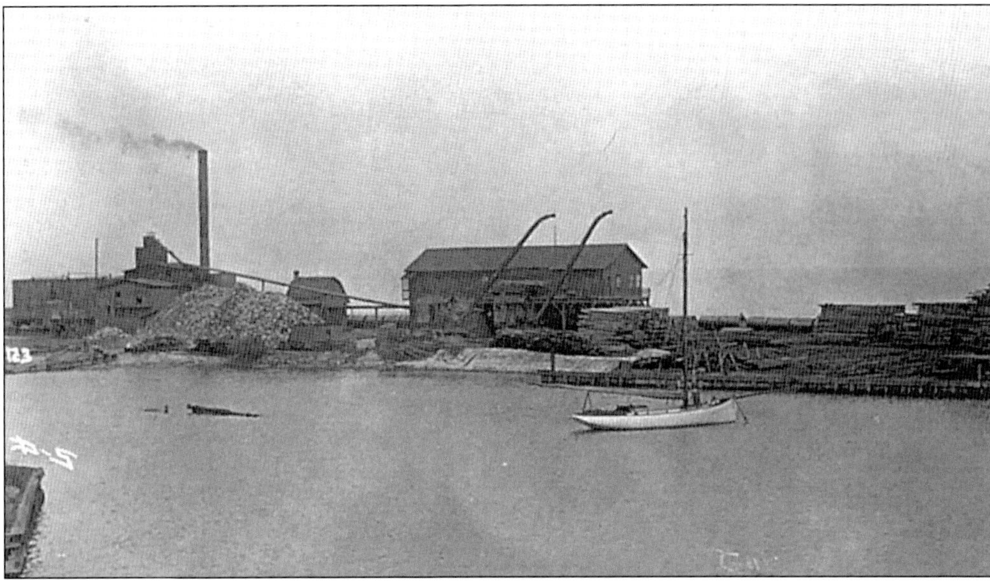

Whether called Chicago Creosoting or Chicago Tie and Timber, this business was concerned with treating railroad ties. It operated at the harbor around 1910.

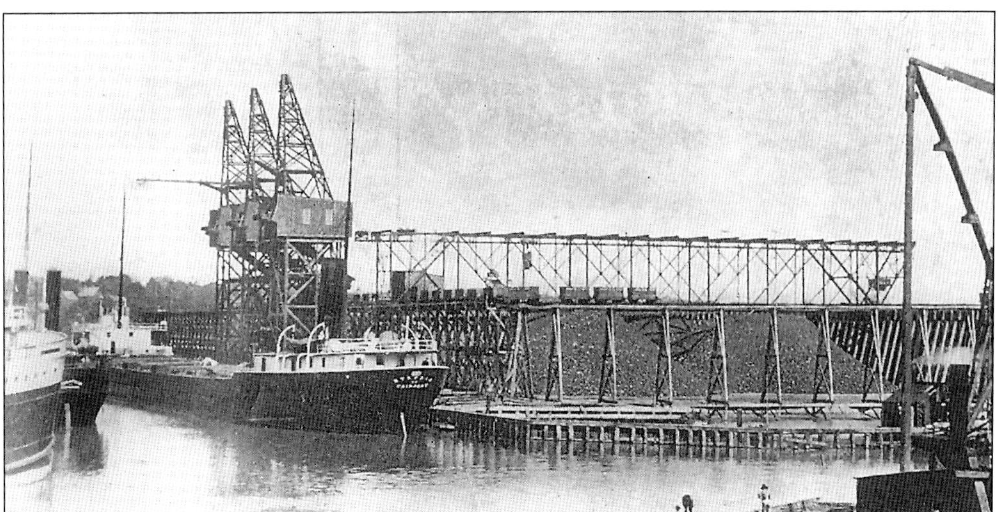

Western Coal and Dock Co. began receiving anthracite coal in 1899 in their private water slip and stored it in their 5-acre storage area before moving it around the country via rail. In 1902 they doubled capacity and began to handle bituminous coal as well.

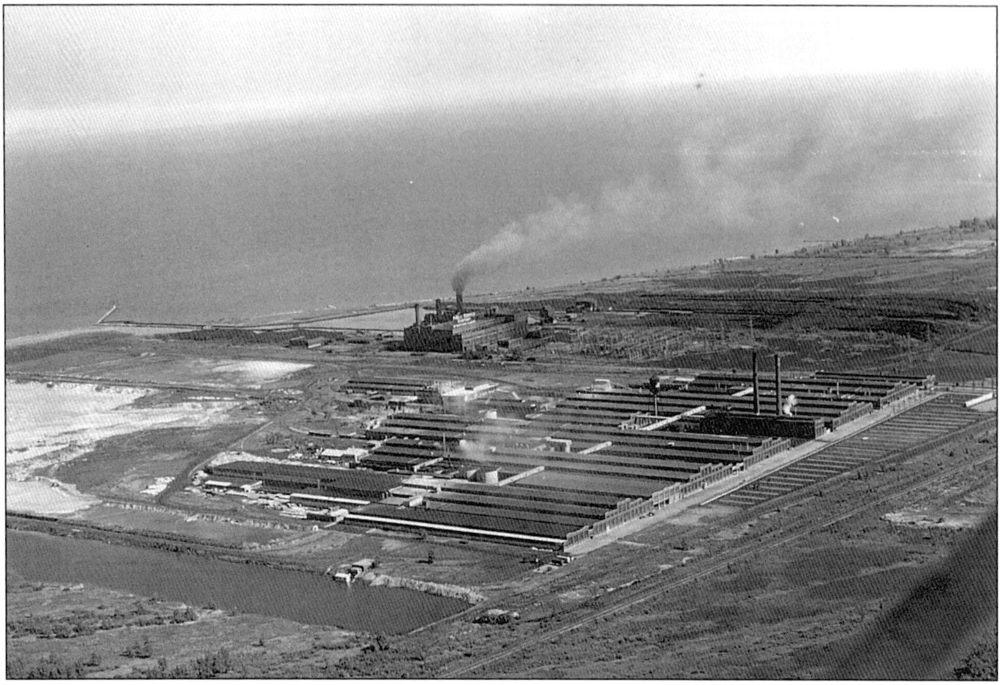

Johns-Manville began building their $15 million plant in 1922. The company was the world's largest manufacturer of asbestos products, such as insulation, roofing, and brake linings. Over 3,000 were employed at the plant's peak, making it one of the largest factories in Waukegan.

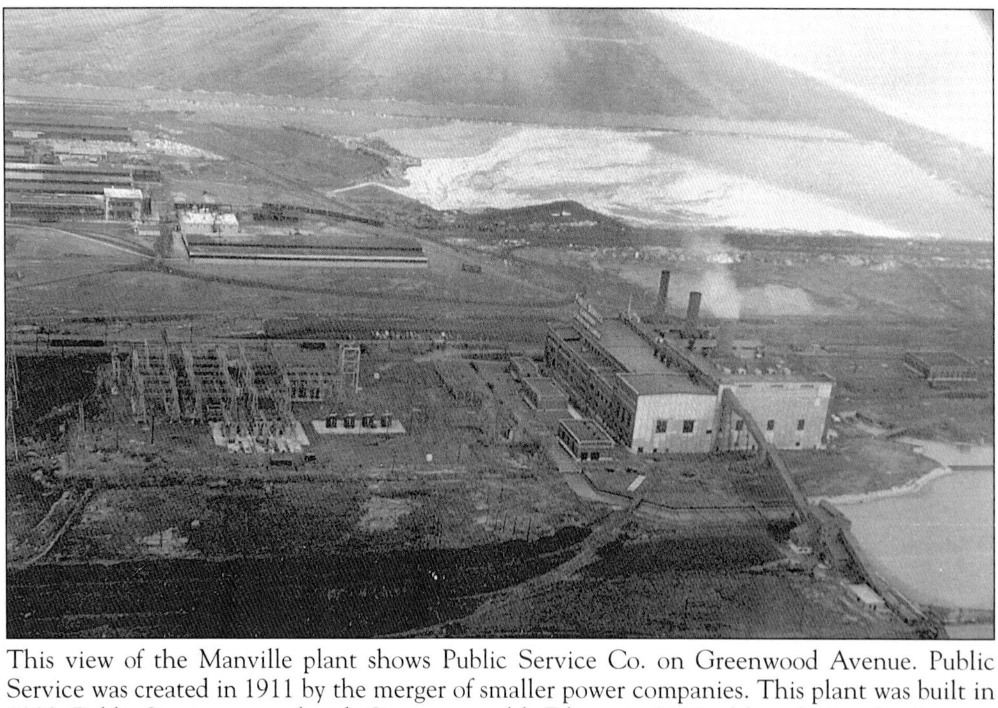

This view of the Manville plant shows Public Service Co. on Greenwood Avenue. Public Service was created in 1911 by the merger of smaller power companies. This plant was built in 1923. Public Service merged with Commonwealth Edison in 1937, although the plant's name wasn't changed until the mid-1960s.

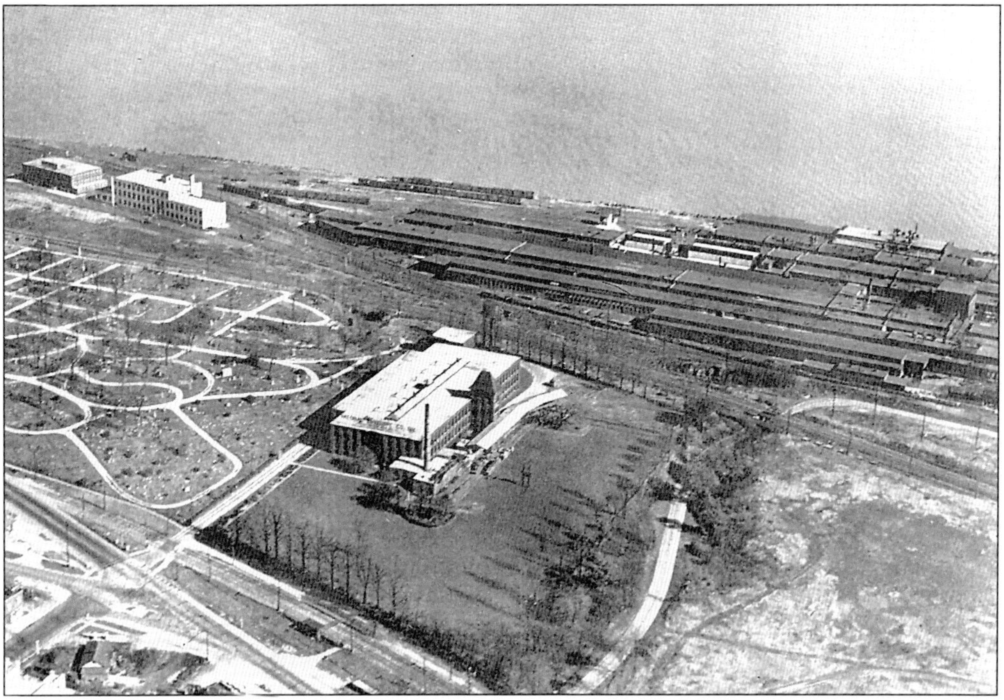

National Envelope came to the area in 1904. Envelopes, stationery, tablets, and school supplies were manufactured at the plant and distributed throughout the southern and western sections of the country. Work continued at the factory until it was closed in the 1990s.

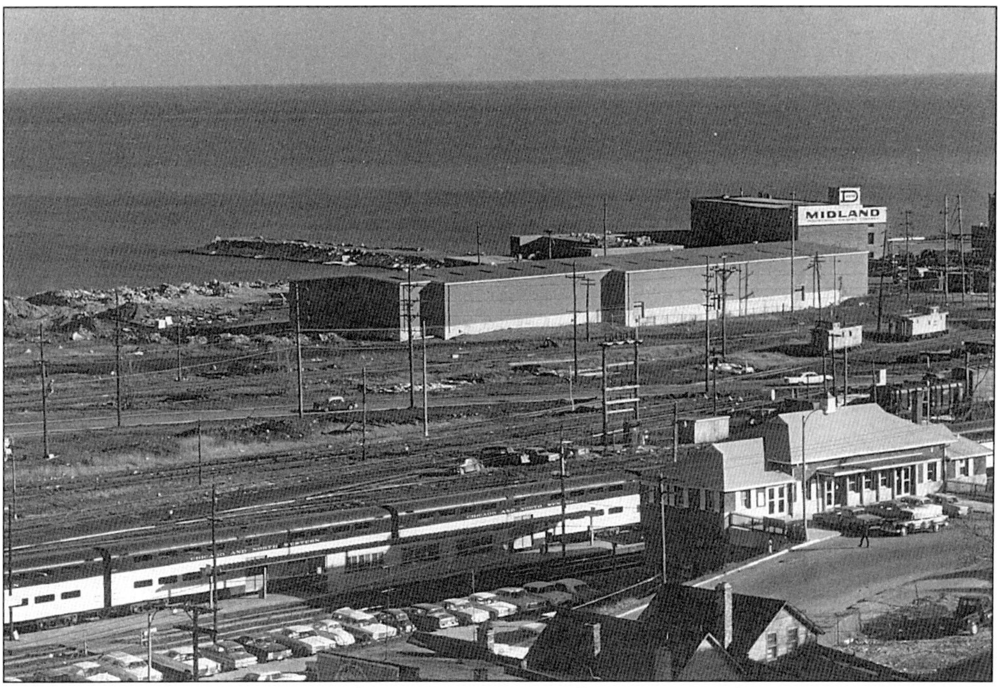

Midland Industrial Finishes Co. began in 1939 to sell coatings to the U.S. Government. It became part of the Dexter Corporation in 1963.

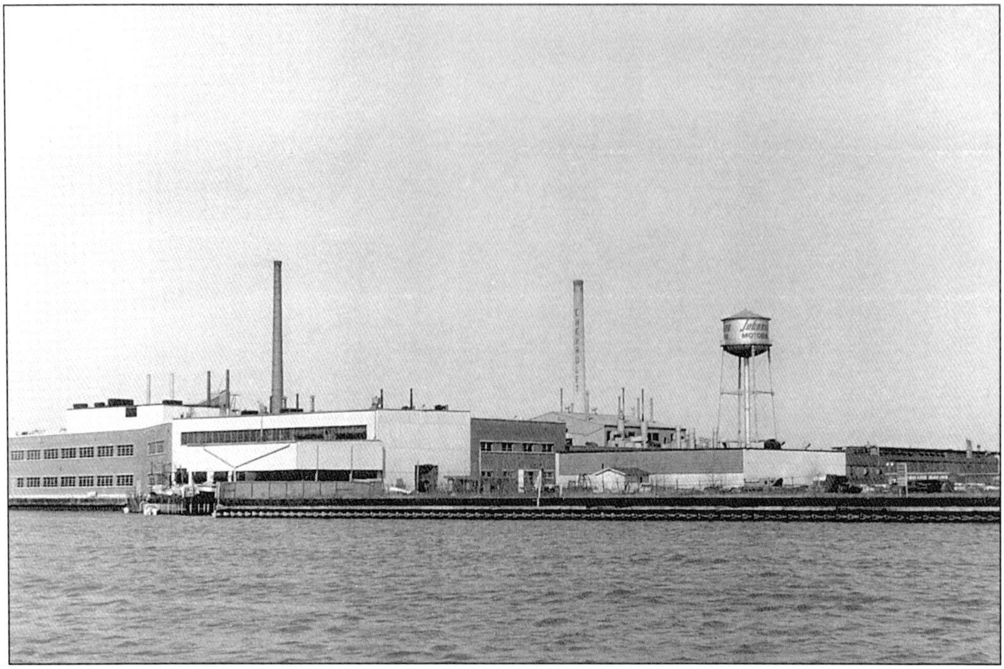

Johnson Motors moved to Waukegan from South Bend, Indiana, in 1927. Outboard Marine purchased the plant in 1936. Outboard motor manufacturing made the plant one of the largest employers in Waukegan. It took until 1952 for the one millionth motor to be made, but only until 1959 for the two millionth.

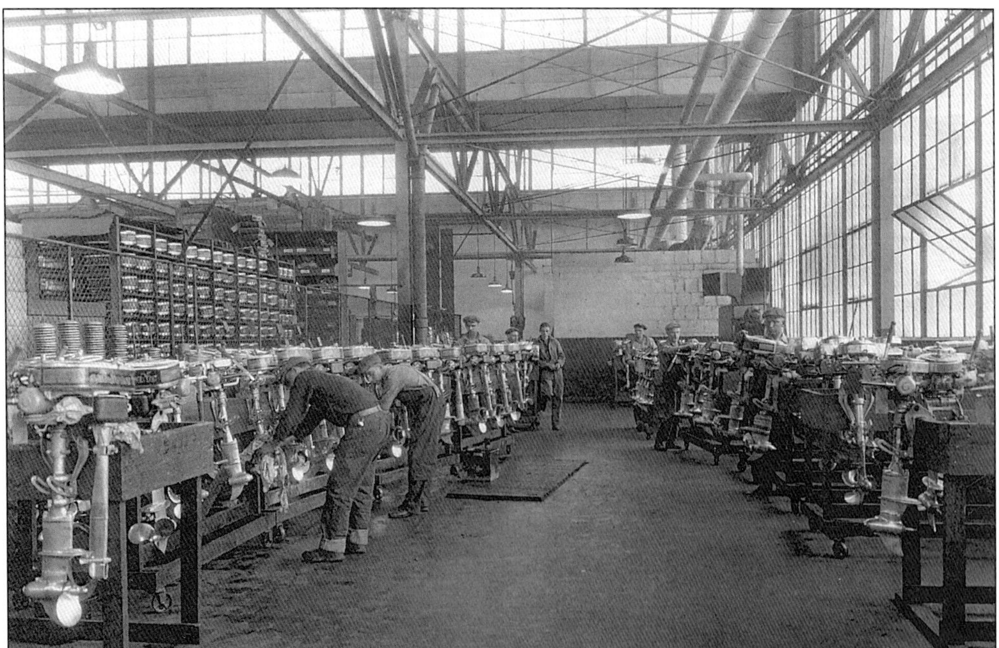

Great care was taken in the manufacture of the motors. Here they are given a final inspection prior to packing for distribution.

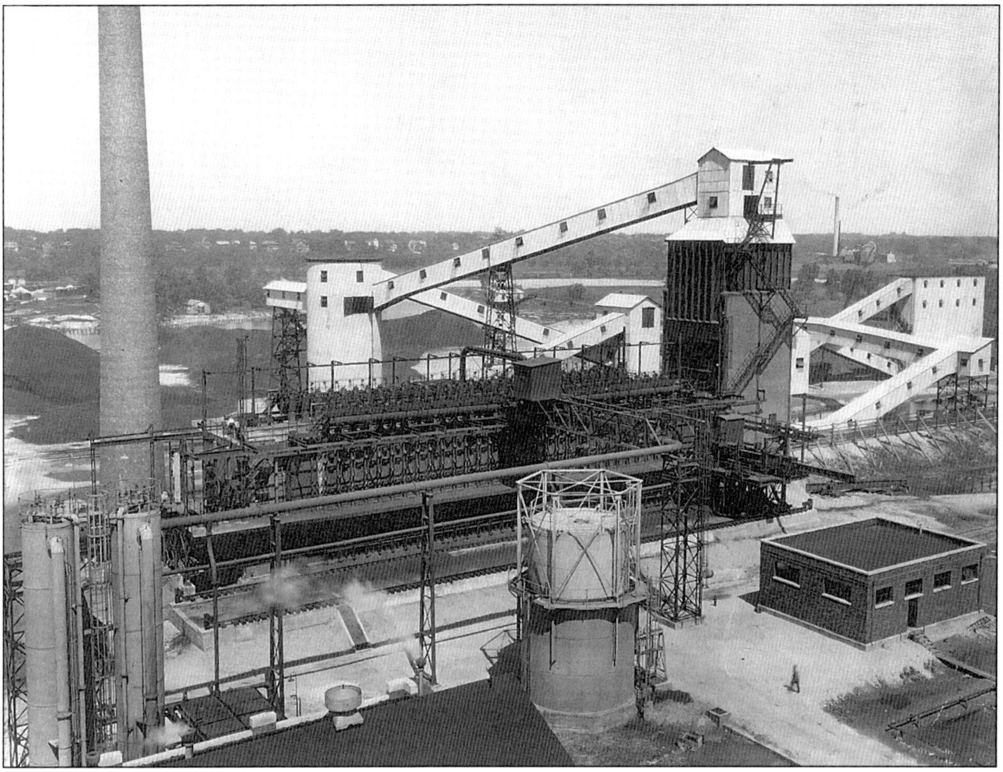

North Shore Coke and Chemical Company began producing coke here in 1928. The property went to North Shore Gas in 1941 and then to General Motors in 1947. Chevrolet-Saginaw continued to produce coke until 1971.

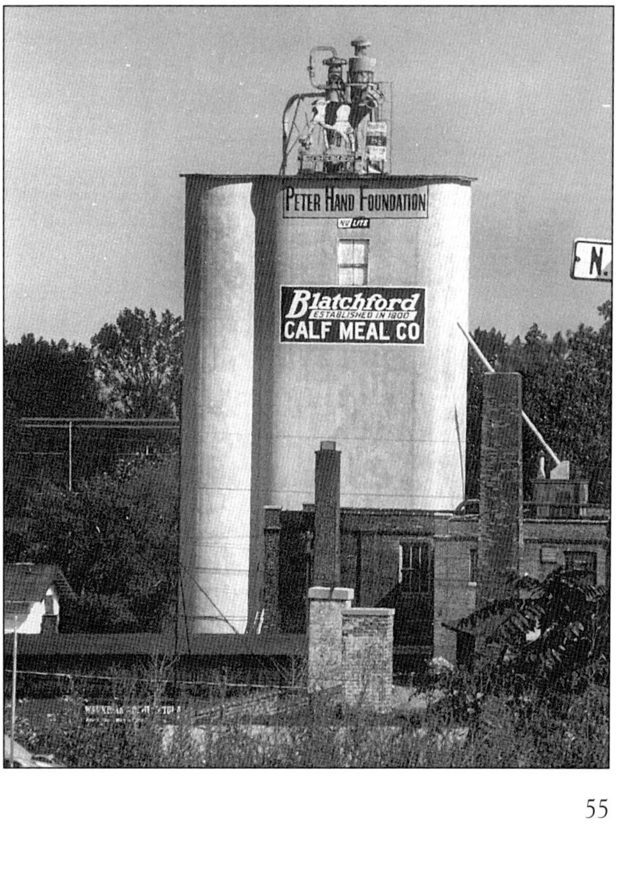

In 1900 John W. Barwell brought his animal food company to Waukegan, a full century after it began in England. Blatchford's Calf Meal was only one of the feeds produced. Poultry, horses, and lambs were also fed from here, and a variety of agricultural products such as fertilizer, grass seed, and sheep dip were produced as well.

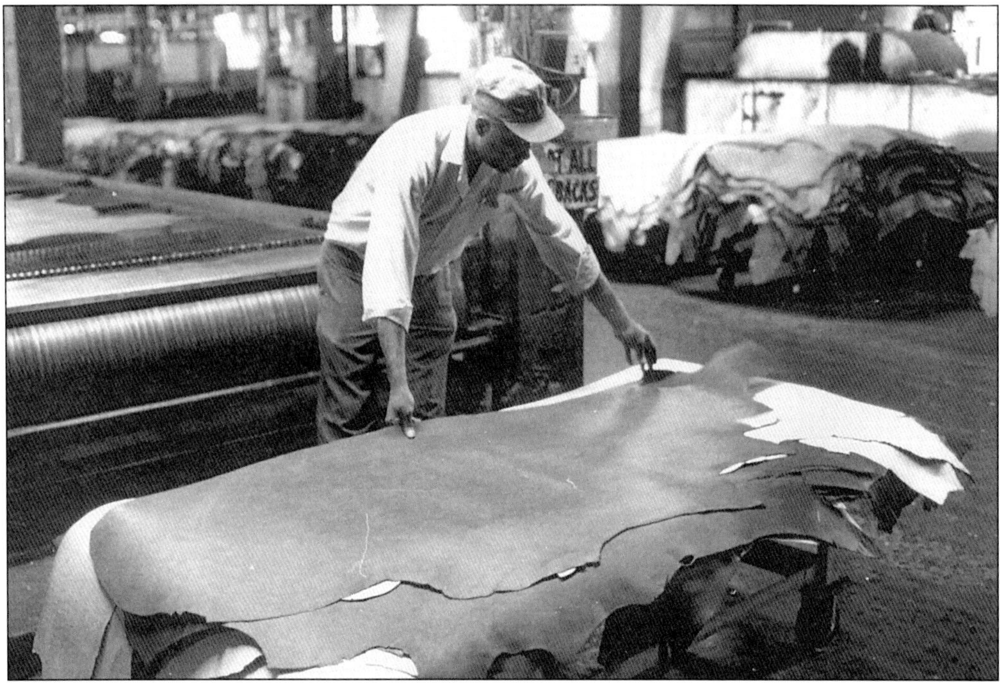

Several tanneries were located on the lakefront over the years, going back to Theobold Herberger in the 1860s. Manning Leather began in Waukegan in 1883 and in 1899 became Wilder-Manning. A new tannery was constructed in 1915 and was taken over by Griess-Pfleger two years later.

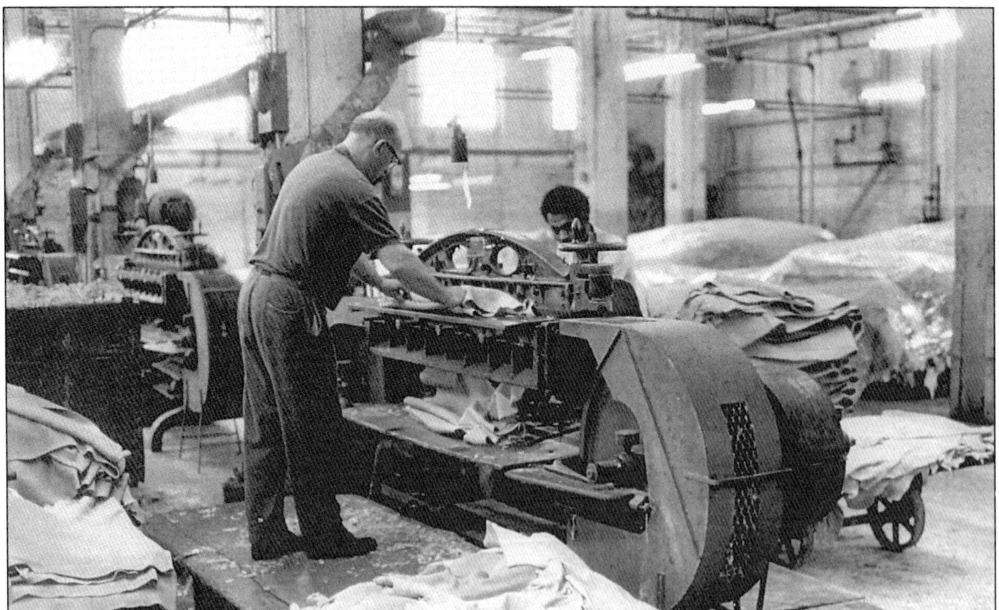

Almost one thousand men were employed at the peak of production. Five thousand cowhides and 2,500 calf hides were processed daily, and the hides were turned into leather in five to six weeks. The plant ceased operations in 1973.

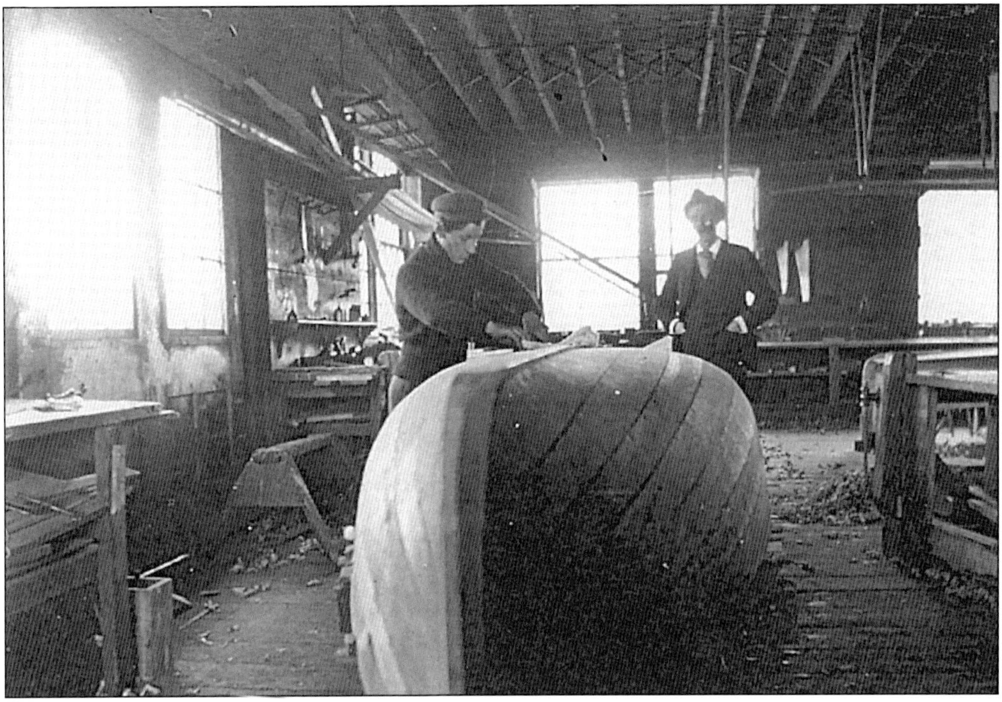

At the end of Madison stood the Douglas boat works. Before 1900 the company claimed to be the builder of the greatest number and variety of boats in the U.S.

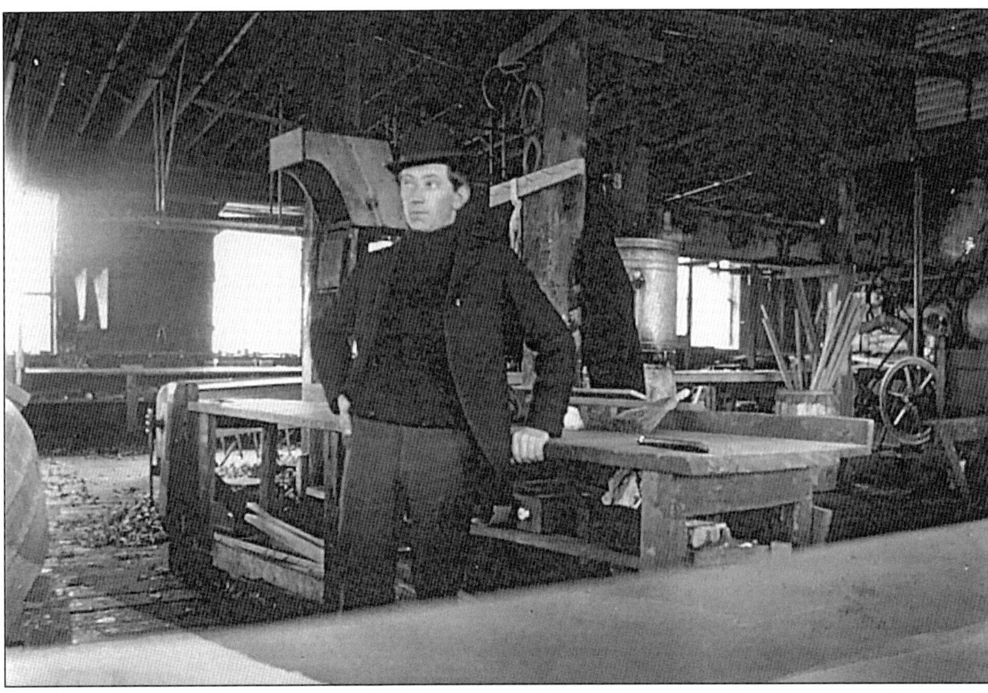

For 15¢ a boat catalogue was available. It was probably quite extensive since Douglas carried three hundred to one thousand boats, from canoes to steam launches. Whether the customer wanted a boat powered by coal, wood, or oil, it was not a problem for the R.J. Douglas Co.

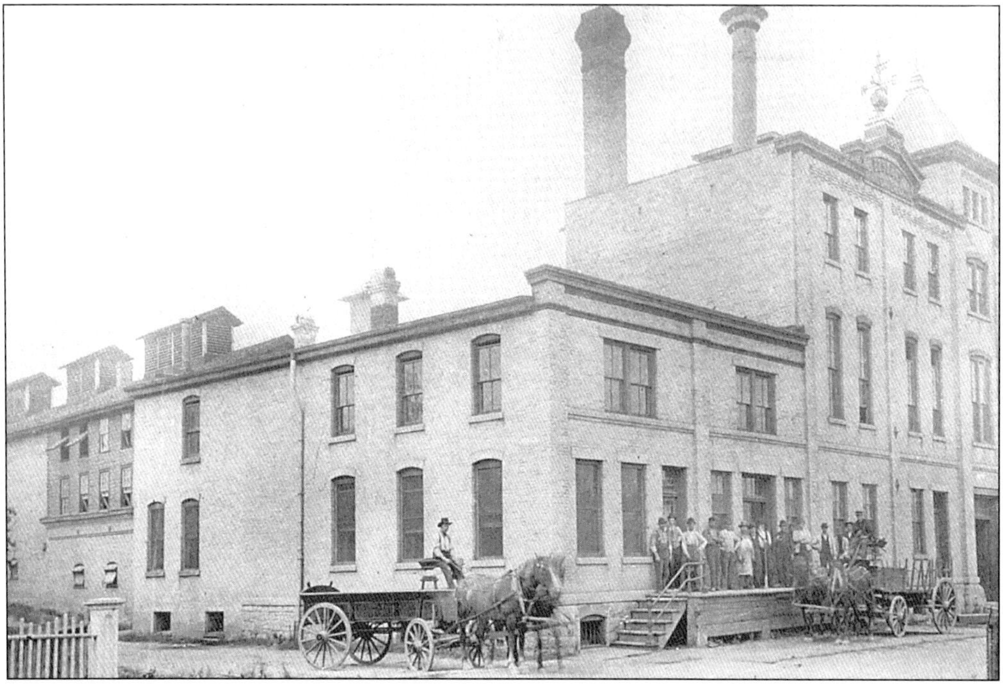

William Besley began the Waukegan Brewing Company in 1853 in a building along Belvidere Road. He was born in England and his father was also a brewer. Porter and ale were the primary products, and even elicited testimonials for their medical benefits.

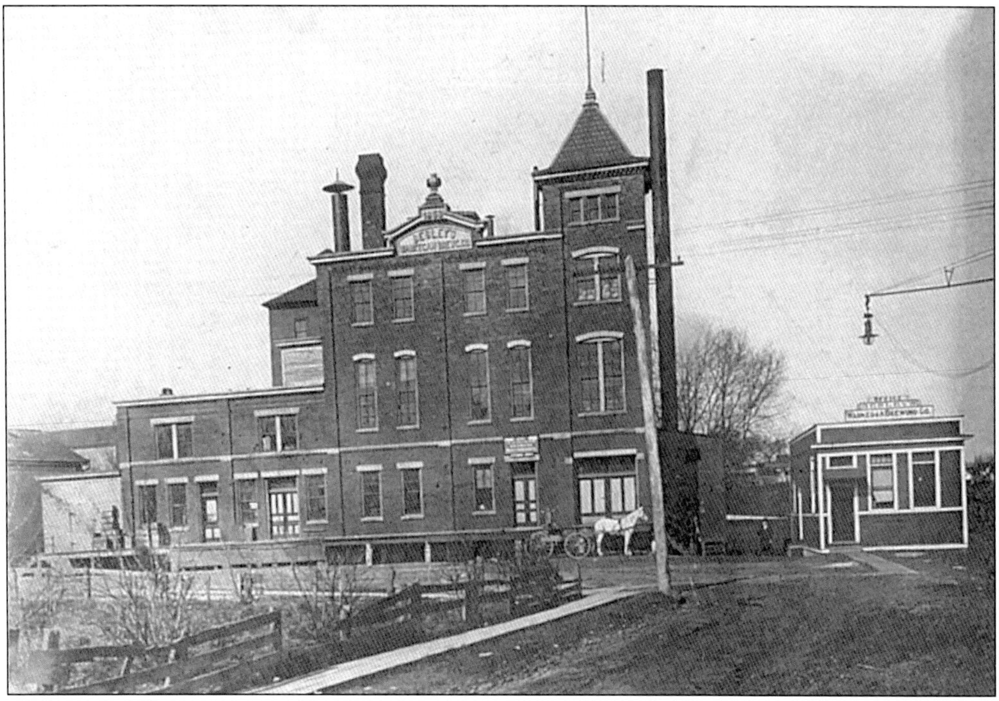

Besley expanded into a new brewery on Utica Street and a malt house on Sheridan Road, while the Belvidere site became a bottling house. In 1897 it cost $4.75 for a case of two dozen quarts.

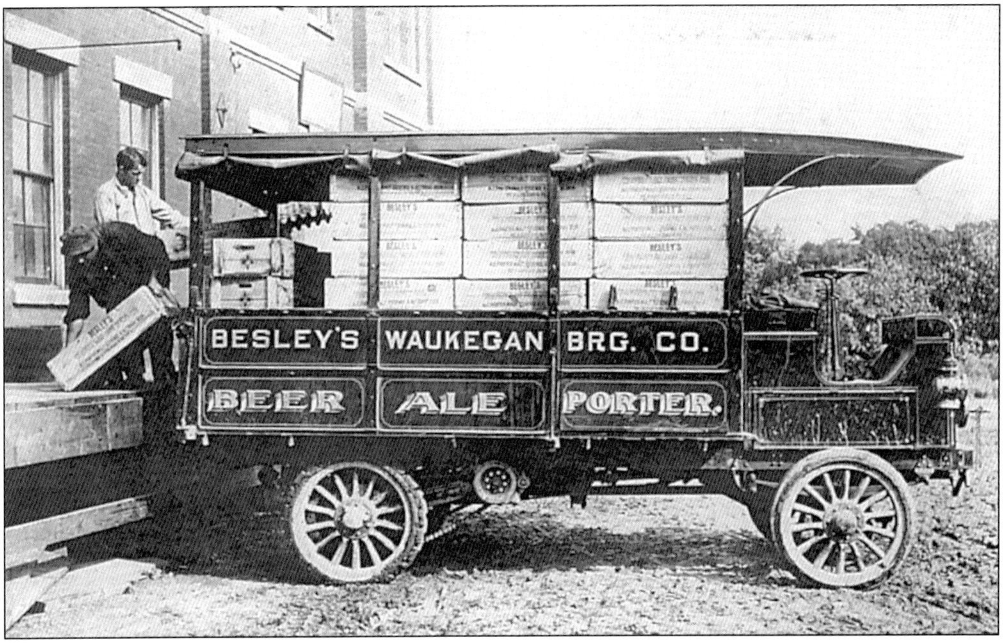

The Besley family ran the brewery until selling it in 1912. The coming of Prohibition forced the closing of the business in 1916, and it never re-opened.

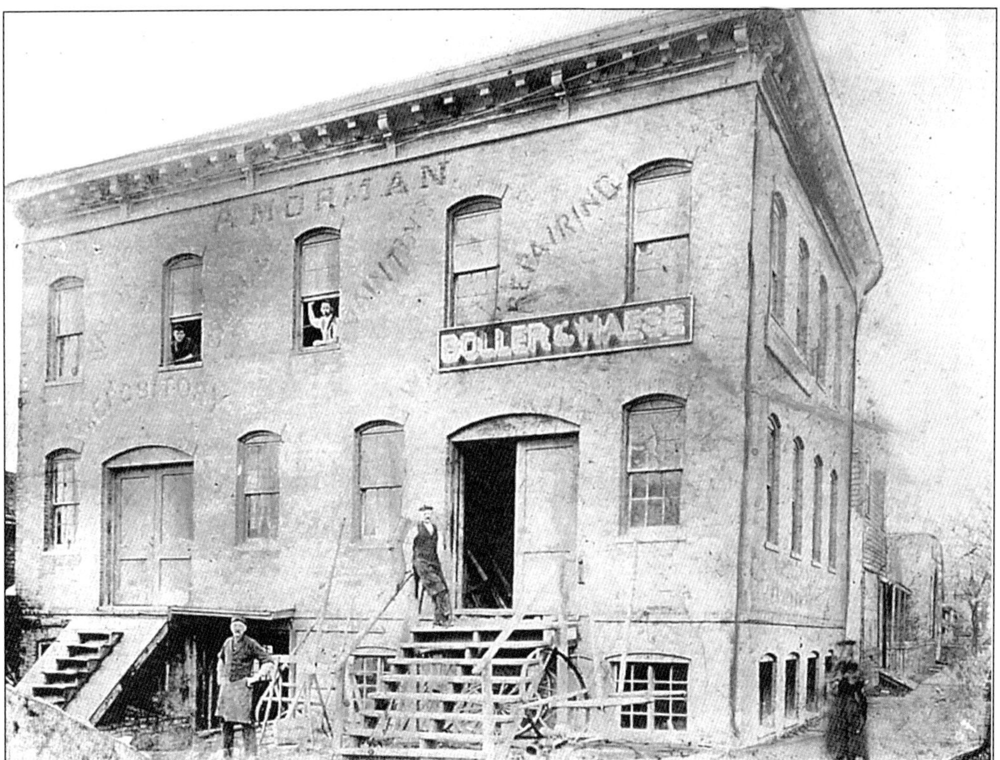

All your carriage, wagon, and sleigh needs could be handled by Frederick Boller and John Haese in their shop at Washington and County. Their partnership ended by 1900.

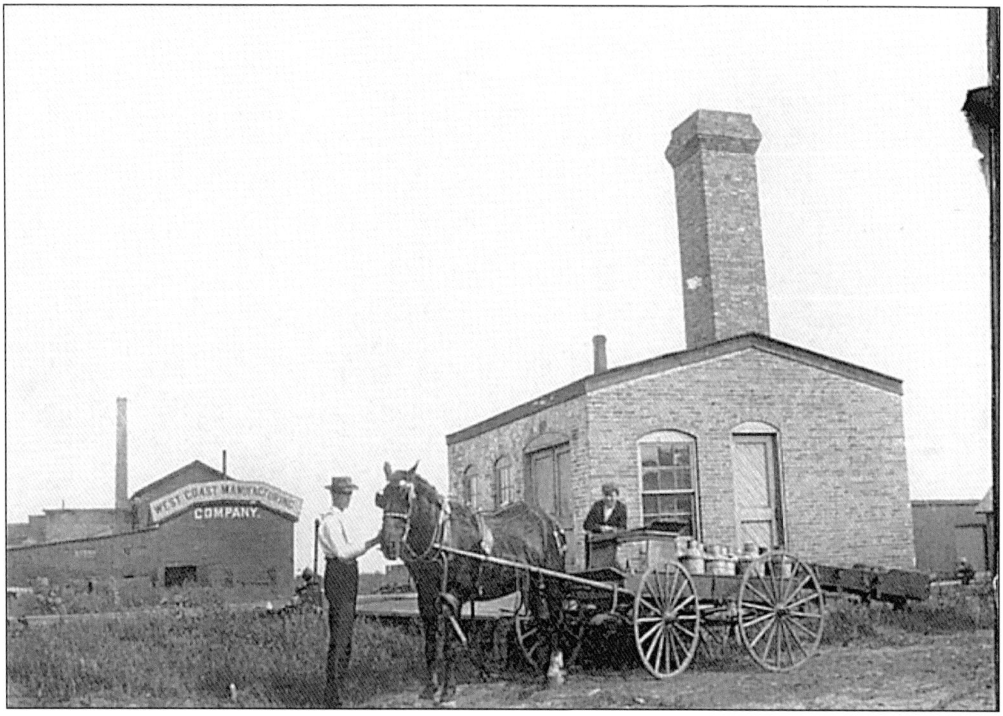

West Coast Manufacturing came to the area around 1897, but didn't stay too long. It produced roofing materials.

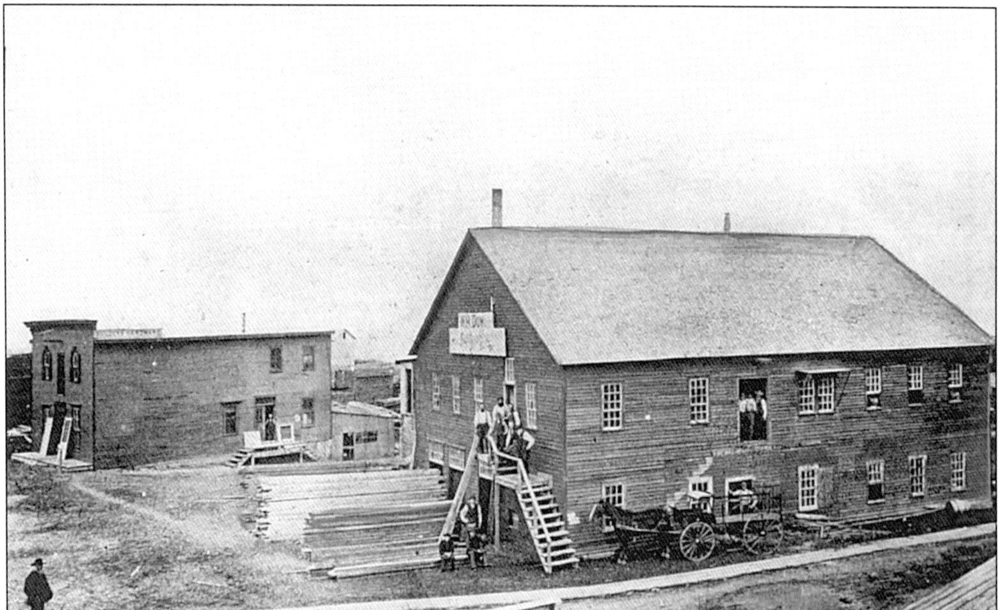

W.H. Dow manufactured sashes, doors, blinds, and mouldings at their factory in Waukegan. The location did change over the years, but always remained near the lakefront. One move was necessitated because the plant was in the way of the EJ & E Railroad. The company produced much of the material used in developing Waukegan.

Five

TRANSPORTATION

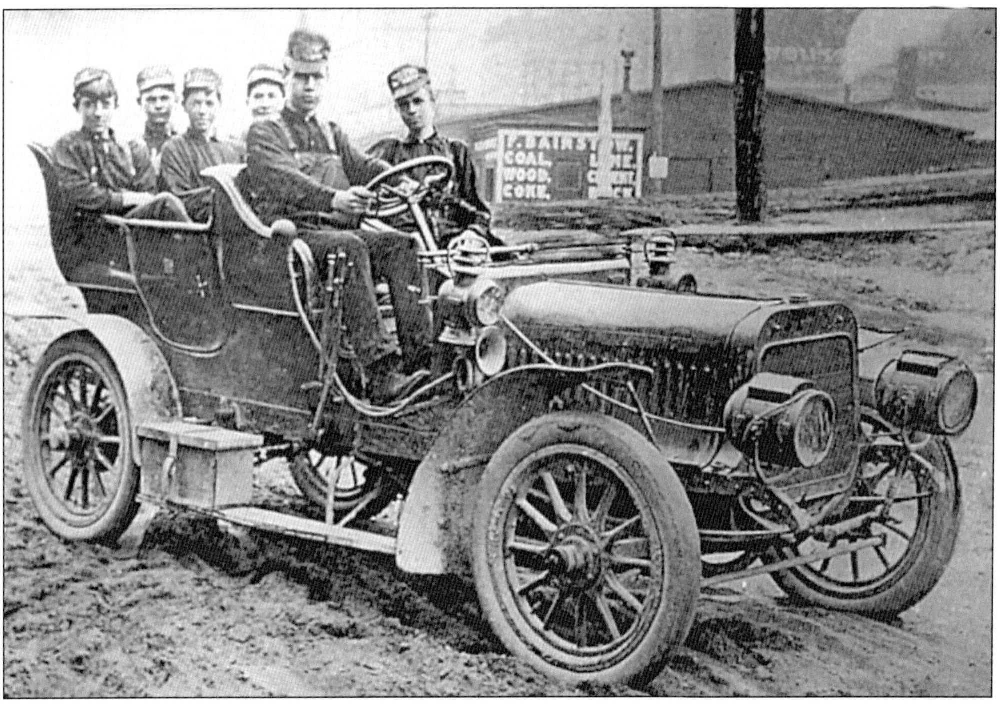

Waukegan had its own automobile in the early part of the 1900s. The Apollo was made at the Chicago Recording Scale Co. at Spring and Madison. It was built to hold five persons and its design allowed for speeds up to 60 miles per hour. Success of the venture was doubtful since the manufacturing lasted only a couple of years.

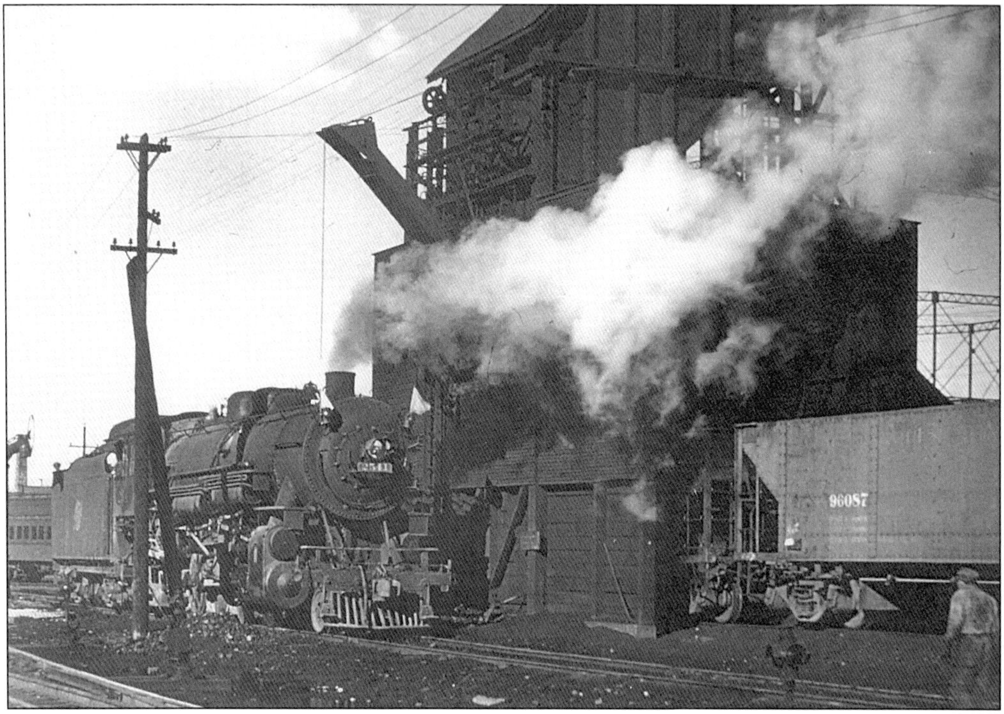

Railroads were an essential part of Waukegan's industrial development. Supplies for the factories and the finished products moved in and out of the city via the EJ & E or Chicago and Northwestern railroads.

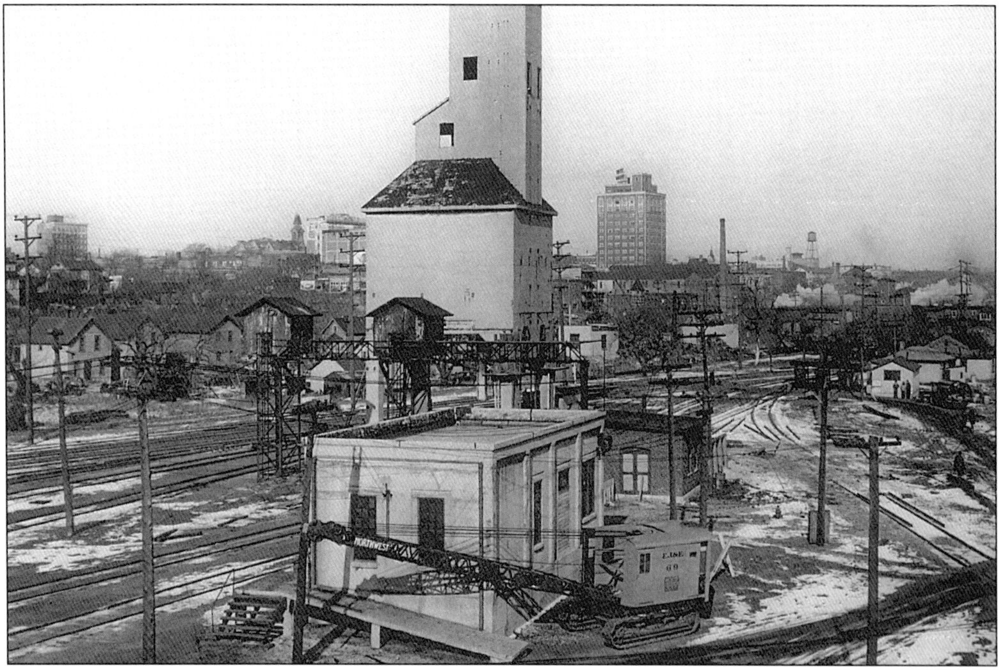

The rail yards could seem to be a confusing maze of tracks, but it worked for the railroads. This EJ & E area was watched over by the city's taller buildings.

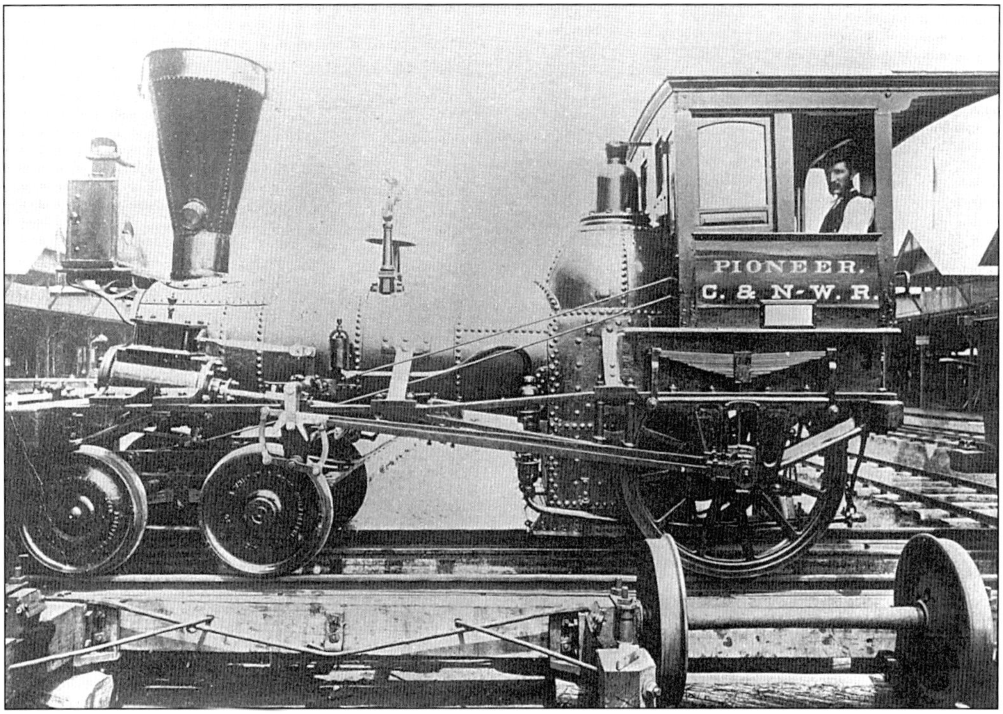

The Chicago & Northwestern RR first entered Waukegan on January 11, 1855, even though the line was still called the Chicago and Milwaukee RR. That was a significant milestone for the city and was probably powered by an engine much like this recreation.

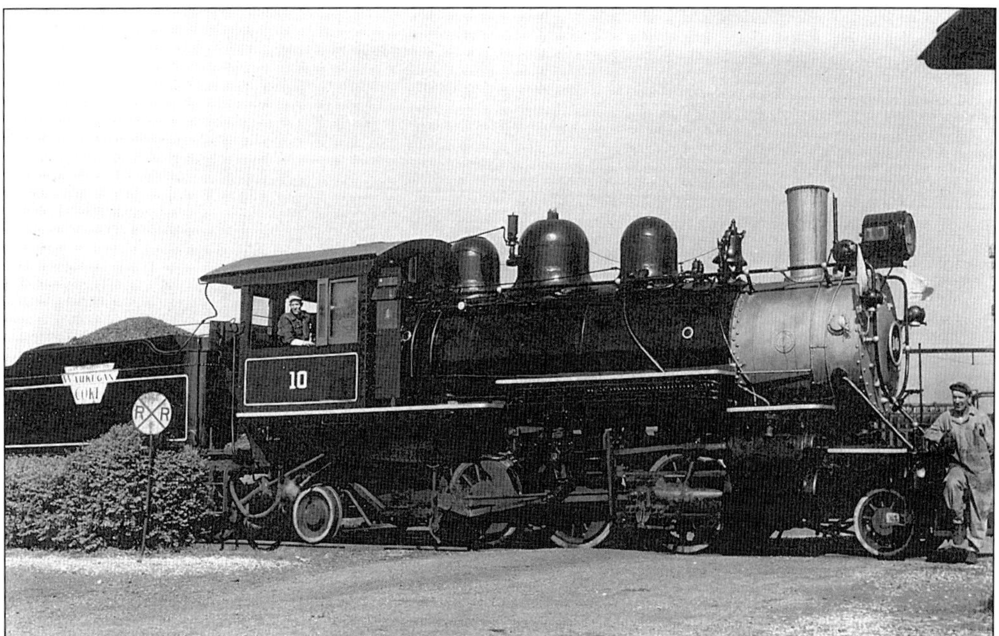

Trains could use the coke produced in Waukegan to power the engine because it was a "clean, smokeless fuel."

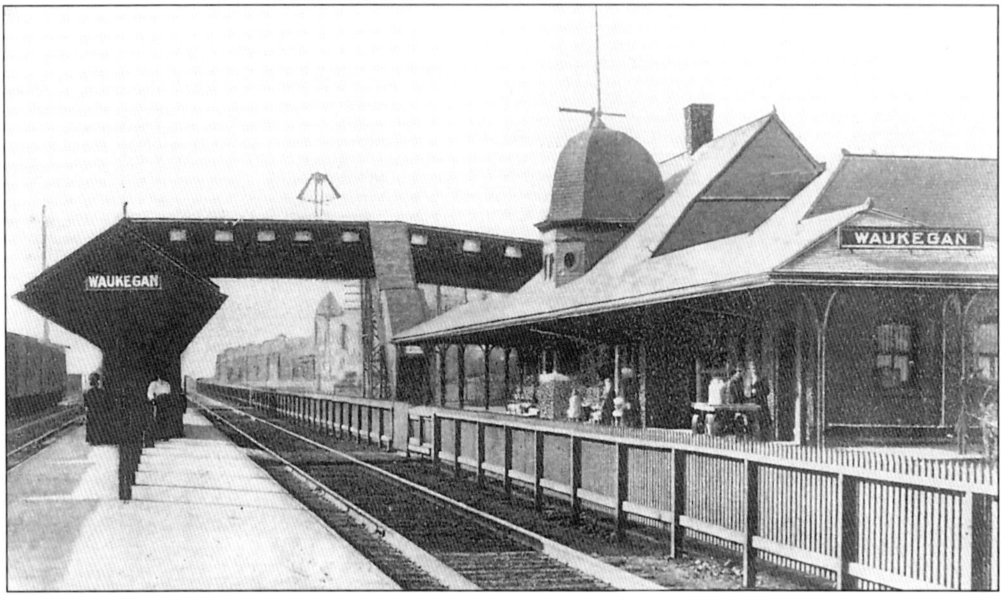

The Northwestern station has had several variations. This picture is dated 1911, but it is uncertain when the overhead walkway was constructed.

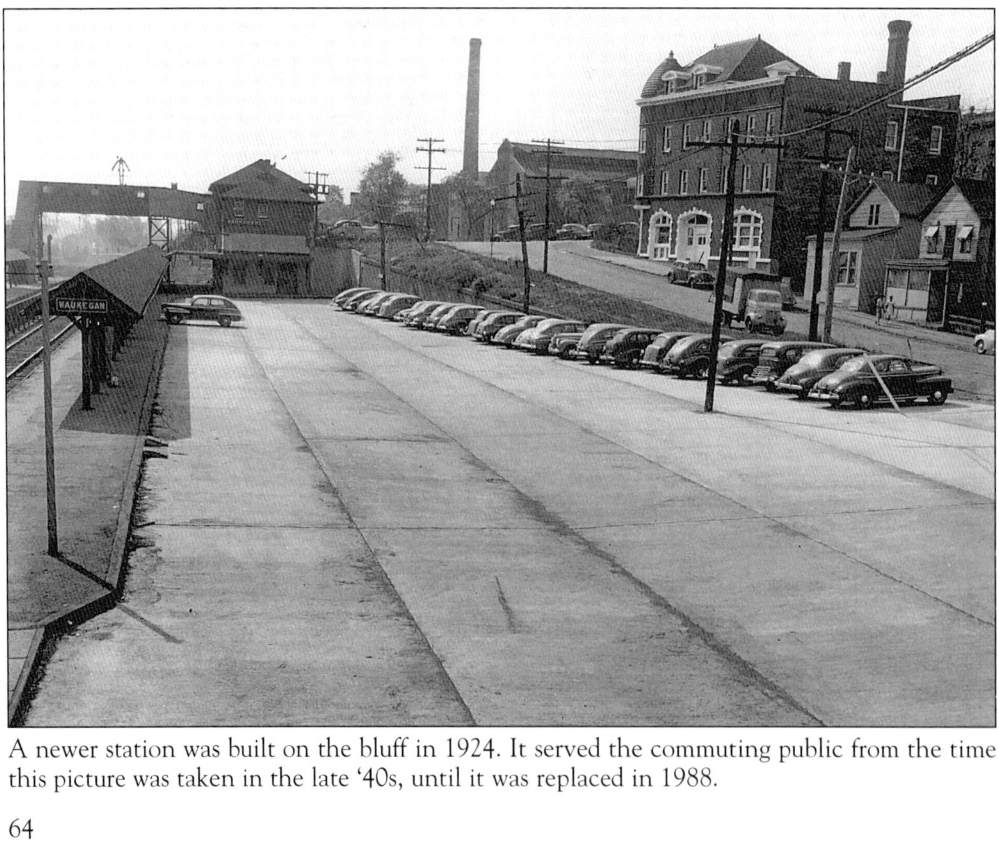

A newer station was built on the bluff in 1924. It served the commuting public from the time this picture was taken in the late '40s, until it was replaced in 1988.

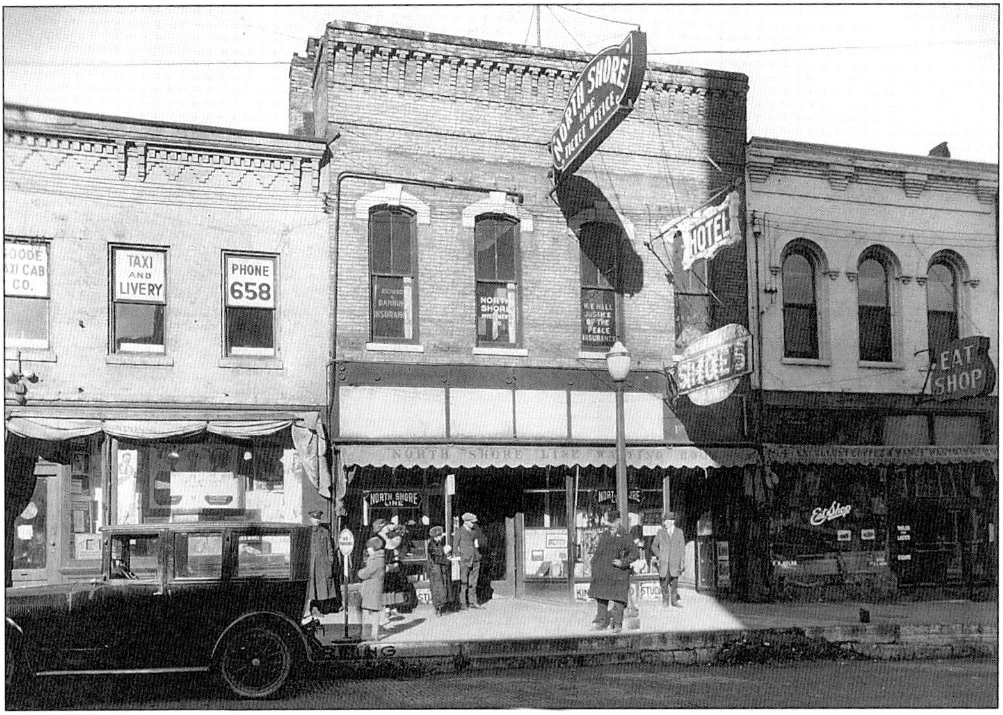

The Chicago, North Shore & Milwaukee RR ticket office was on Washington west of Genesee. It was nestled between Nolan's Eat Shop and Goode Taxi Cab Co. in this mid-1920s picture.

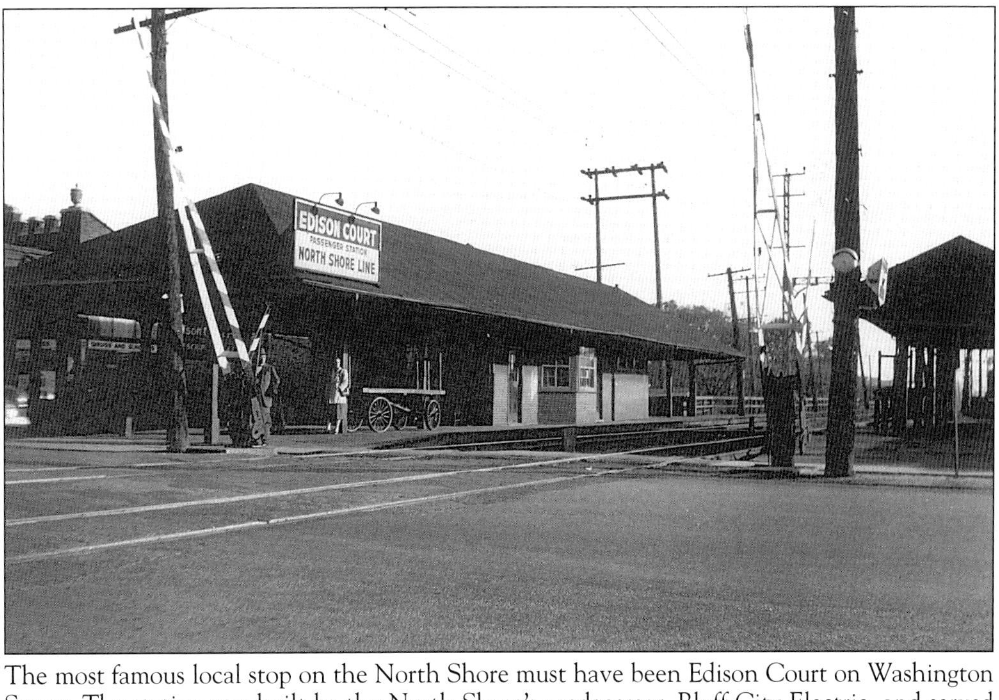

The most famous local stop on the North Shore must have been Edison Court on Washington Street. The station was built by the North Shore's predecessor, Bluff City Electric, and served as the electric railway's freight depot.

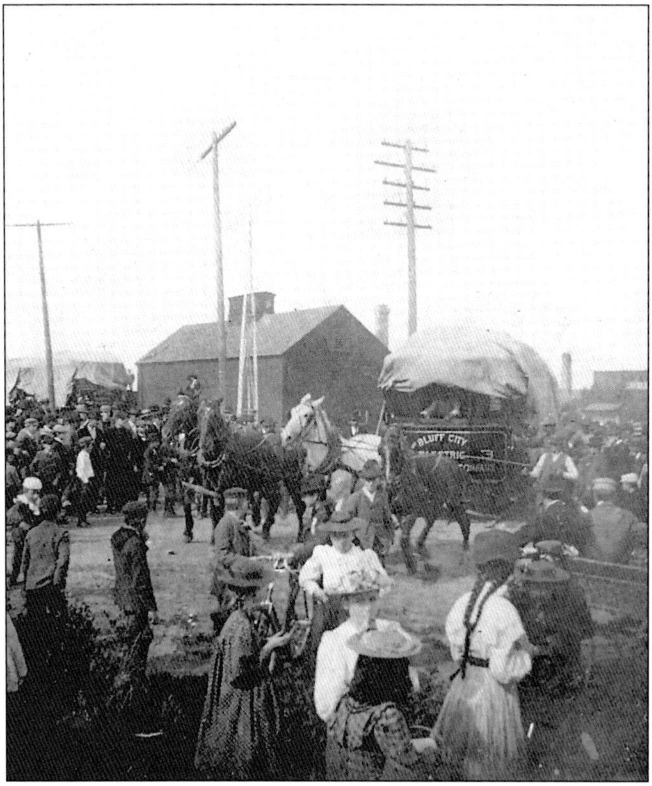

The Bluff City Electric Street Railway Company began in 1894. Here, the first car for that railroad is being delivered in the midst of an obviously interested crowd.

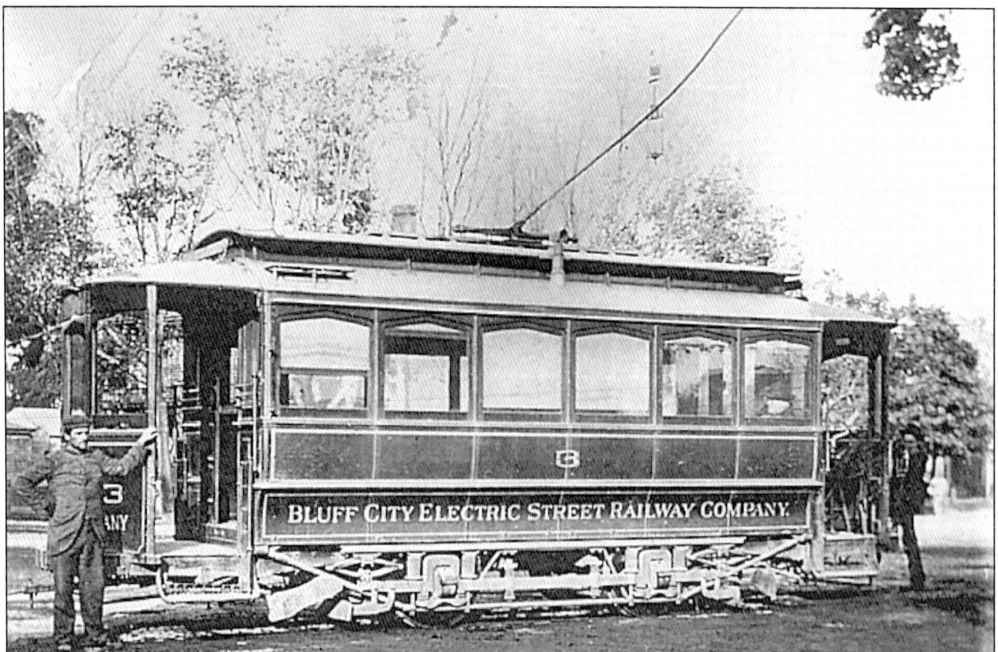

Future name and ownership changes took Bluff City to The Chicago & Milwaukee Electric in 1898, and rail service expanded to Evanston. Subsequently it became the North Shore and service was completed between Chicago and Milwaukee.

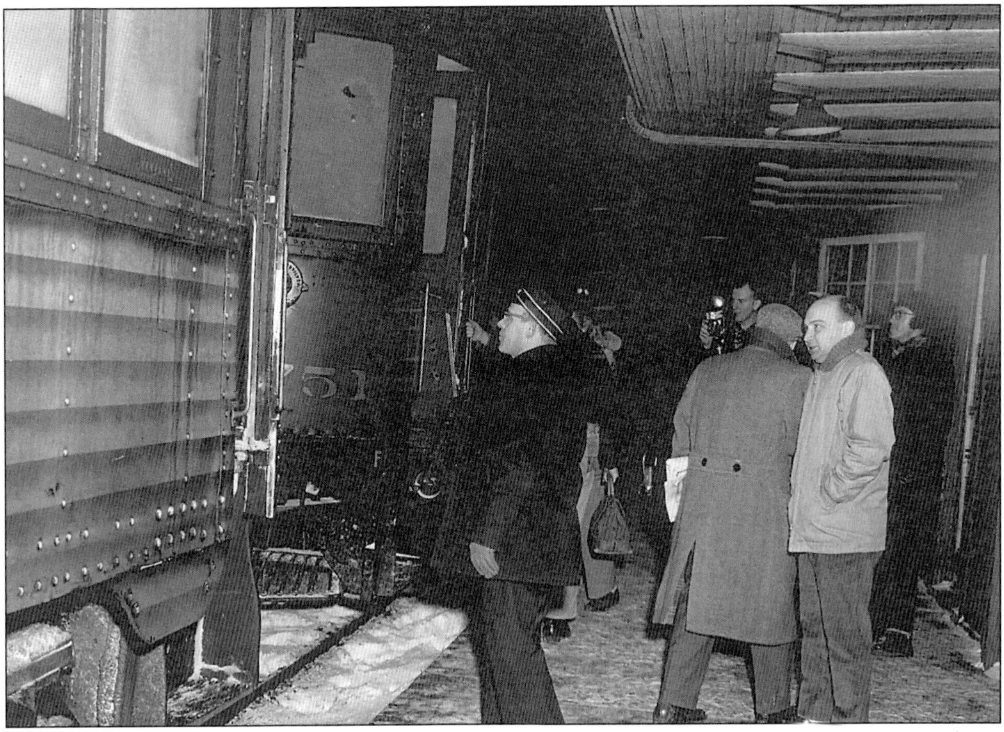

Inter-urban rail service continued via the North Shore. The Skokie Valley Route replaced the Shore Line Route which ceased operation in July 1955.

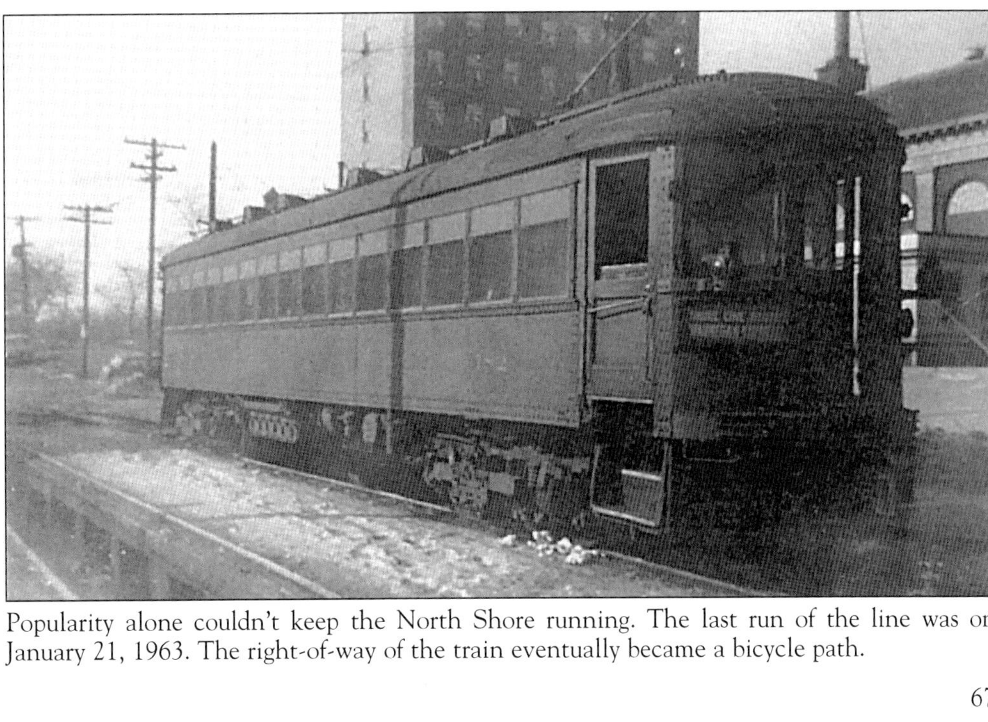

Popularity alone couldn't keep the North Shore running. The last run of the line was on January 21, 1963. The right-of-way of the train eventually became a bicycle path.

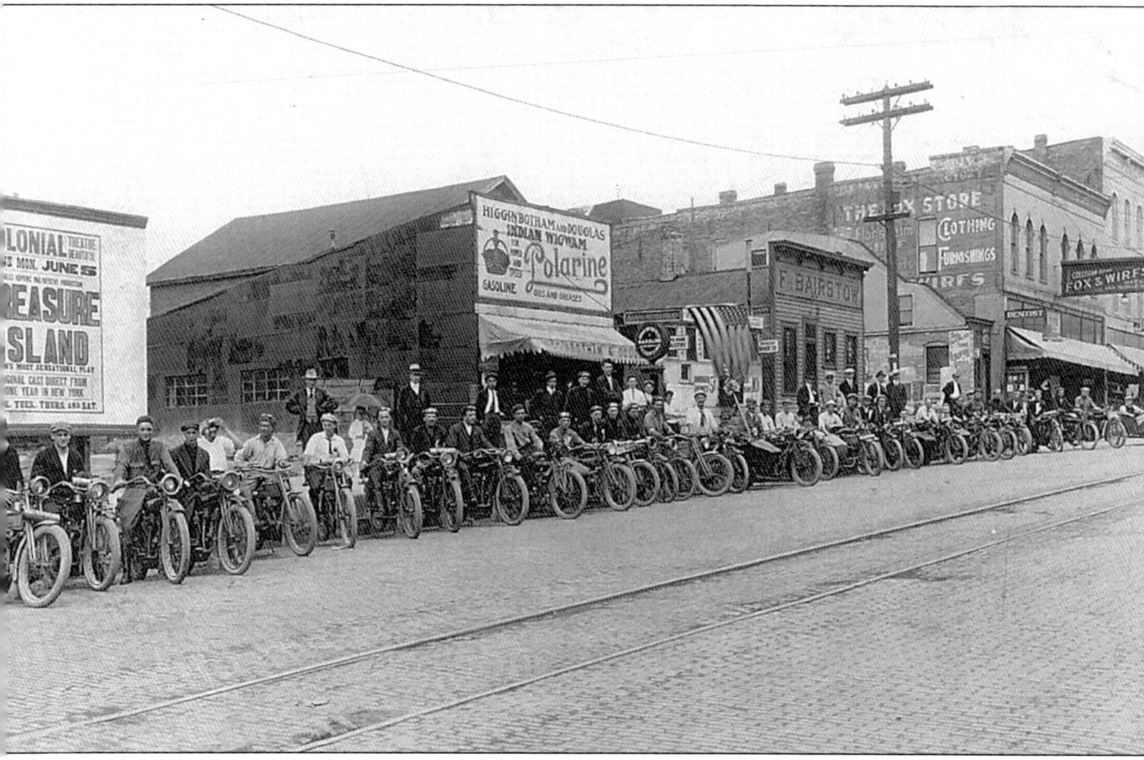

Between Washington and Water, on the west side of Genesee, Thomas Higginbotham and Delbert Douglas operated an Indian Motocycle agency from 1903 until the mid-1920s. It clearly was a popular place in 1916 when this picture was taken.

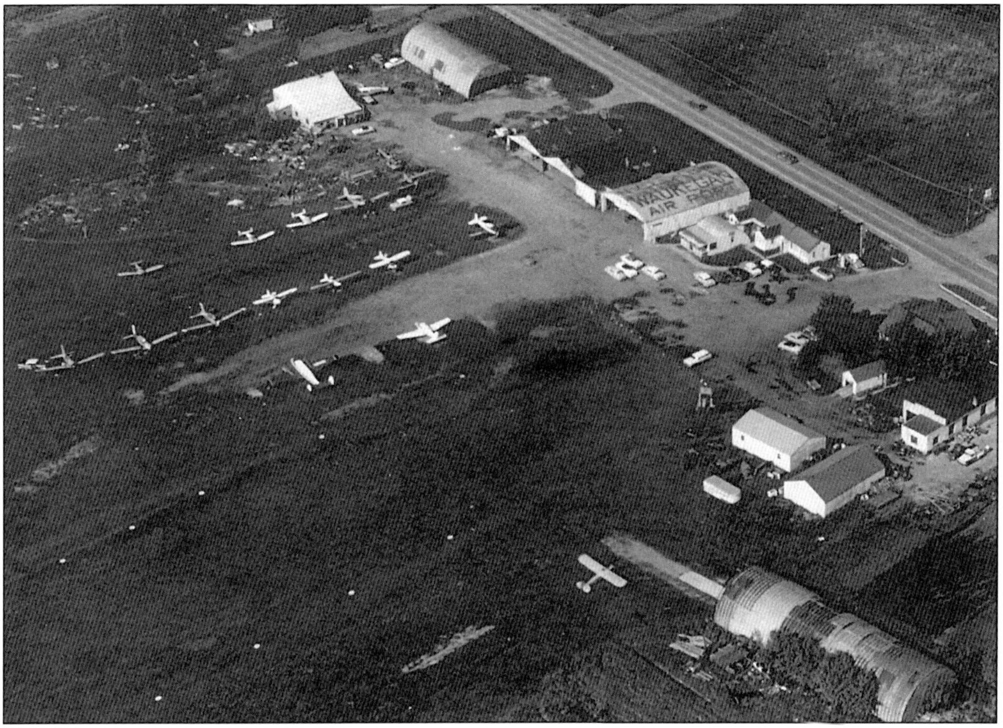

It is hard to imagine that there was once an airport at Green Bay and Sunset. Waukegan Airport operated at that location from 1927 to 1965.

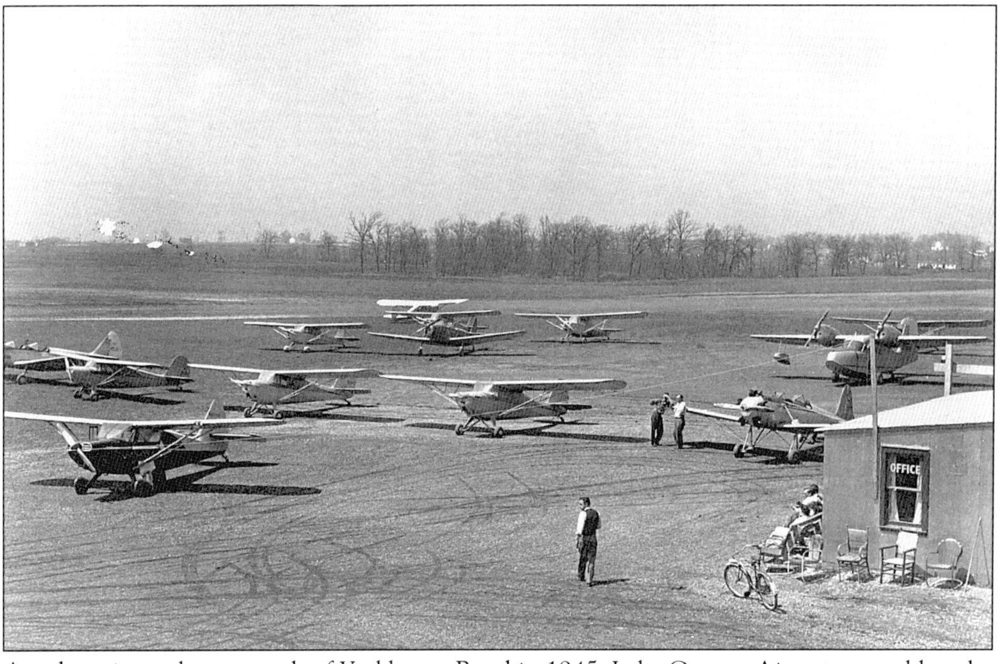

Another airport began north of Yorkhouse Road in 1945. Lake County Airport was sold to the Waukegan Port District in 1957 and was eventually re-named Waukegan Regional Airport.

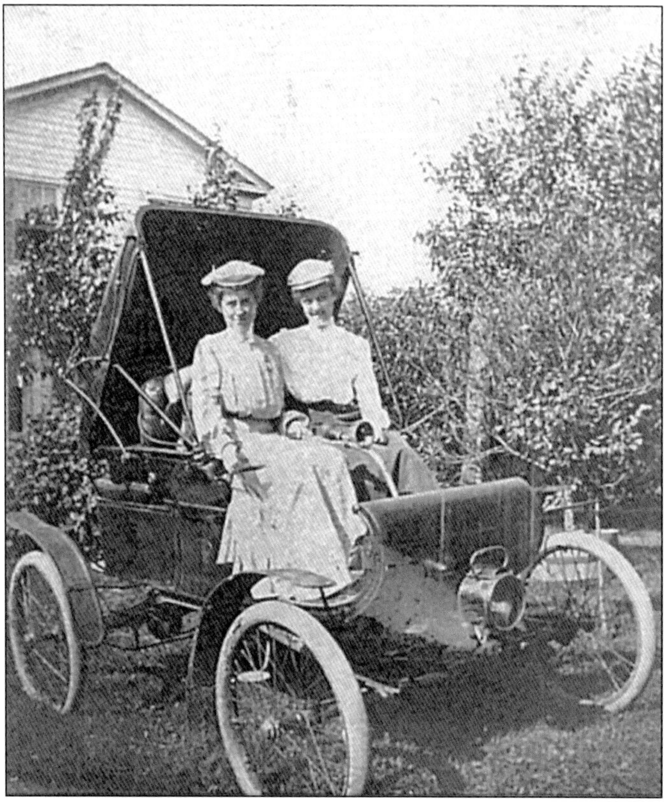

A local physician, Dr. R.H.T. Nesbitt, was the owner of the first car in Waukegan. His purchase on June 5, 1899, even pre-dated this early auto, shown in 1903.

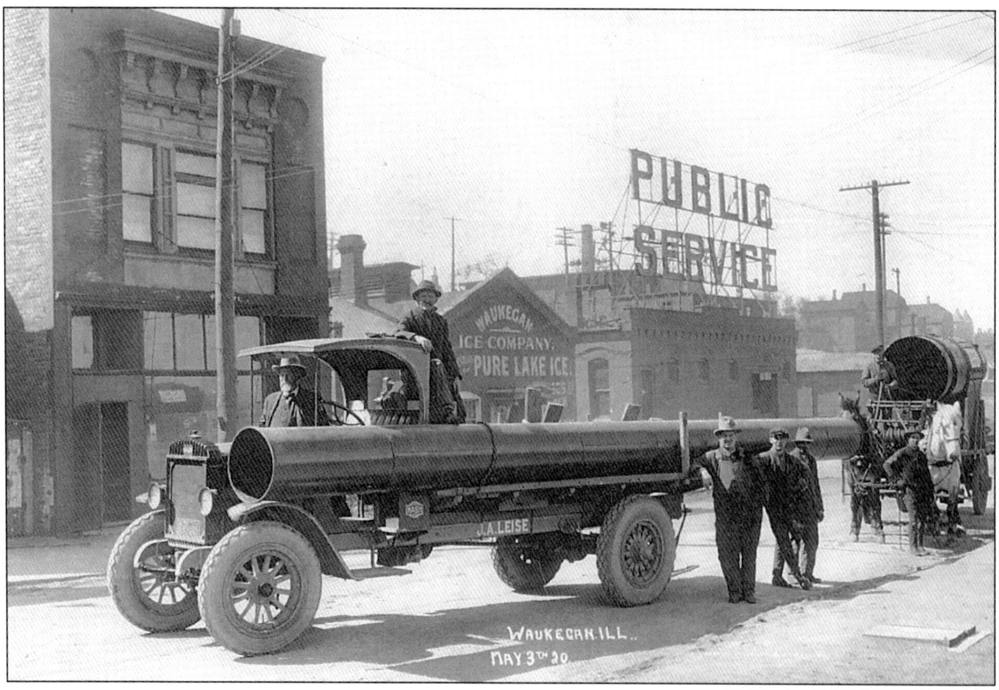

Trucks eventually replaced horses for heavy duty hauling. John Leise demonstrated this in 1920 in his drive down Spring Street.

Six

SERVICES

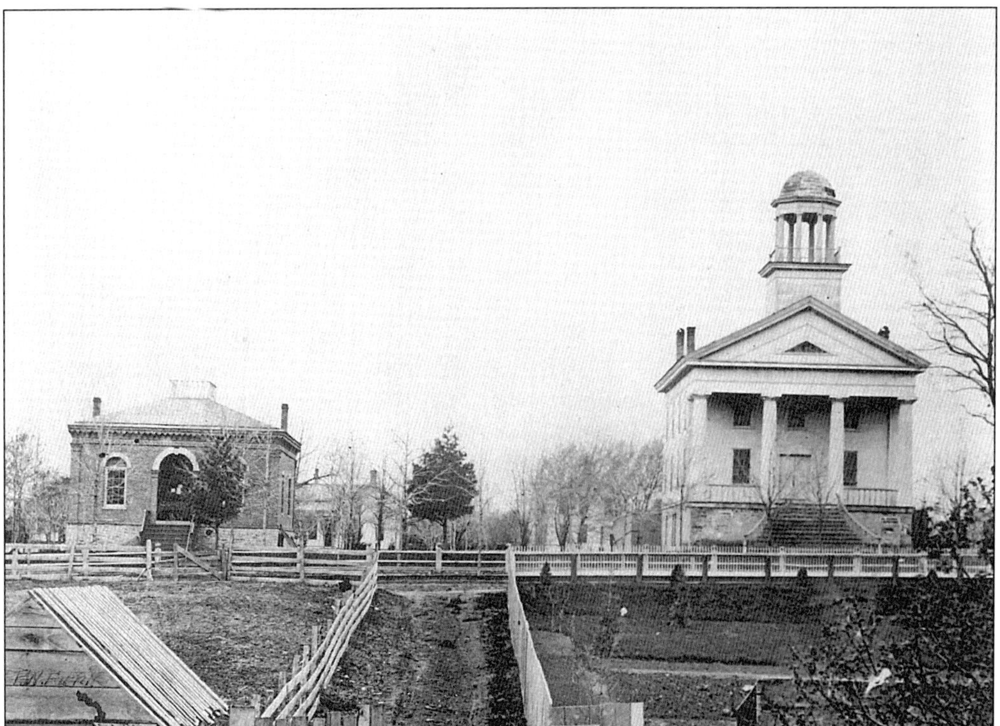

When the county seat was moved to Little Fort a courthouse was needed. Elmsley Sunderlin loaned $200 to the county for the purchase of 160 acres. The commissioners bought the property in April 1841. The courthouse was finally ready for occupancy on December 4, 1845. The grounds were the site of the first Lake County Fair held in September of 1852.

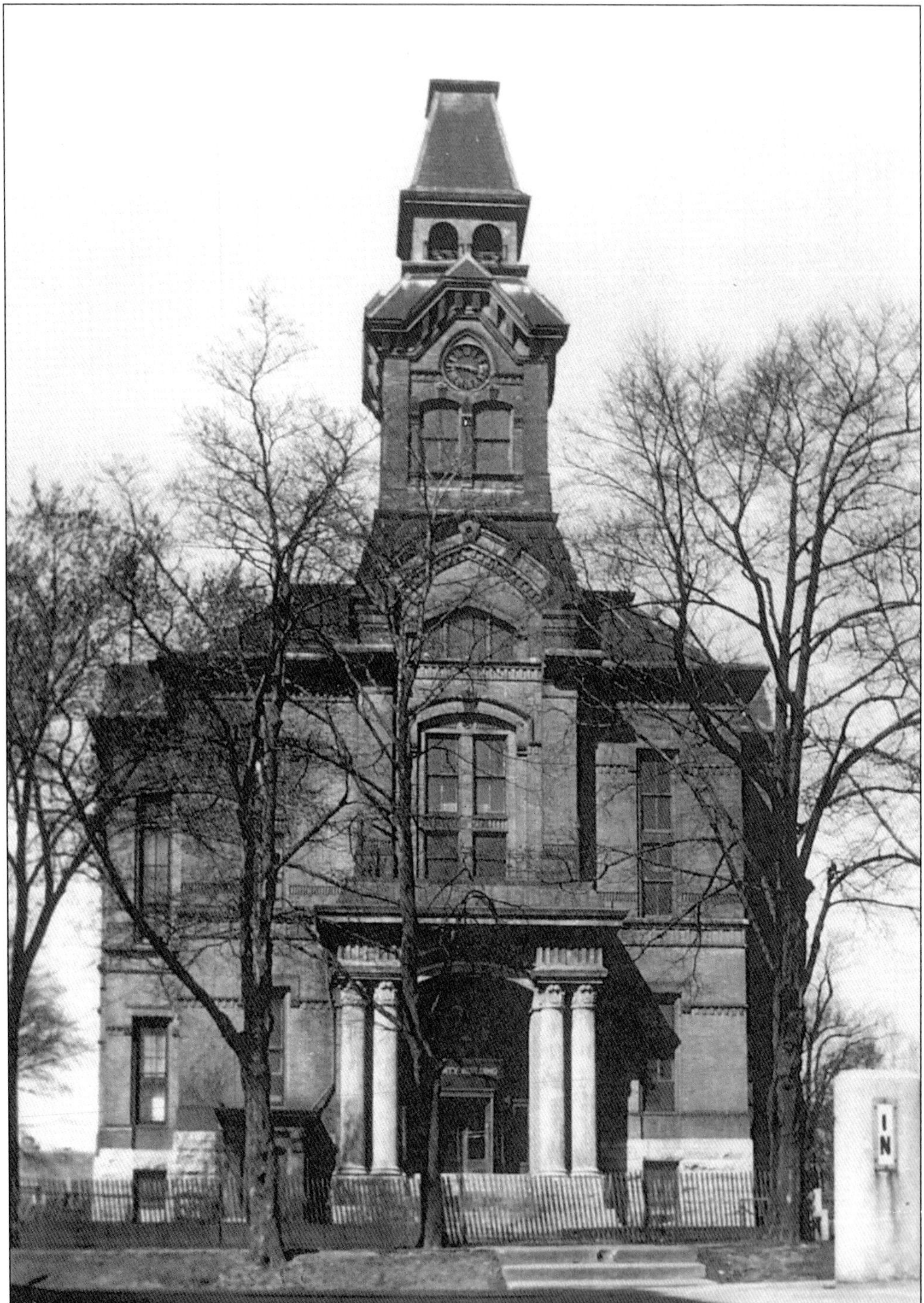

The original courthouse burned down October 21, 1875, despite the efforts of a largely volunteer fire department. A new courthouse was built and occupied on November 6, 1878. A new jail was built in 1895. Fire struck the courthouse clock tower in June 1955. Construction of a new courthouse prompted the demolition of this one in 1967.

August of 1899 saw the dedication of the Soldiers and Sailors Monument on the courthouse grounds. The idea for the monument originated immediately after the Civil War to honor those who took part in that conflict. The monument was moved to its new location in 1968 in conjunction with the building of a new courthouse complex.

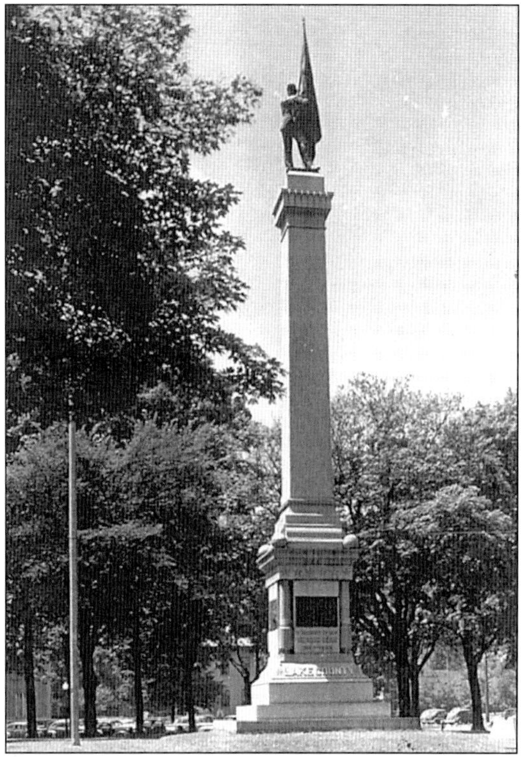

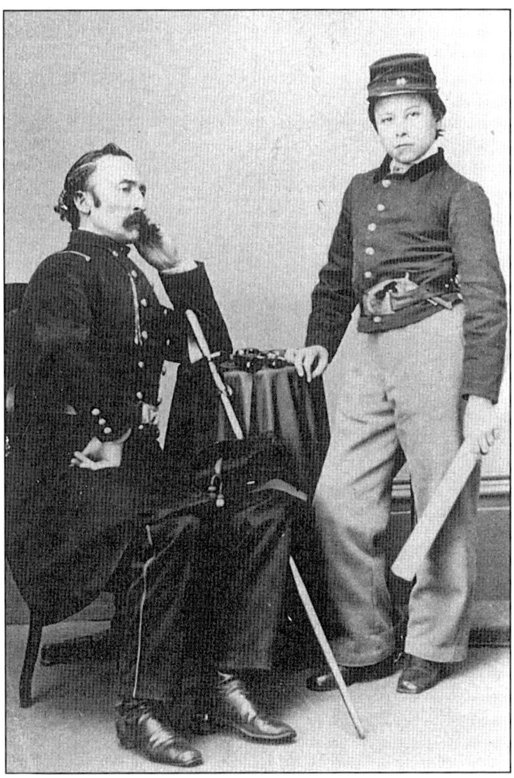

Among those honored by the monument was Orion P. Howe, the youngest recipient of the Medal of Honor. Although a 14-year-old drummer boy during the Civil War battle of Vicksburg, he demonstrated great heroism and suffered severe wounds. For whatever reason, however, his medal was not issued to him until 1896.

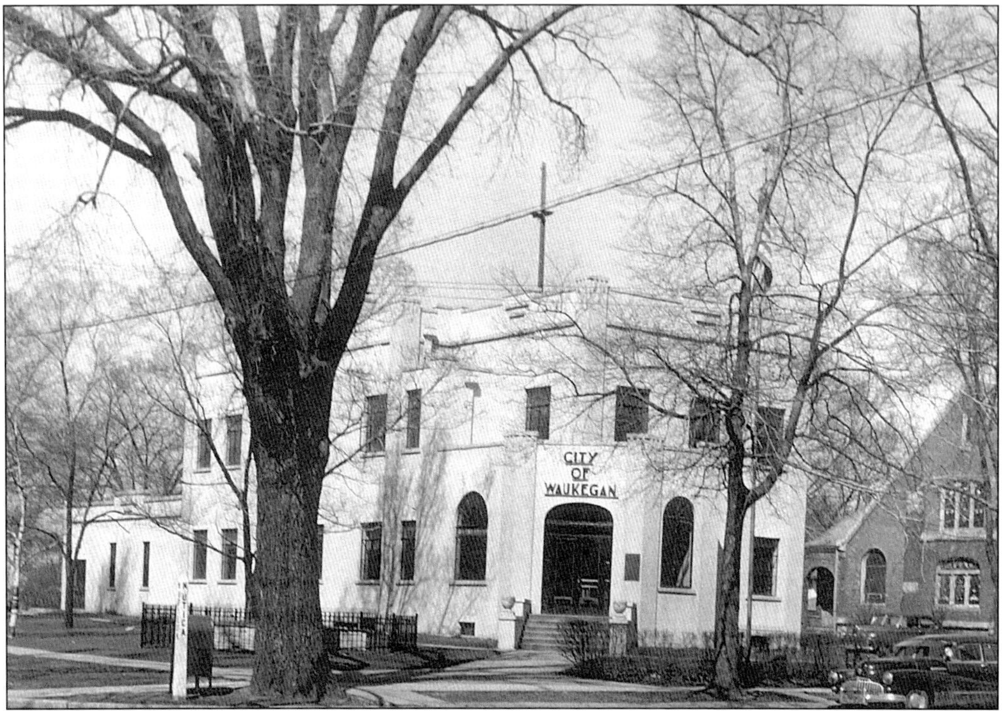

This is how City Hall looked prior to its remodeling in 1961.

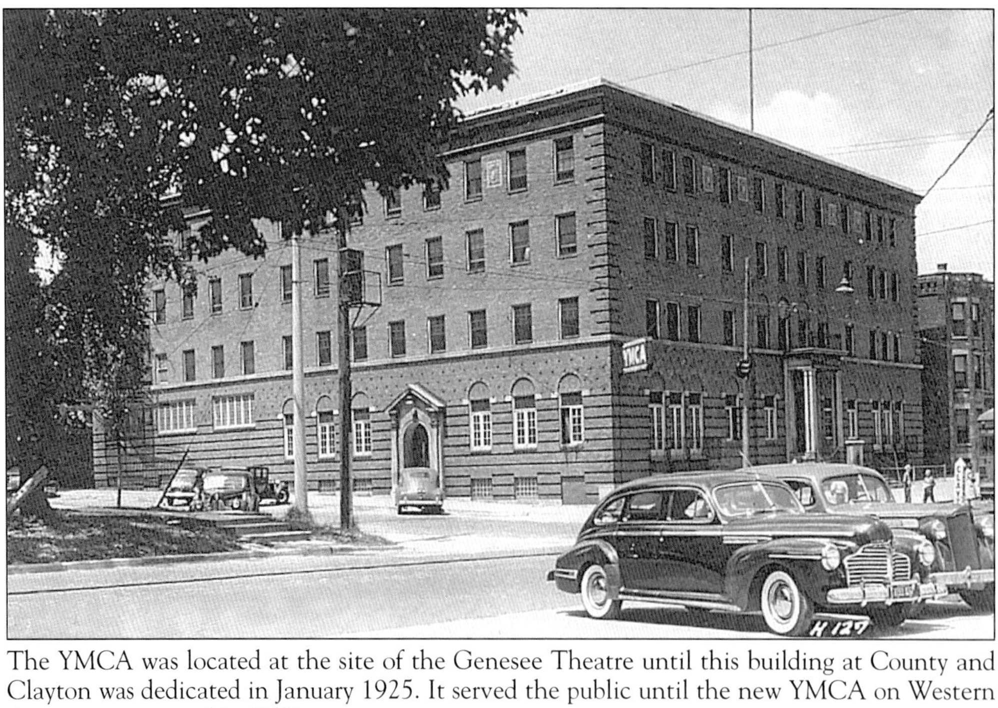

The YMCA was located at the site of the Genesee Theatre until this building at County and Clayton was dedicated in January 1925. It served the public until the new YMCA on Western Avenue was opened in 1987.

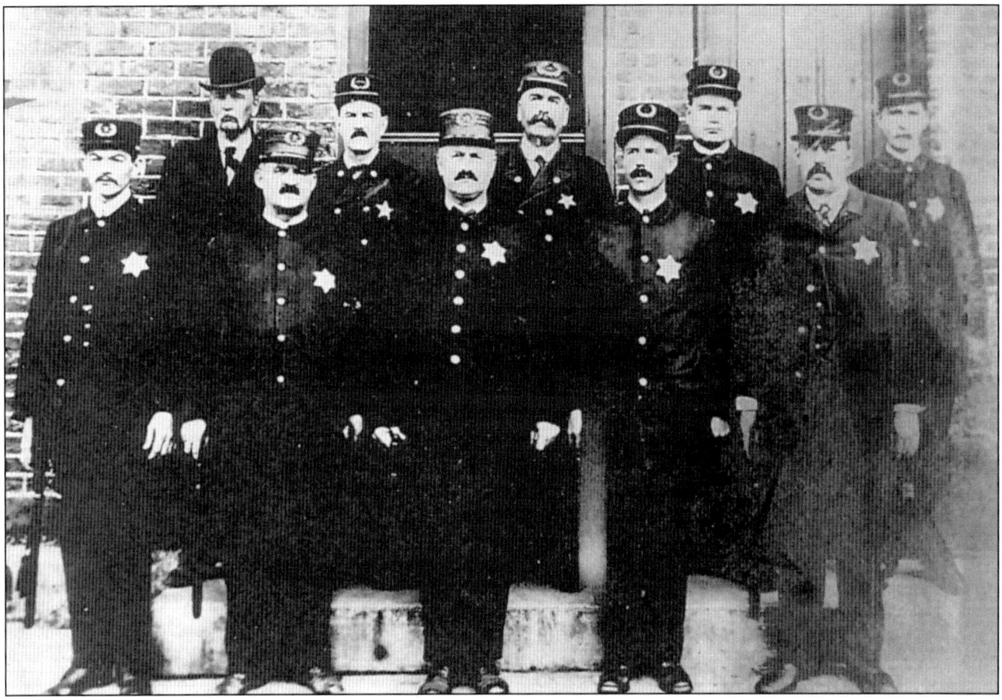

In 1908 the Police Department was ably served by the pictured men. Above, from left to right, are as follows: (front row) Matt Stocker, Bill Davis, Frank Tryon, John Metz, and Phil Michels. In the back row are John Maynard, Adam Vogel, Tom Tyrell, John Nemi, and Pat Salmon.

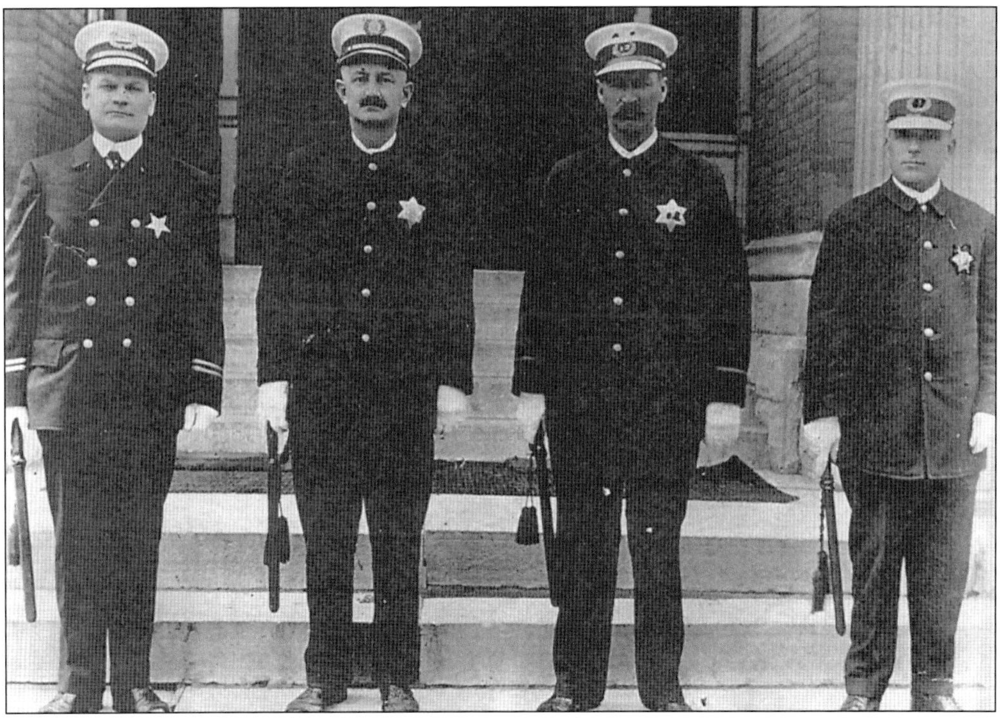

The uniforms may change but the mustaches remain the same.

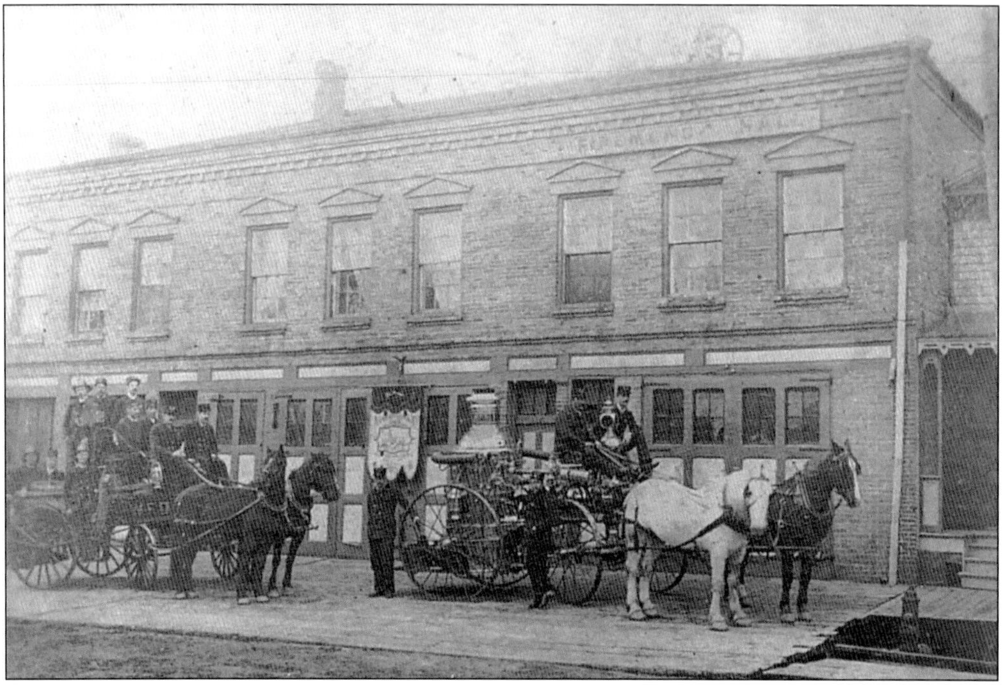

Waukegan Hook and Ladder Co. No. 1 was organized in 1849. The Fire Department was headed by a foreman and/or a chief engineer until 1882 when the first fire chief appeared. Horses, obviously, pulled the early equipment.

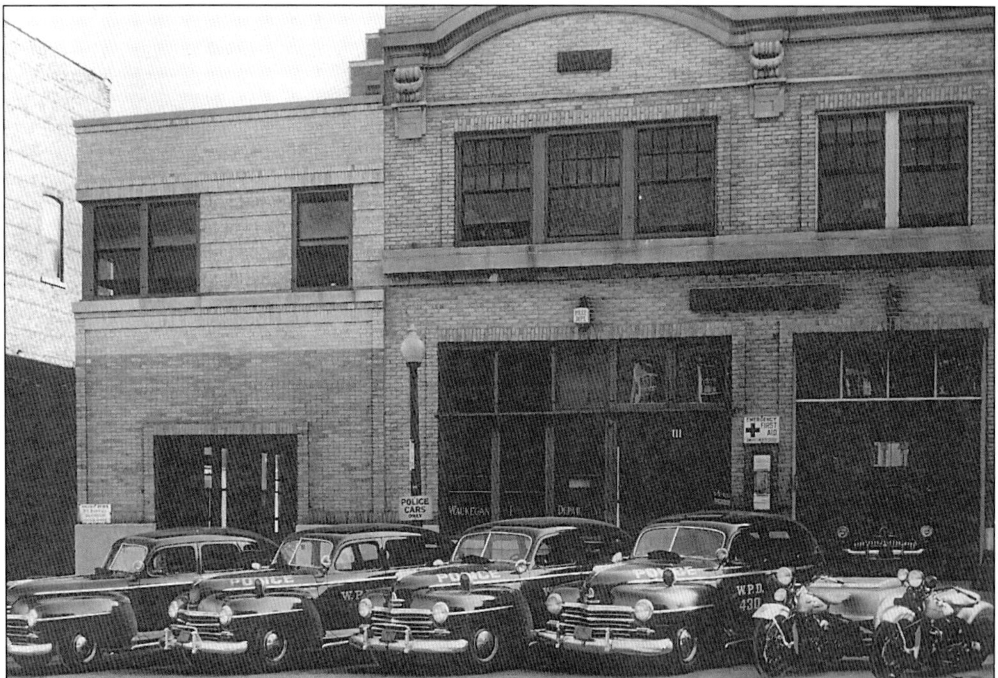

Police and fire departments shared space downtown on Madison Street until it was vacated in 1962. The building was demolished in 1978.

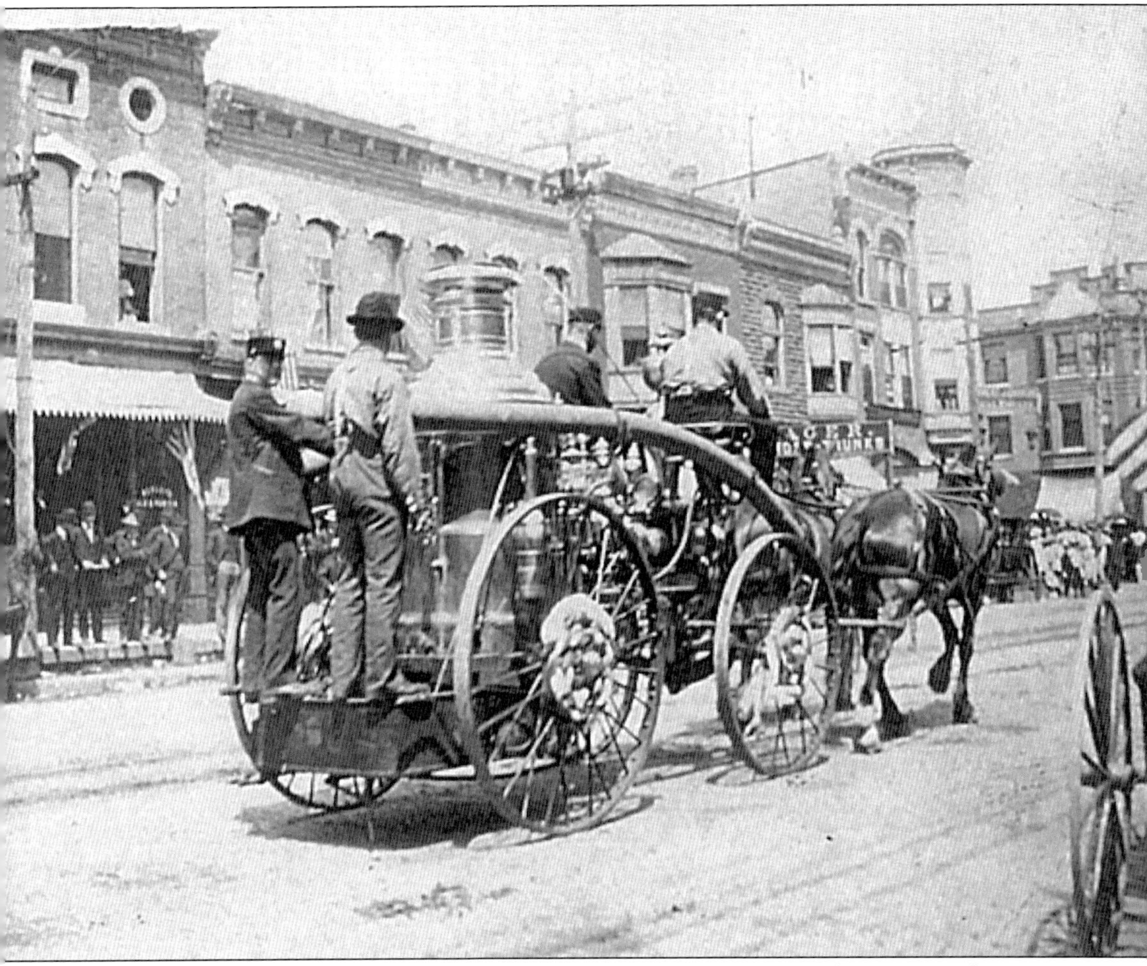

The nickeled steam water pumper was the pride of the fire department when it arrived. It was badly damaged on its first run when the horses pulling it ran away. The pumper was repaired and gave many years of service.

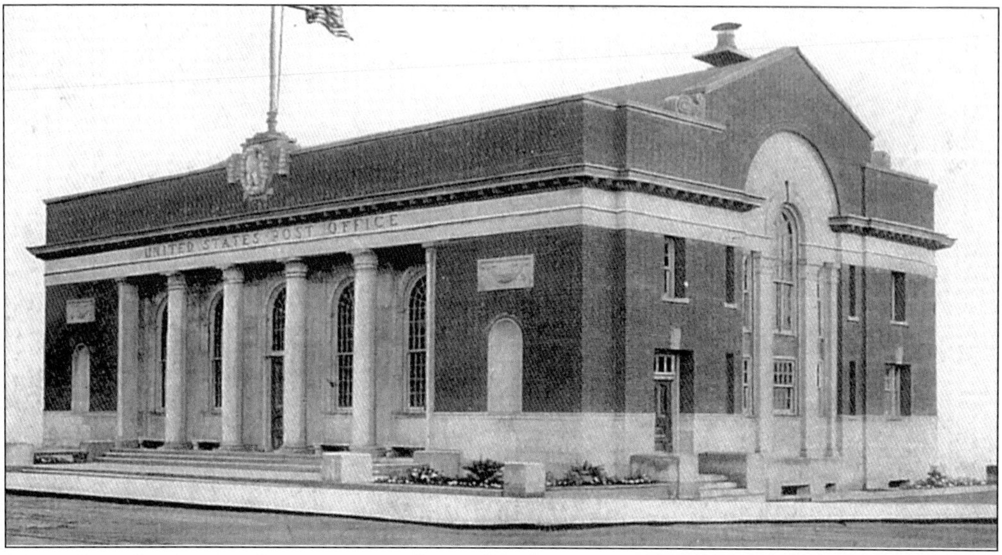

Ground was broken for the new post office at Washington and Utica on March 1, 1912, and it was completed in 1914.

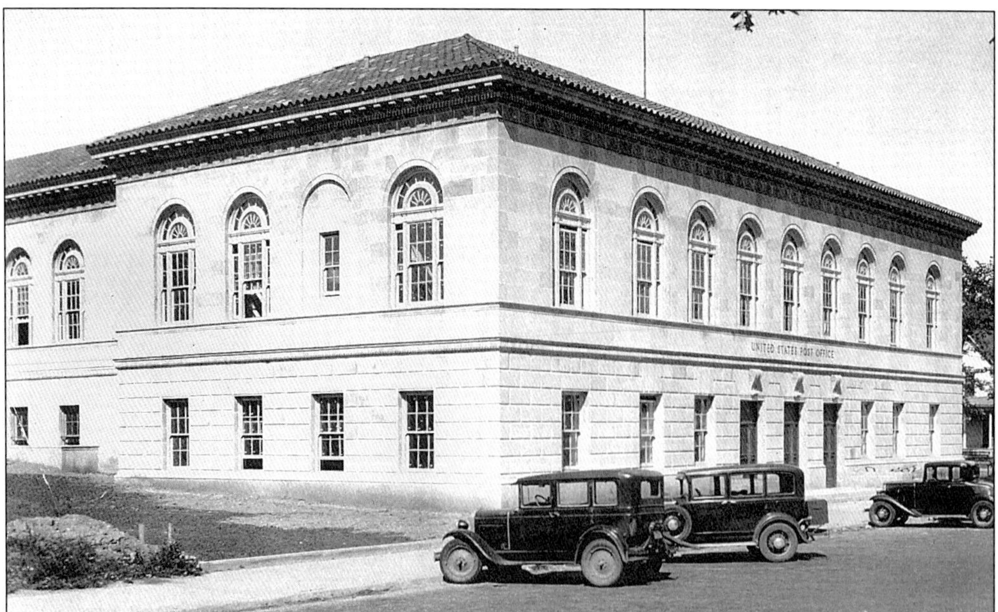

The new post office at Julian and Genesee was dedicated October 18, 1933. The former location remained as a federal building until its demolition in 1971.

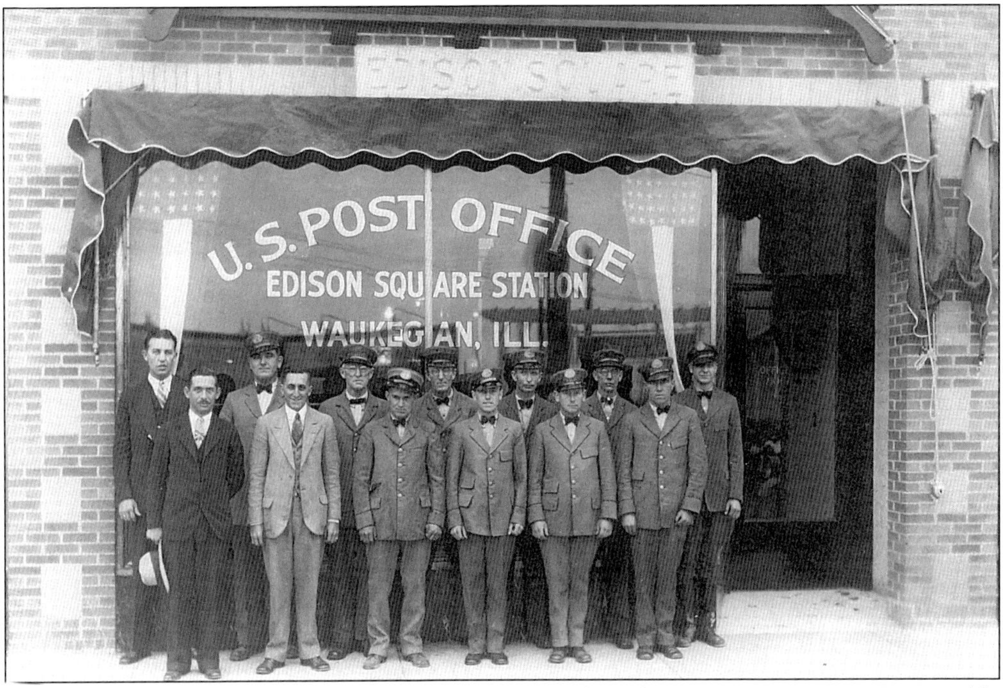

An important adjunct to the main post office was the Edison Square Station. It was ably manned by the men above. Pictured, from left to right, are as follows: (front row) M. Talcott, F. Offenlock, ? McDonald, R. Gustie, H. Palmer, and G. Graham. In the back row are C. Gelling, E. Quedenfeld, S. Burnett, C. Barnstable, E. Loftus, H. Babcox, and J. Jackson.

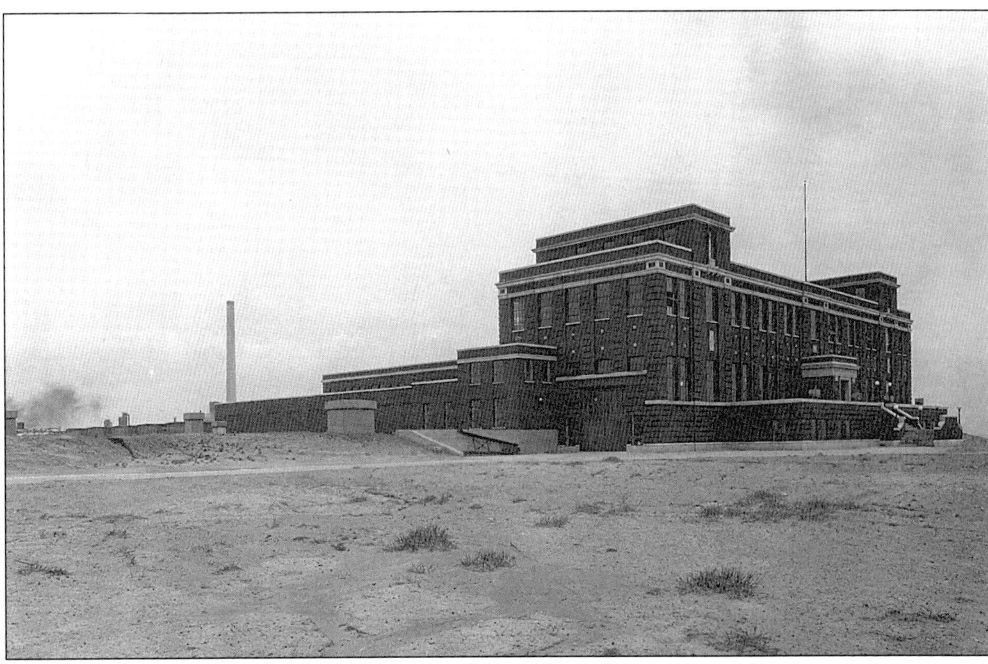

The city's water needs were met first by a public well in 1849 and later by a pumping station in 1895. This pumping and filtration plant was built across from the harbor in 1929.

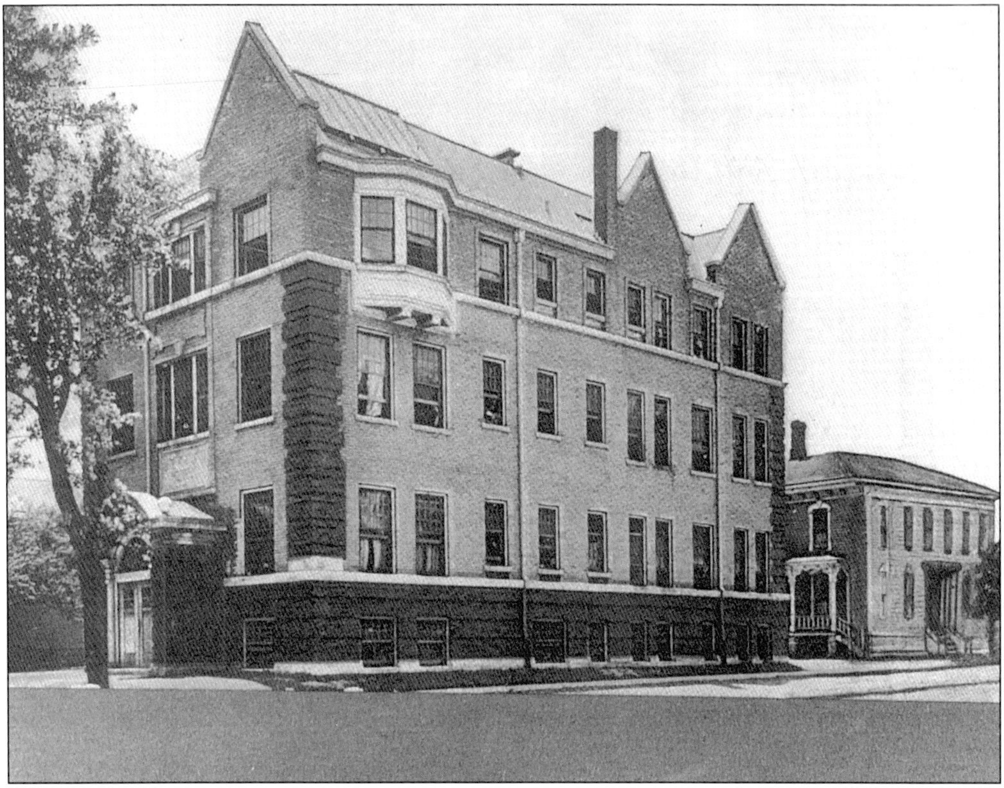

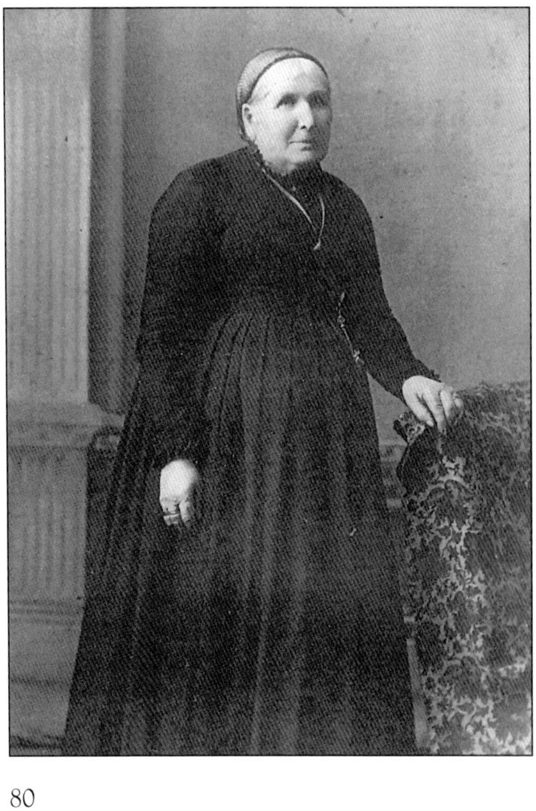

At the end of the 19th century, Waukegan acknowledged the need for a hospital by opening a small facility on North Avenue. Later more space was gained in a house at North and Franklin. The first real hospital, built for that purpose, was the 34-bed Jane McAlister Hospital which admitted its first patient September 24, 1904.

That hospital could not have been built without the generosity of this woman. Jane McAlister and her husband moved to Waukegan later in her life. In the summer of 1903, shortly before her death, Jane donated $20,000 for the purpose of building a hospital.

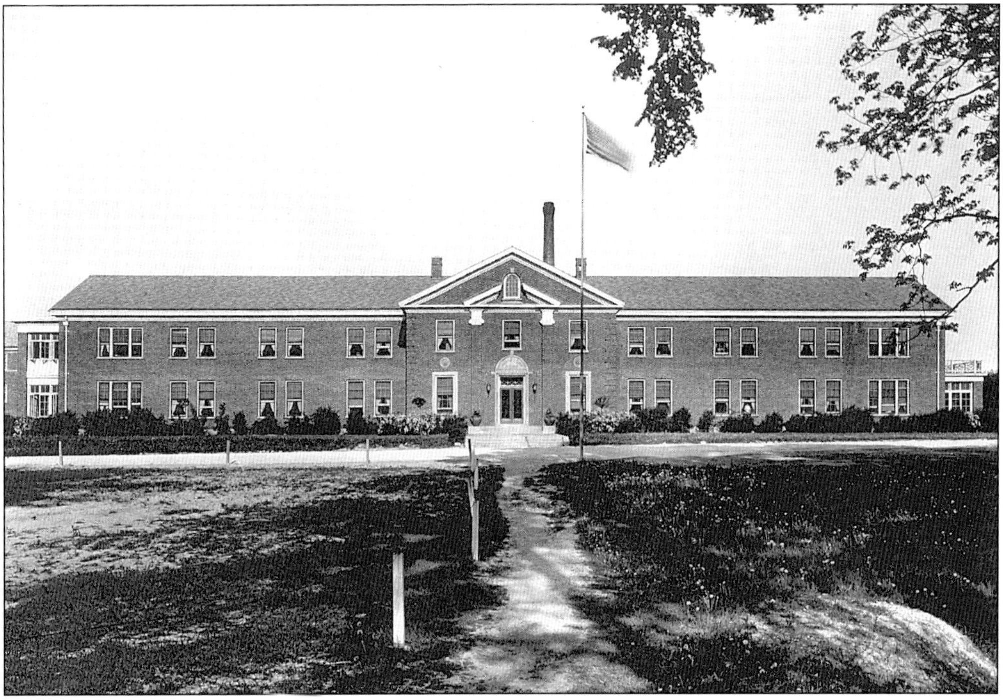

Victory Memorial Hospital was begun after, and in honor of, World War I. A cornerstone contained material from the Jane McAlister Hospital. The 75-room hospital opened its doors to the public on November 23, 1923.

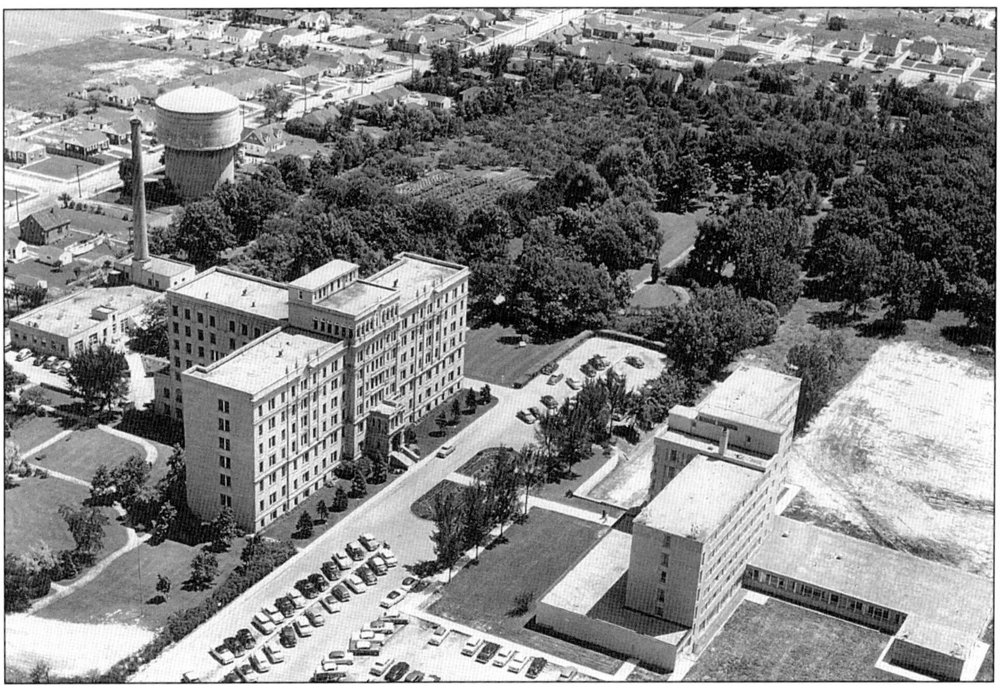

The Missionary Sisters bought property on Washington Street in 1927 and opened St. Therese on April 28, 1929. That hospital began with 180 beds.

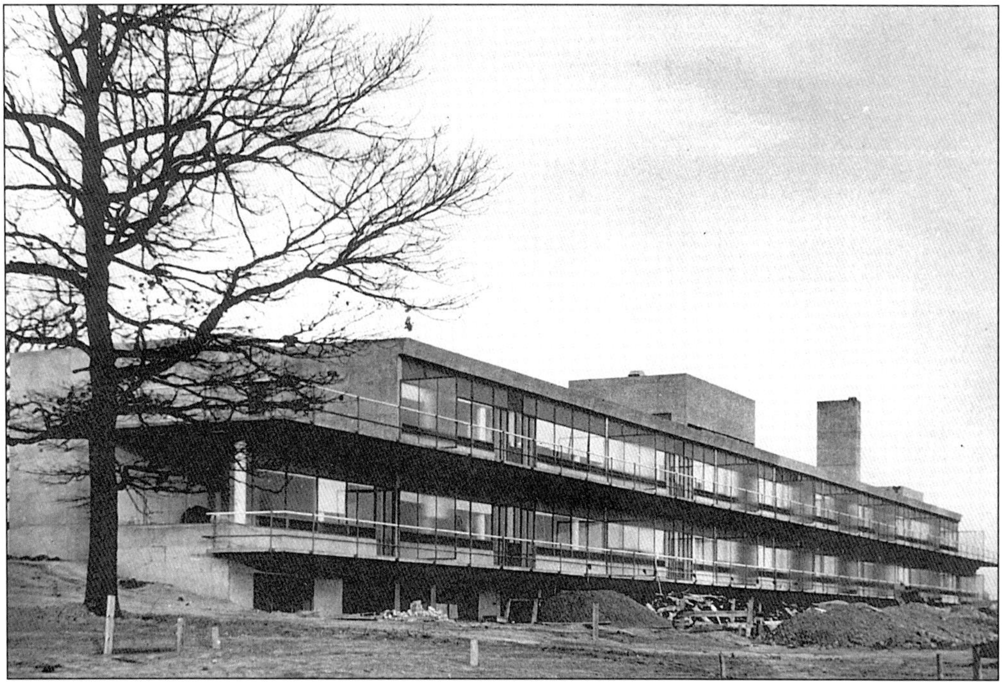

Lake County Tuberculosis Sanatorium opened in September 1939, on Belvidere Street. It became part of the Lake County Health Department in 1974.

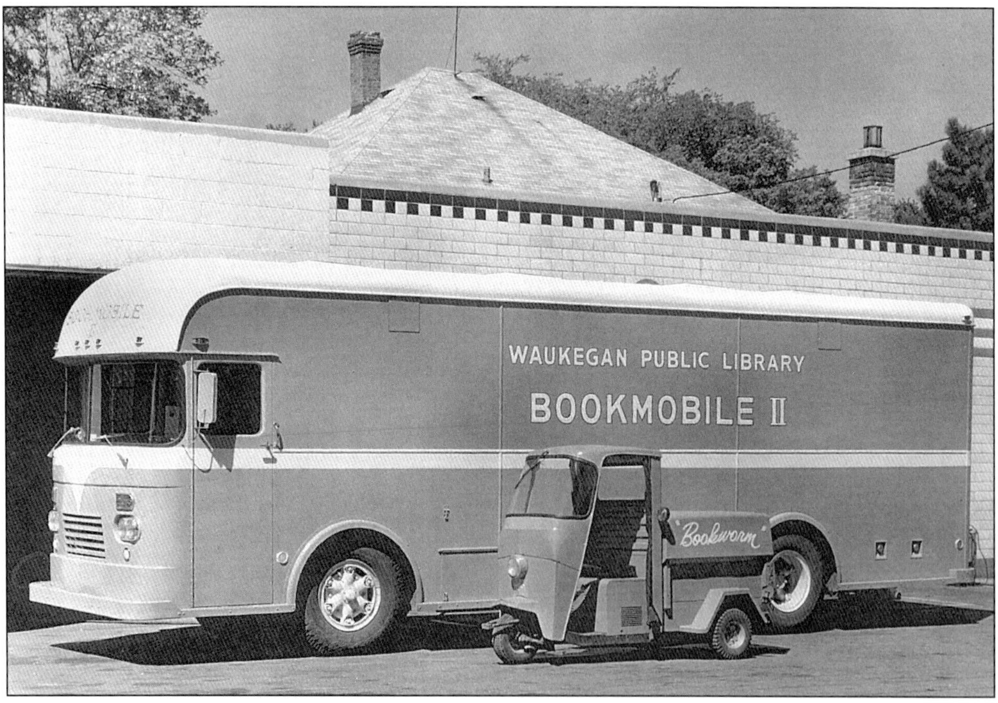

The Waukegan Public Library began in 1898 and was housed in the Carnegie Building starting in 1903. It moved to its current location in December 1965. Waukegan's first bookmobile went into operation in April of 1956.

Seven

CHURCHES

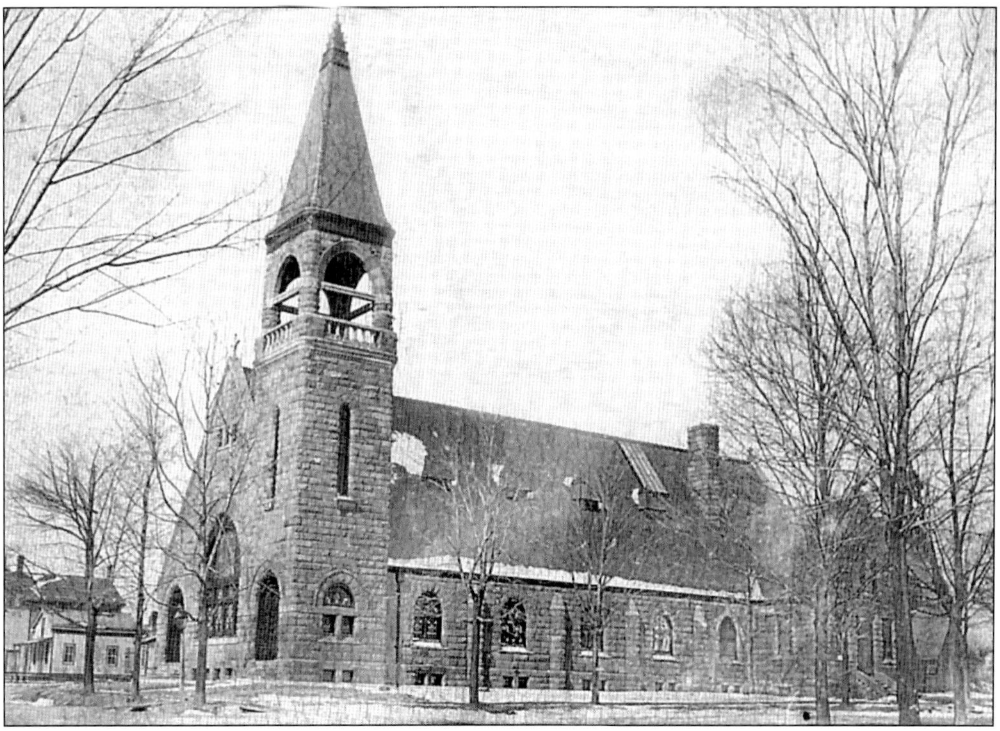

Churches are an important part of the fabric of Waukegan. Many different faiths are represented and the congregations often followed the clustering of immigrants as they settled in the area. Christ Episcopal Church was organized in 1846. This church opened in 1889 and is listed in the National Registry of Historic Buildings.

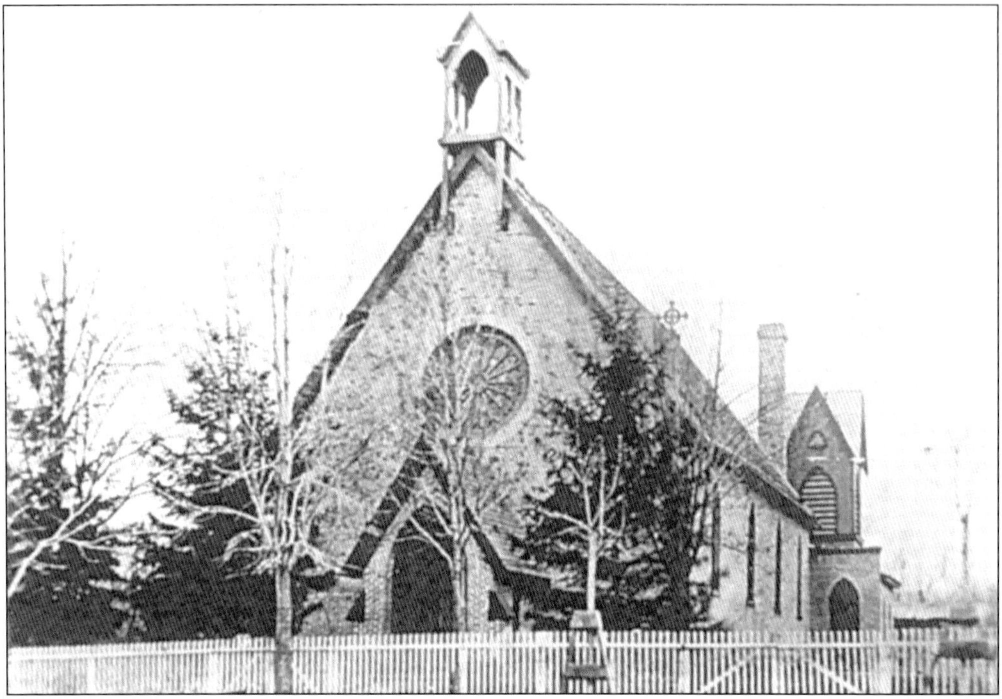

The earlier Episcopal Church was built in 1851 and served until the present one was completed.

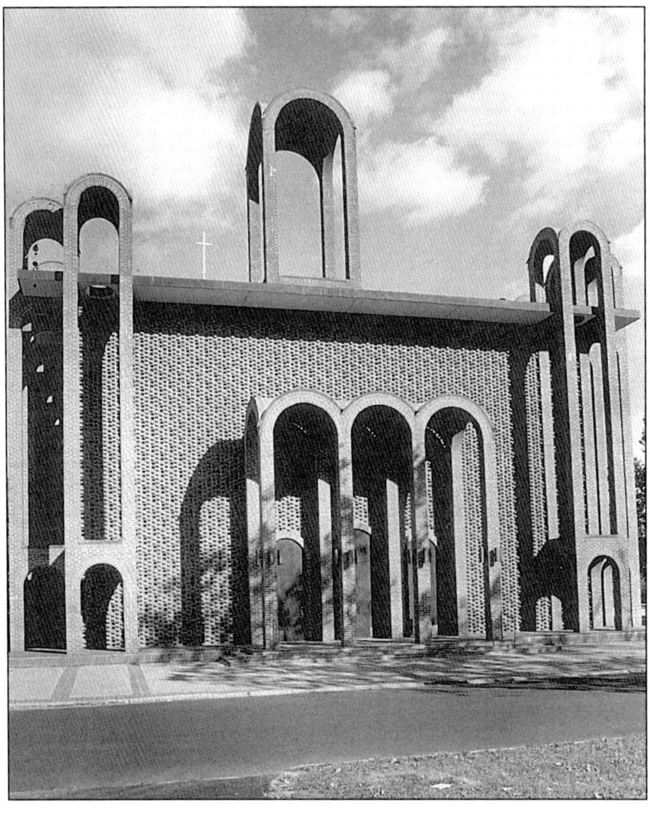

St. Anastasia Catholic Church on Glen Flora opened in 1926. The new church was dedicated December 6, 1964.

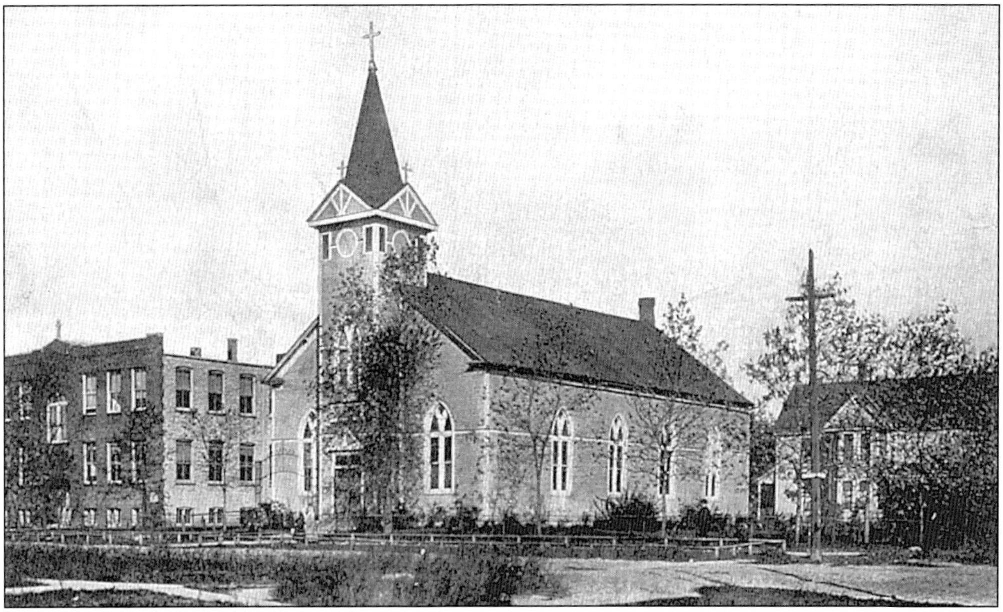

St. Bartholomew's was the second Lithuanian parish in the Chicago Archdiocese. It was established in 1896 and this church was used from 1904 to 1937, when a new church was built. In 1996 the parish was merged with St Joseph's to form Holy Family.

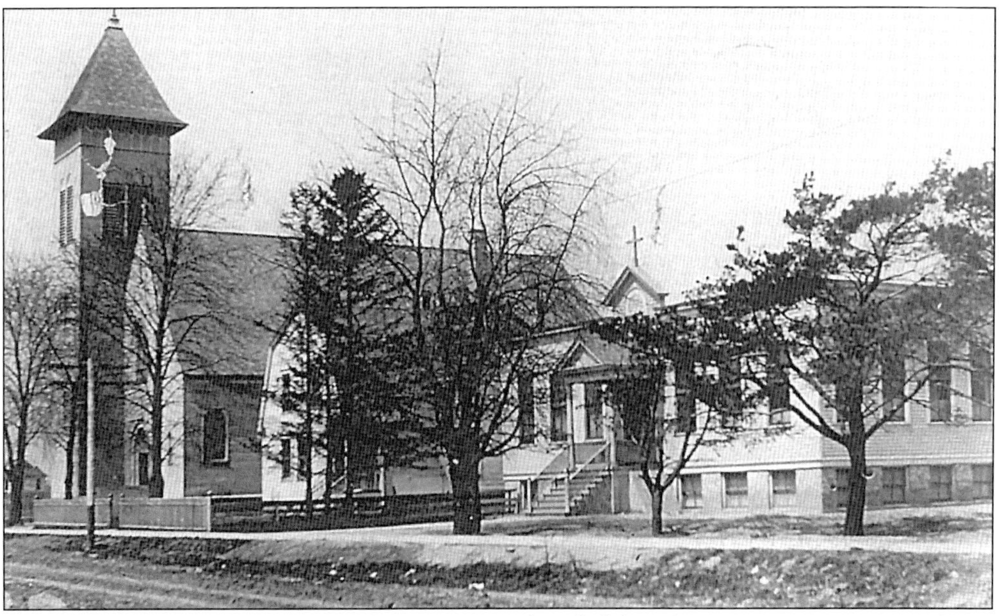

Mother of God Church on Tenth Street was founded by Slovenian immigrants and was dedicated November 27, 1903. The parish merged into Queen of Peace in 1991.

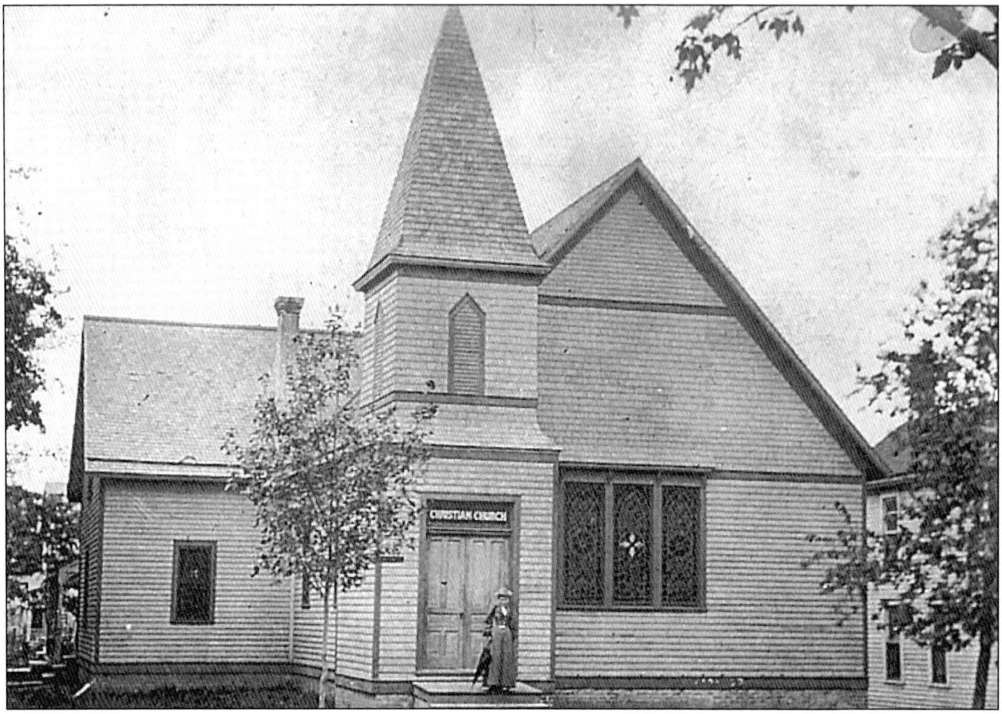

The First Christian Church dedicated this building at Clayton and Utica in 1890, and it served until destroyed by fire in 1940.

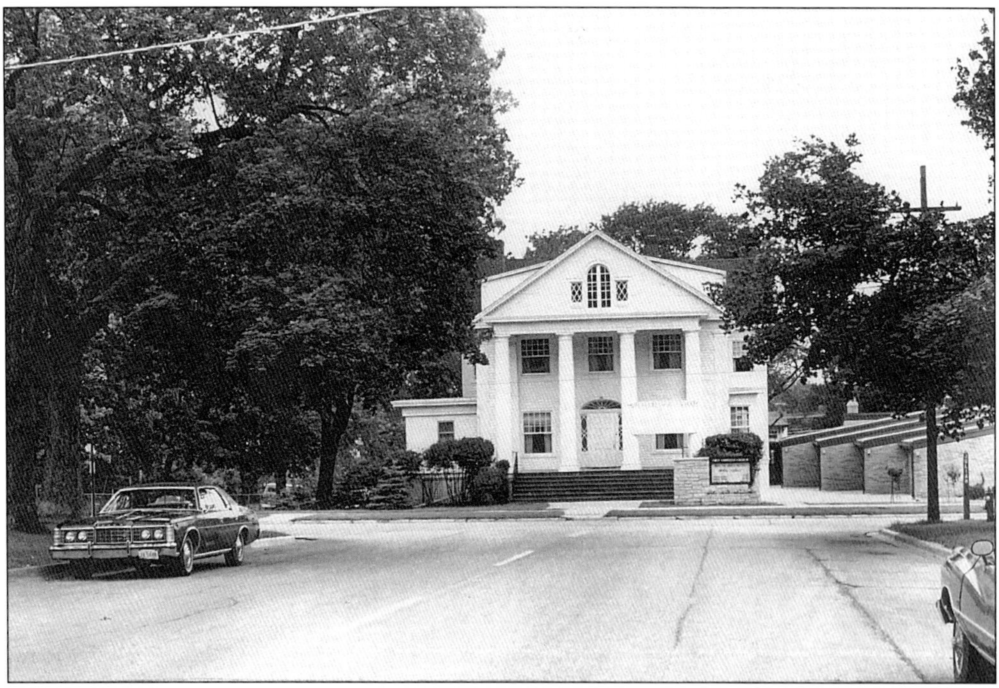
Following the fire the congregation moved to the north end of Utica Street. That building was demolished in 1983.

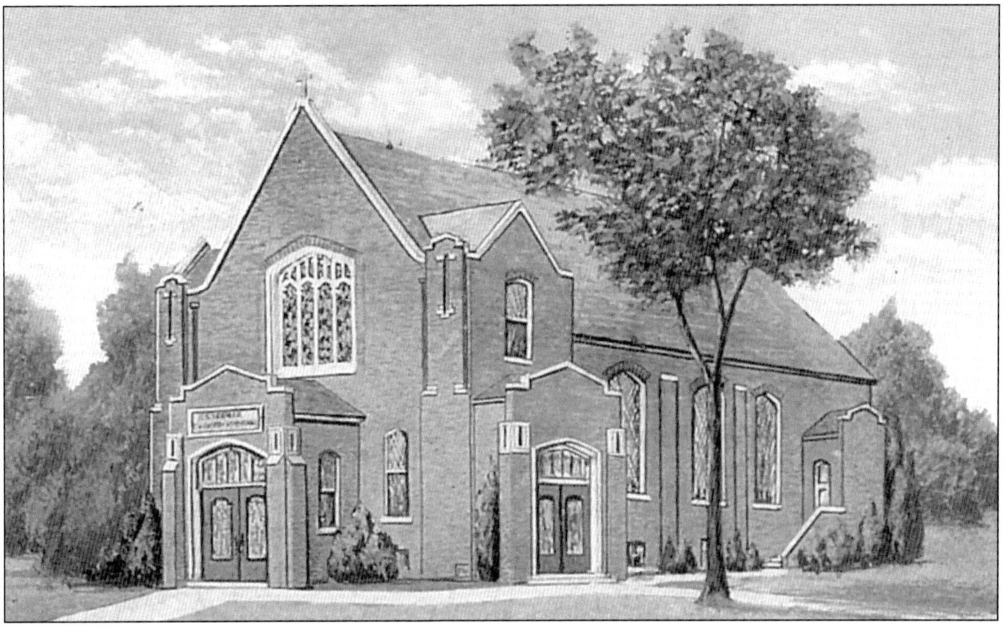

Redeemer Lutheran Church was organized in 1927 and the church was dedicated in 1929. It received a new façade in 1964.

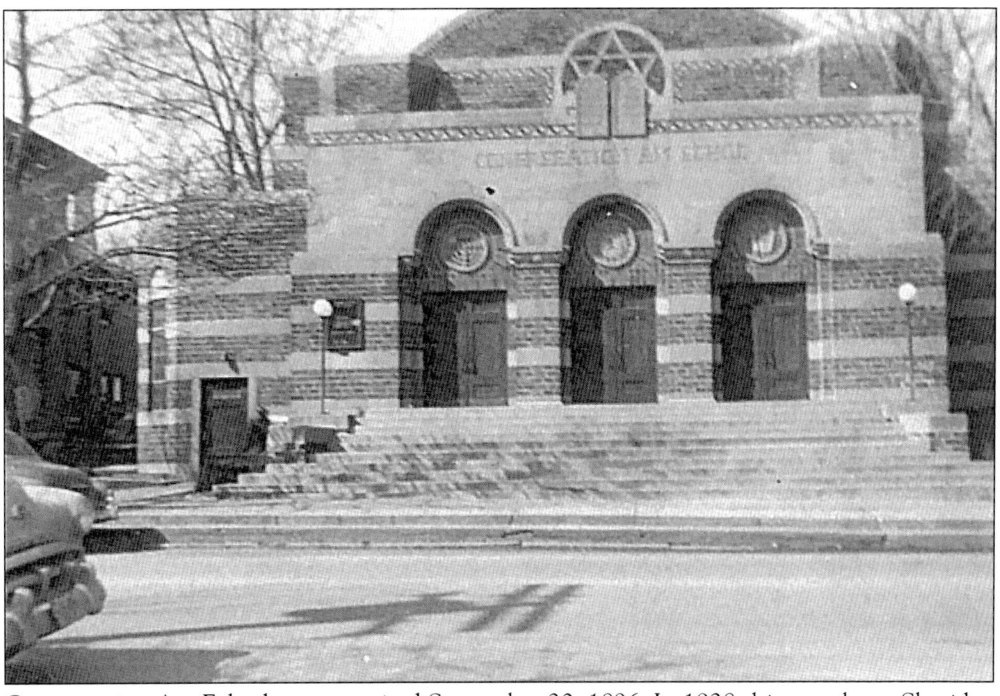

Congregation Am Echod was organized September 20, 1896. In 1928 this temple on Sheridan Road was opened. It served the congregation until a new temple on Sunset was dedicated in 1968. This building was razed in 1973.

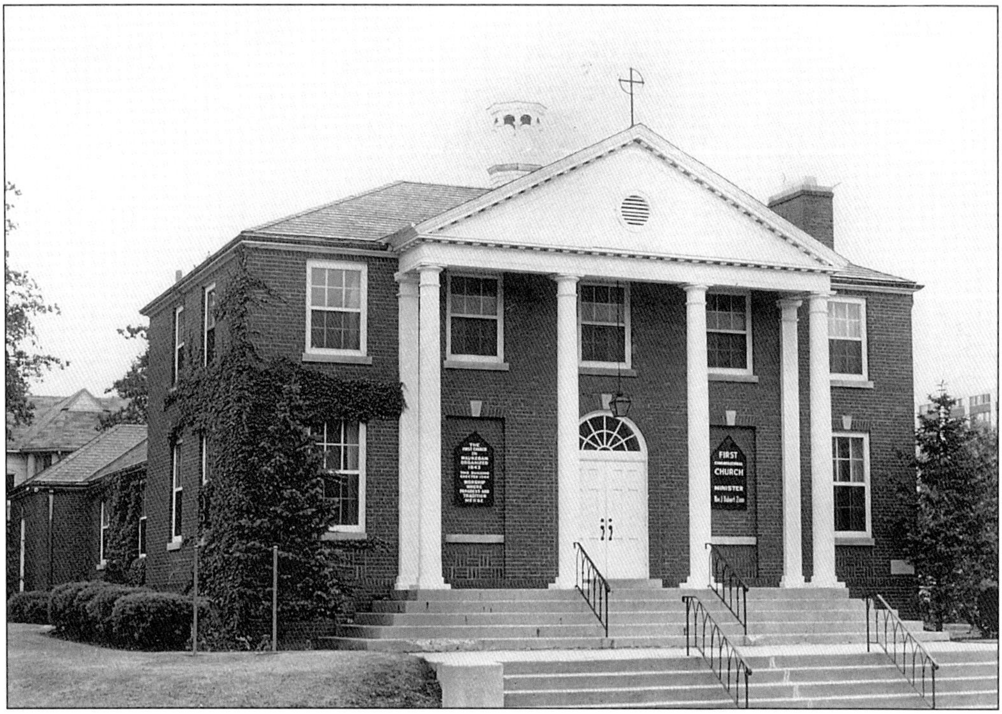

The Congregational Church was organized in 1843 at the home of Waukegan pioneer D.O. Dickinson. The first church was built in 1862 and lasted until destroyed by fire in 1939. A new church was built at the same location in 1940.

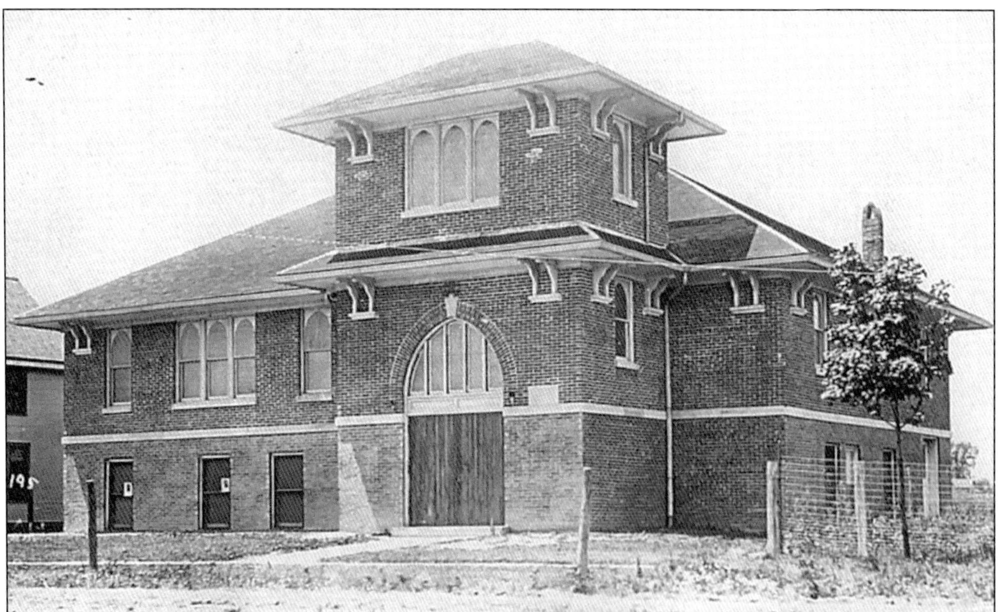

Chapel Street Christian Church was organized in 1905. The ground floor of the edifice was dedicated in 1907 and the superstructure completed in 1913. The name was changed to Central Christian Church in 1941.

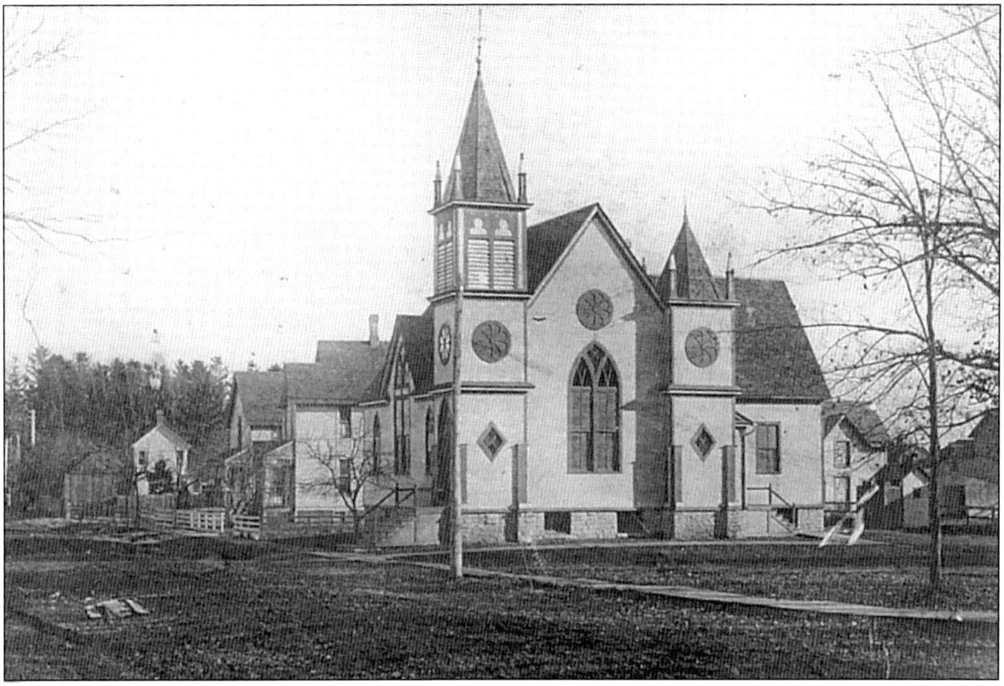

Many Swedish immigrants arrived here to work at Washburn and Moen. Like many others they typically lived in their own enclaves and began their own congregations. One example would be the Swedish Methodist Church at South Avenue and Utica.

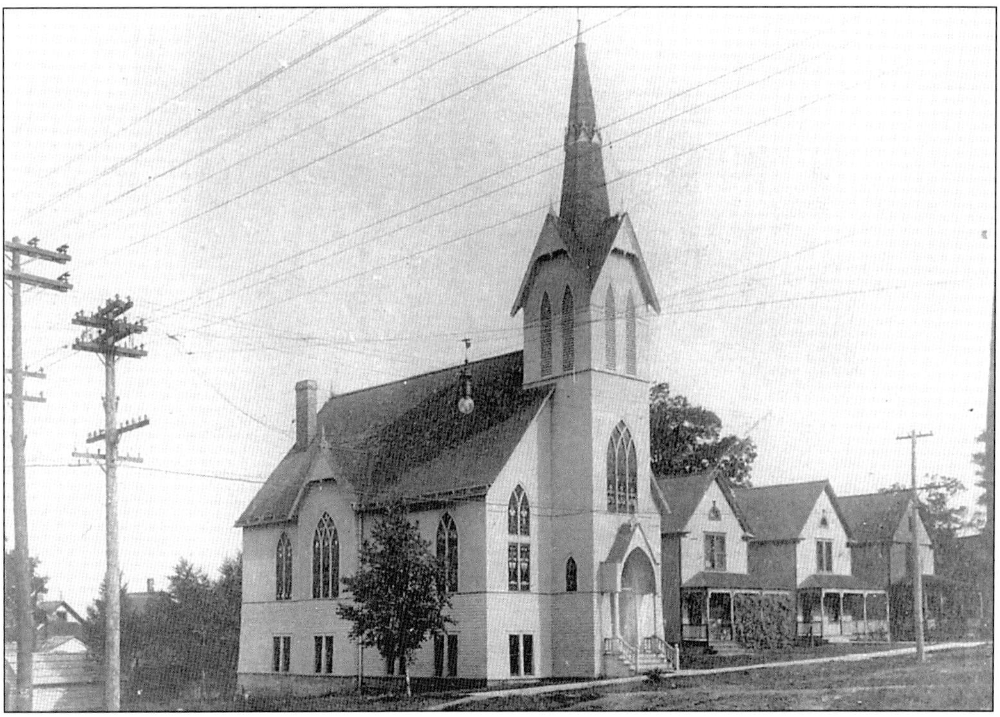

Other immigrants would worship at the Swedish Lutheran Church at Oak and McKinley.

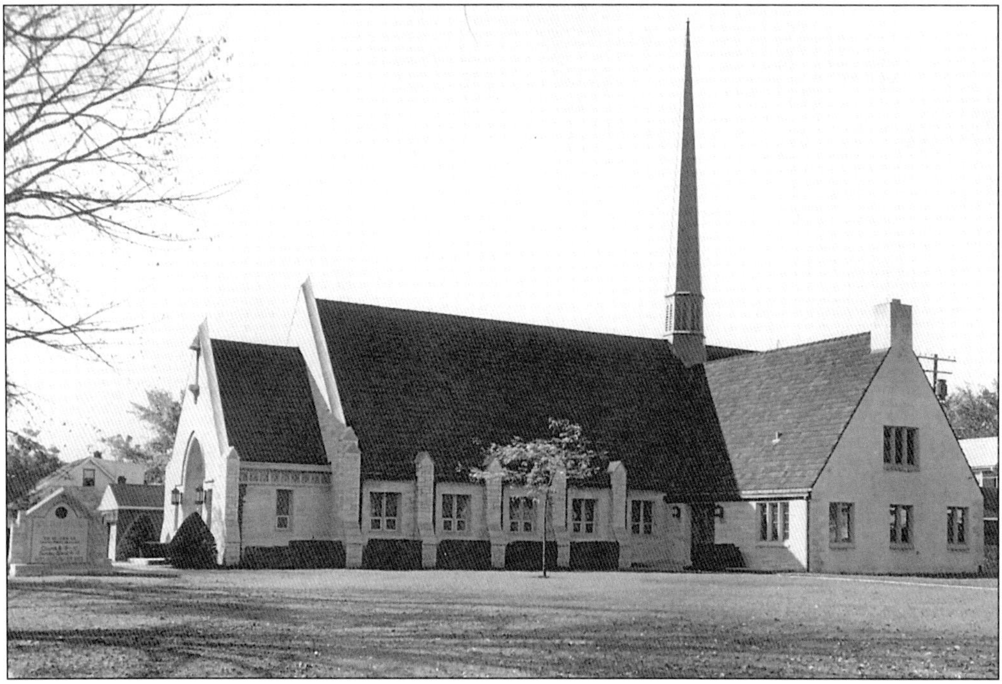

St. Paul's Lutheran Church was founded in 1930 and services were held in a prefabricated building on the east side of Lewis Avenue. The current church was built across the street in 1955.

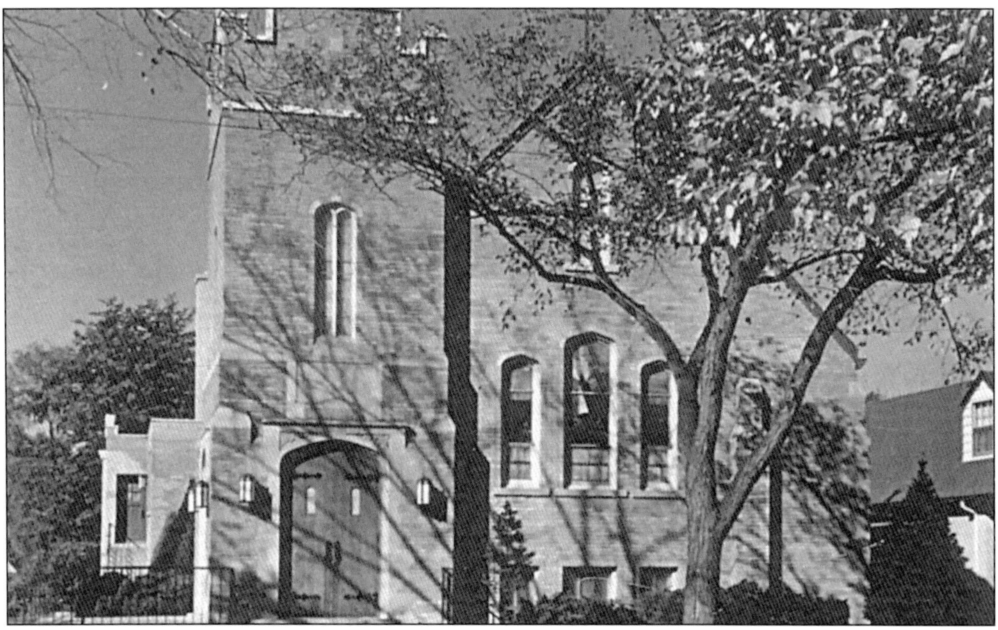

In 1891 Immanuel Evangelical Lutheran Church was organized as the first Lutheran church in Waukegan. Their first church was on Lake Street. This church, at Glen Rock and Chapel, was dedicated in 1924. A new church at Glen Flora and Frolic opened in 1995.

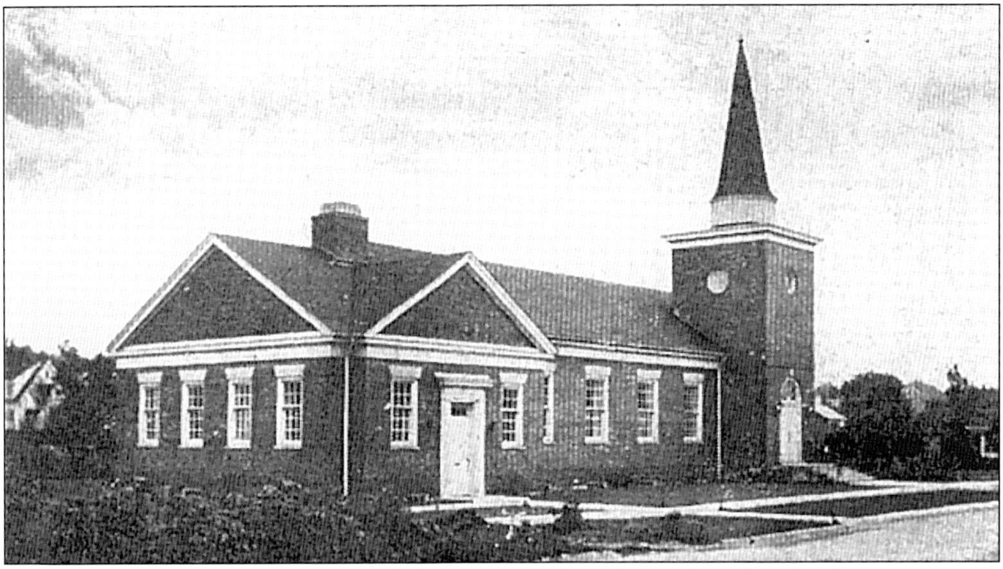

St. Mark's Lutheran Church was founded in 1893 as a Finnish-speaking church. The congregation first met on South Genesee Street. This church was dedicated in 1951 and served the congregation until it was sold prior to the church's move to Yorkhouse and Delaney in 1987.

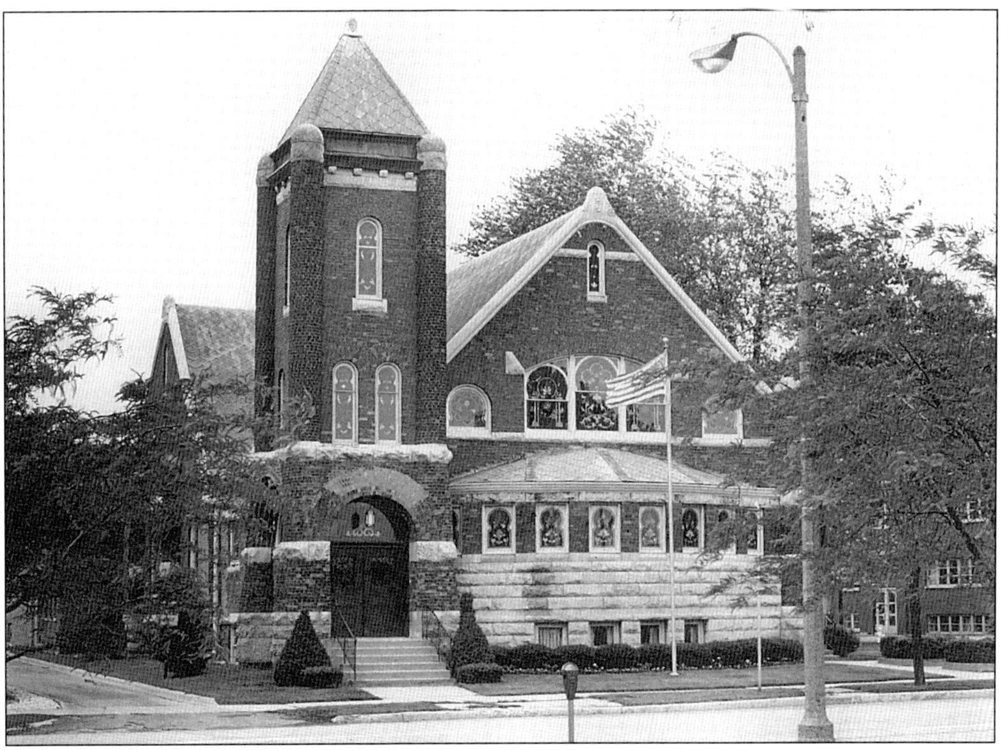

The First Presbyterian Church of Waukegan was formed in November 1857, and a church was built the following year. The cornerstone for the current building on Utica Street was laid November 18, 1893.

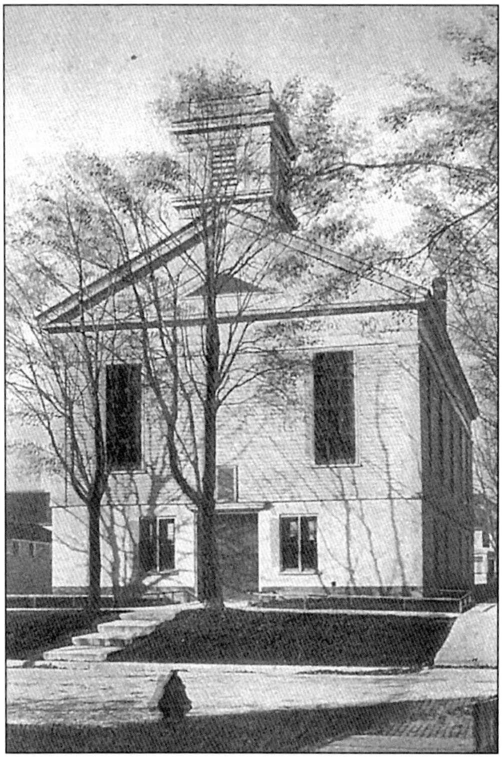

The First Methodist Church built its first church at Utica and Clayton in 1849. It was refitted and reopened in 1867.

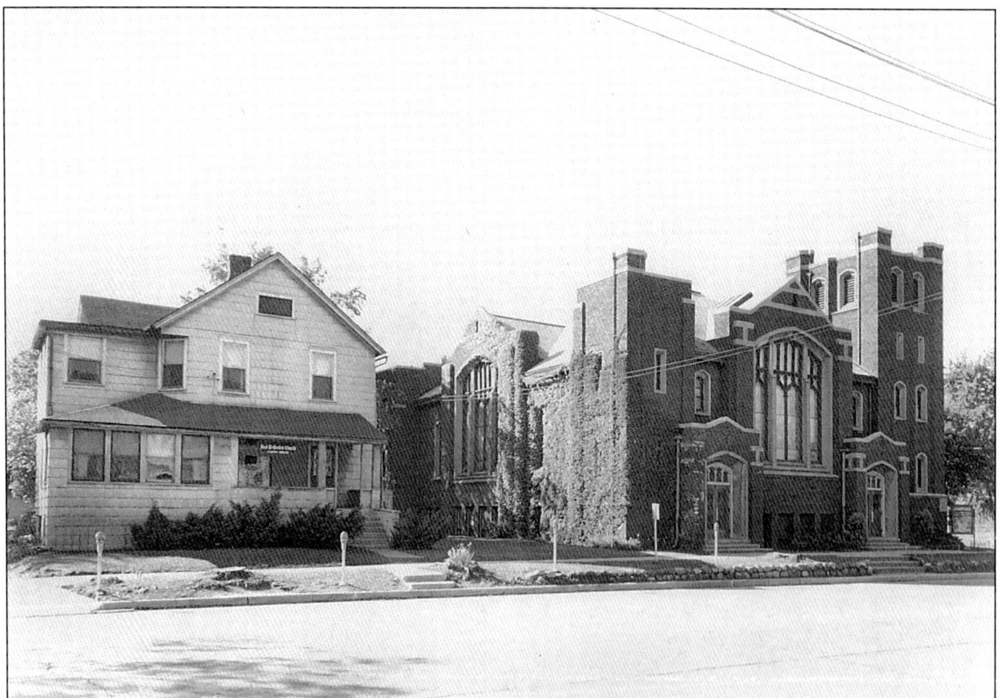

The present church, at the same location, was built in 1917 to meet the growing needs of the congregation.

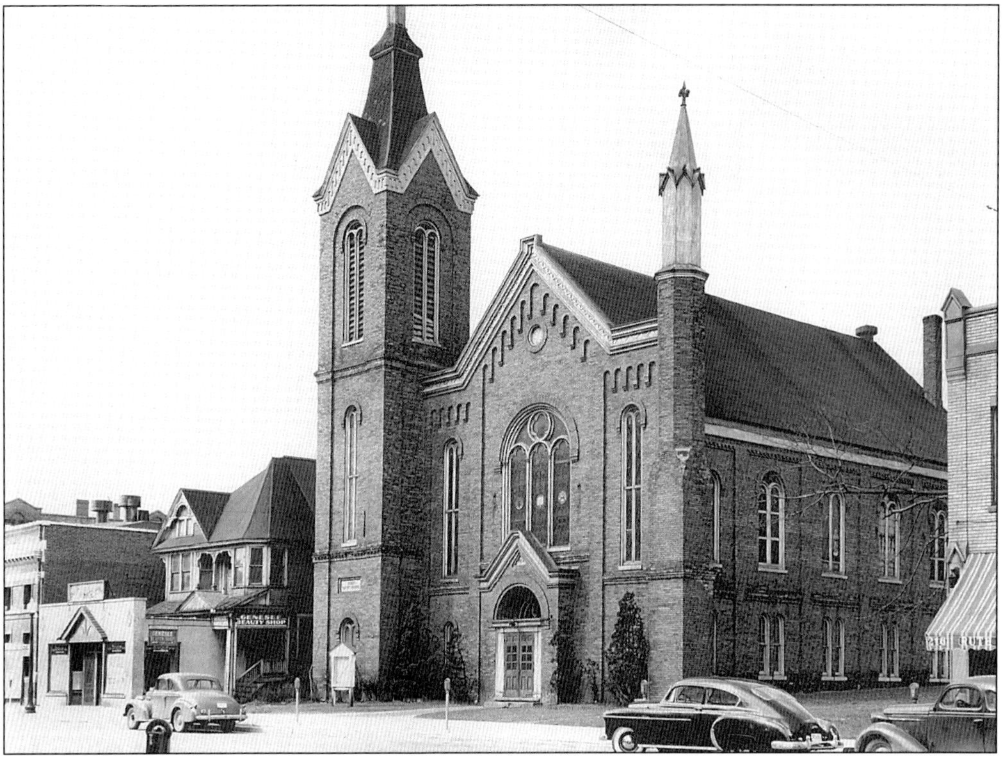

First Baptist Church was organized in 1846 and built its first building in 1849. Pictured is the second church, which was dedicated in 1866. The building was demolished in 1950.

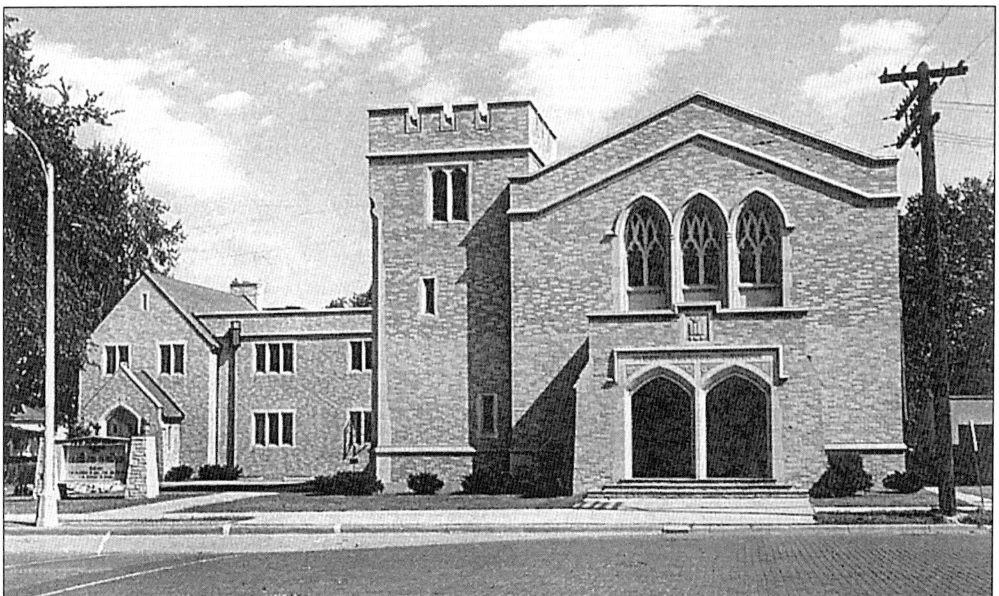

The new building, on the east side of Genesee Street, was dedicated September 10, 1950. Expansion of the church building was completed in 1982.

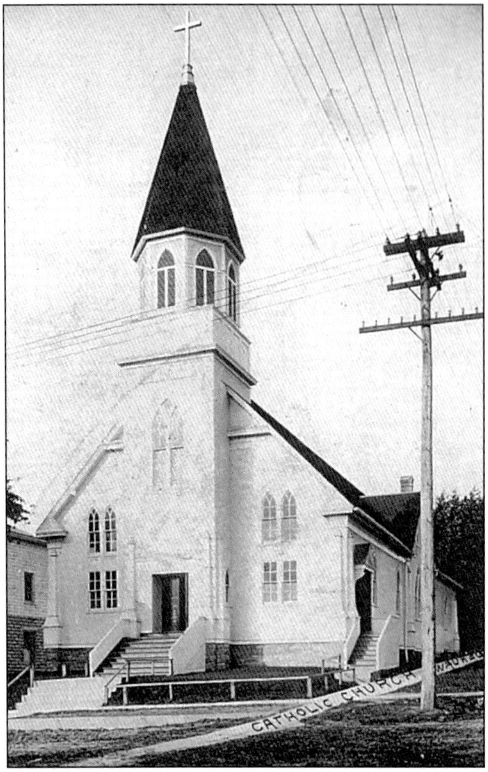

Immaculate Conception parish had its beginnings in 1844 when the Little Fort Church was the earliest in Lake County to become a parish. A church at County and Water was built in 1846, and its name became Immaculate Conception in 1864.

The new church, at Grand and West, had its dedication on May 11, 1930.

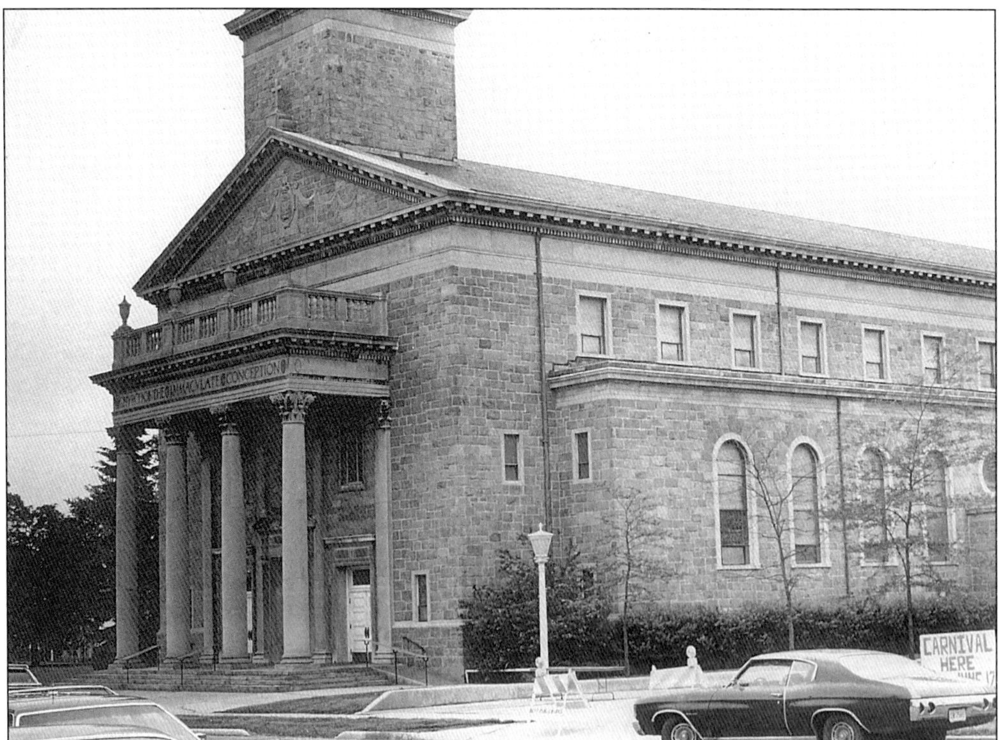

Eight

RECREATION

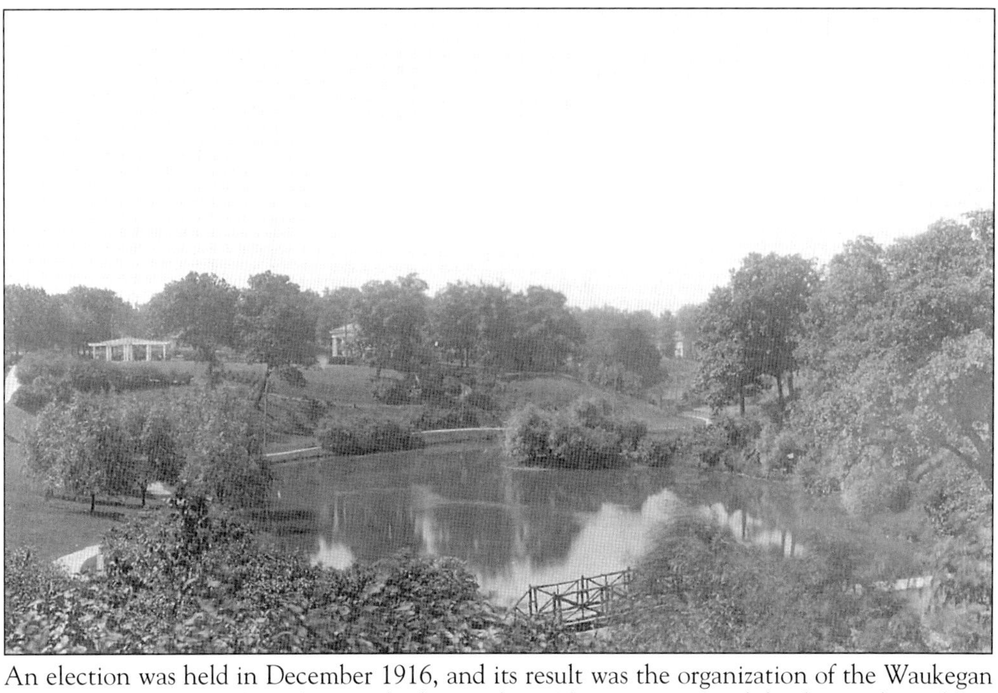

An election was held in December 1916, and its result was the organization of the Waukegan Park District. Roosevelt Park, at Belvidere and McAlister, was one of the first parks and was named after President Theodore Roosevelt.

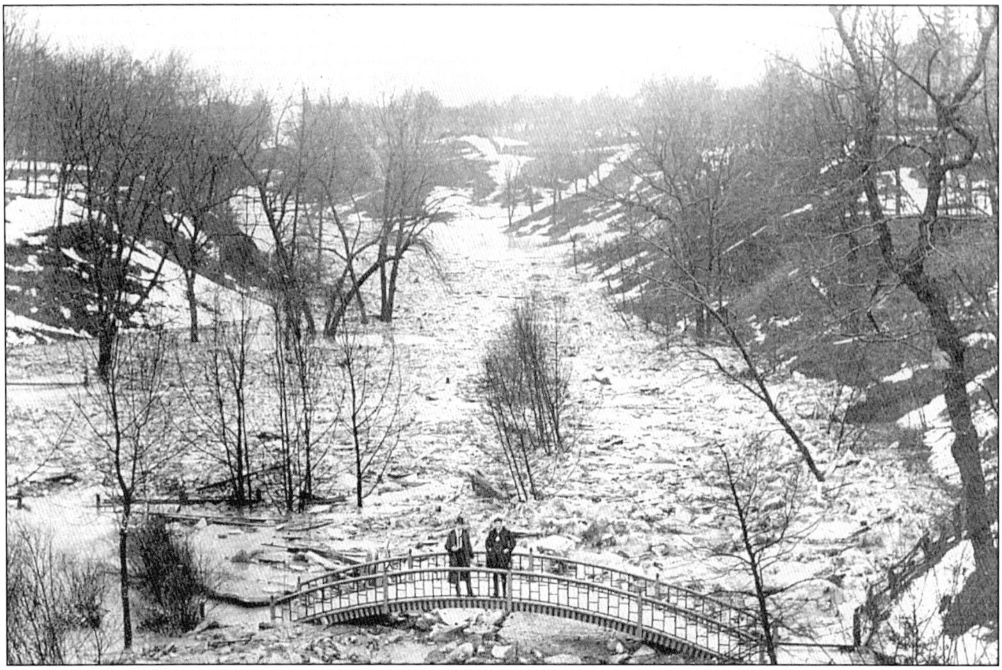

Roosevelt was almost 13 acres in size, and included a large lagoon used for fishing in the summer and ice skating in the winter. A bandstand, field house, and children's wading pool were added attractions.

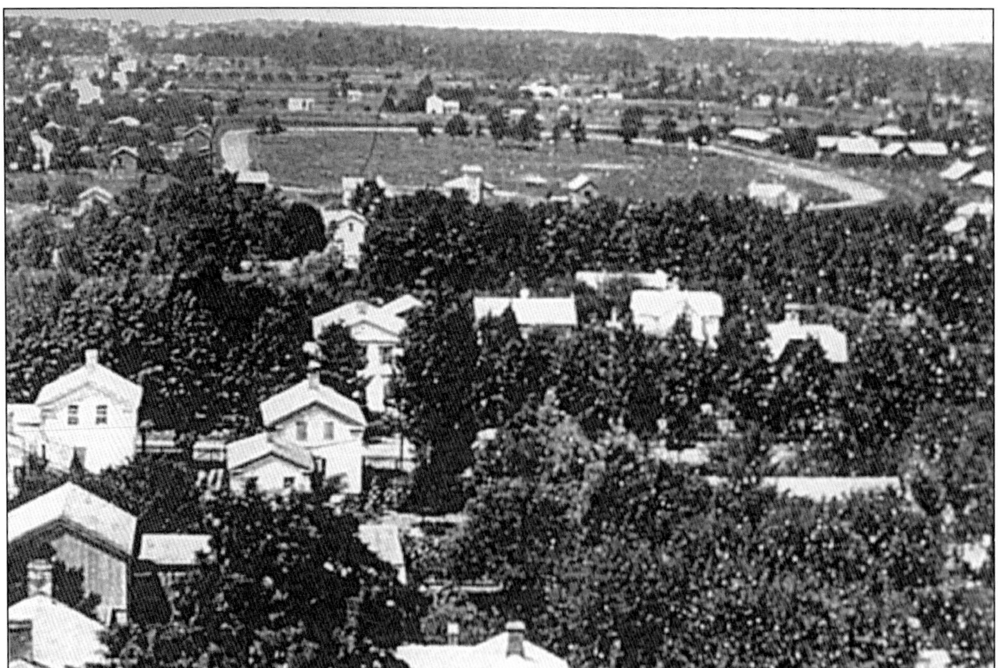

The Waukegan Fair grounds, around Jackson and Washington, operated in the 1870s and '80s. Annual fairs were held, with lots of horse racing featured on the track seen on the upper portion of this photograph.

A major attraction in Waukegan in the 1800s were the mineral springs. The waters from the springs were advertised as having great curative qualities, and there were many testimonials by persons positively impacted by the water. The treatable diseases were numerous and the science of the times supported the claims. Magnesia Mineral Springs, operated by J.F. Powell & Co., was one of several in the city.

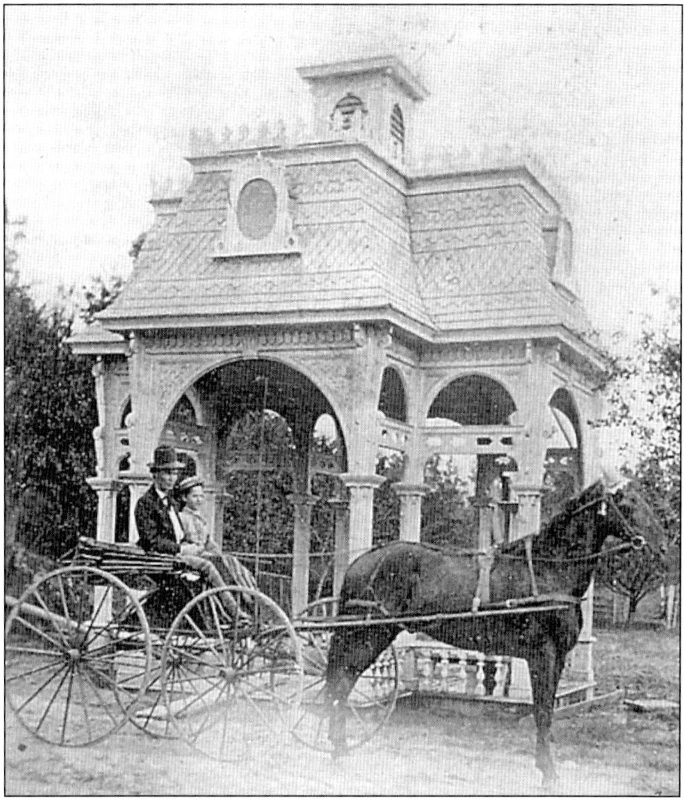

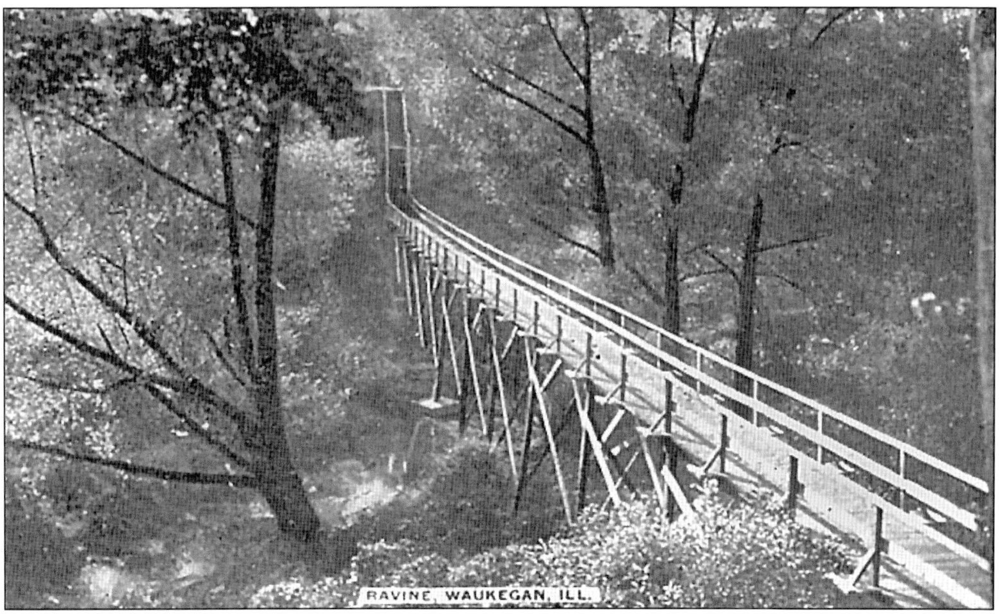

Another major attraction for the city was the ravines. The natural beauty of these areas was appreciated, even if they created natural barriers hemming in parts of the city. Eventually, viaducts, bridges, and land fills solved the transportation issues, but at the cost of some of the ravines' magic.

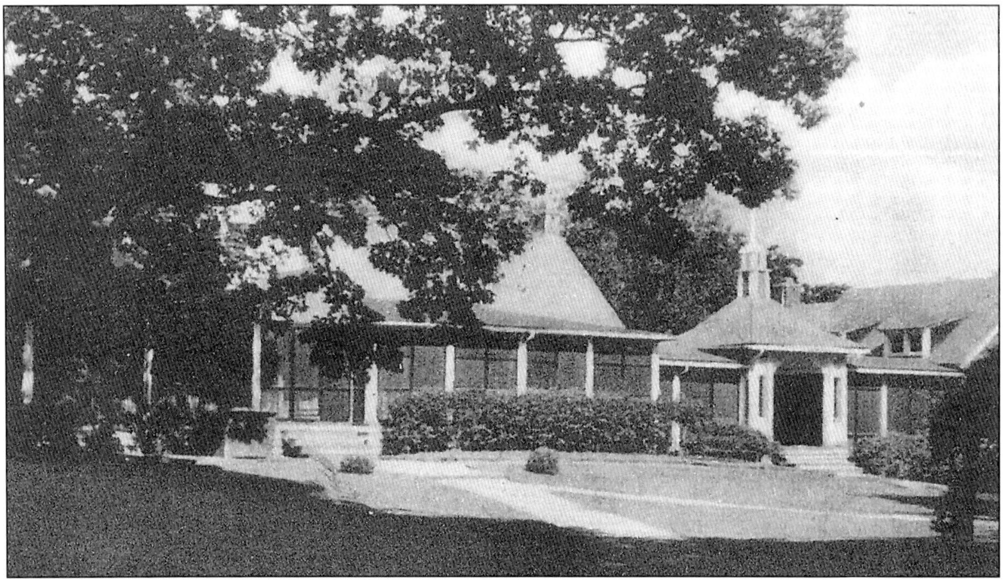

Beginning in 1912, Chicago's Hull House Association took children out of the city for a country vacation in Waukegan. Bowen Country Club was not a country club in the typical sense, but the name helped promote a sense of ownership in the camp. Transportation from Chicago was provided by the Northwestern Railroad.

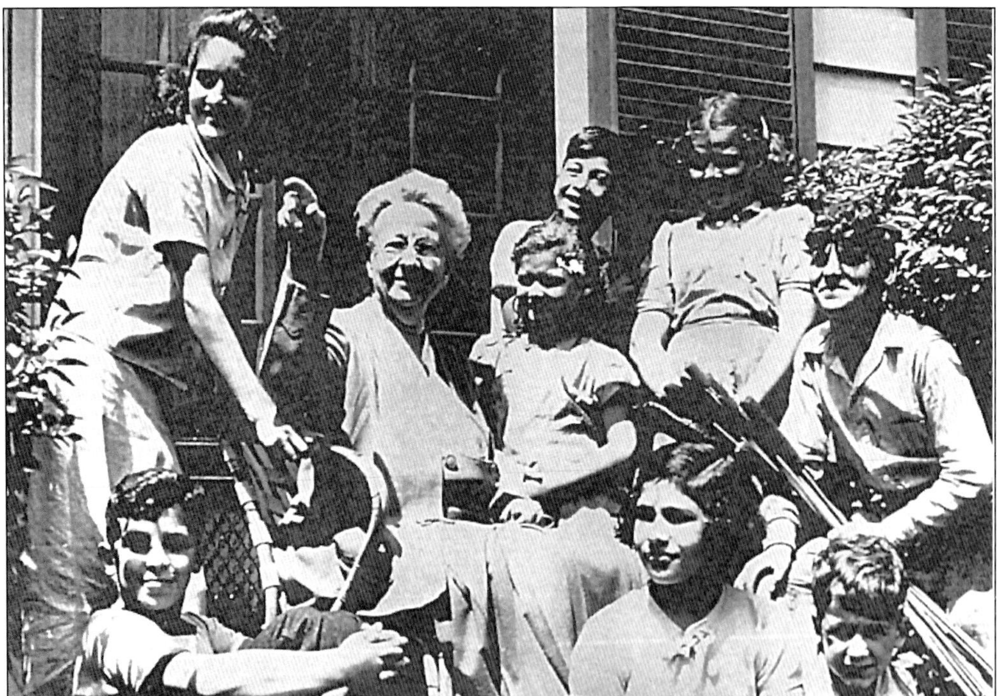

The property, once owned by John Haines, was purchased by Mrs. Louise DeKoven Bowen and named in honor of her husband. She had a house built in 1928. In her later years she spent her summers here. The Waukegan Park District purchased the property in 1963 and turned it into Bowen Park.

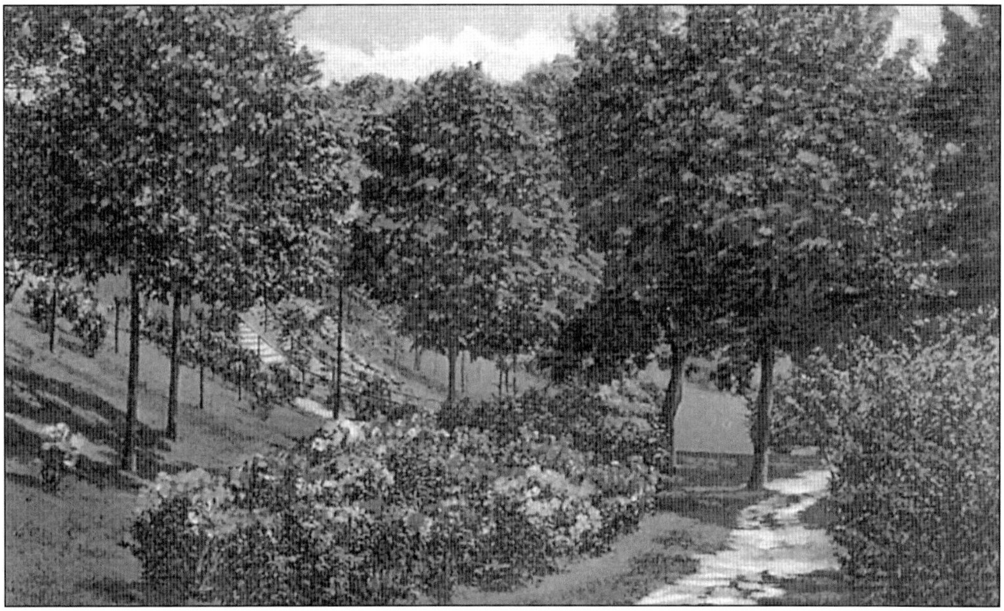

In 1917 the Waukegan Park District purchased 6.5 acres, including part of the Bairstow farm. The subsequent park initially was named Grand Avenue Park. Later the name was changed to Powell Park, named for George N. Powell, Waukegan Chief of Police and Lake County Sheriff.

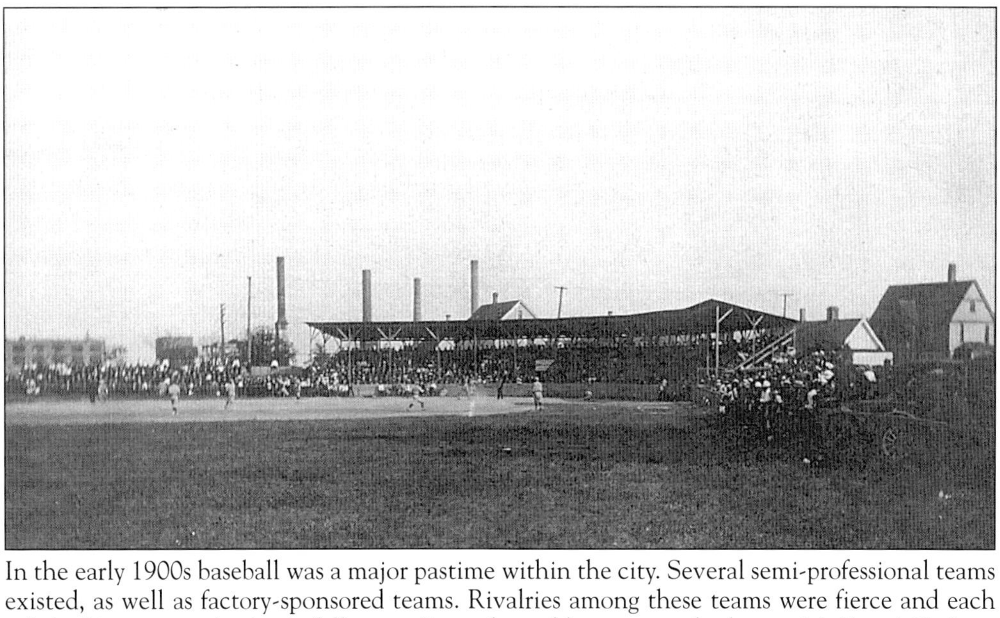

In the early 1900s baseball was a major pastime within the city. Several semi-professional teams existed, as well as factory-sponsored teams. Rivalries among these teams were fierce and each side had its own enthusiastic followers. Several notable games took place at McCann's Park on South Genesee Street.

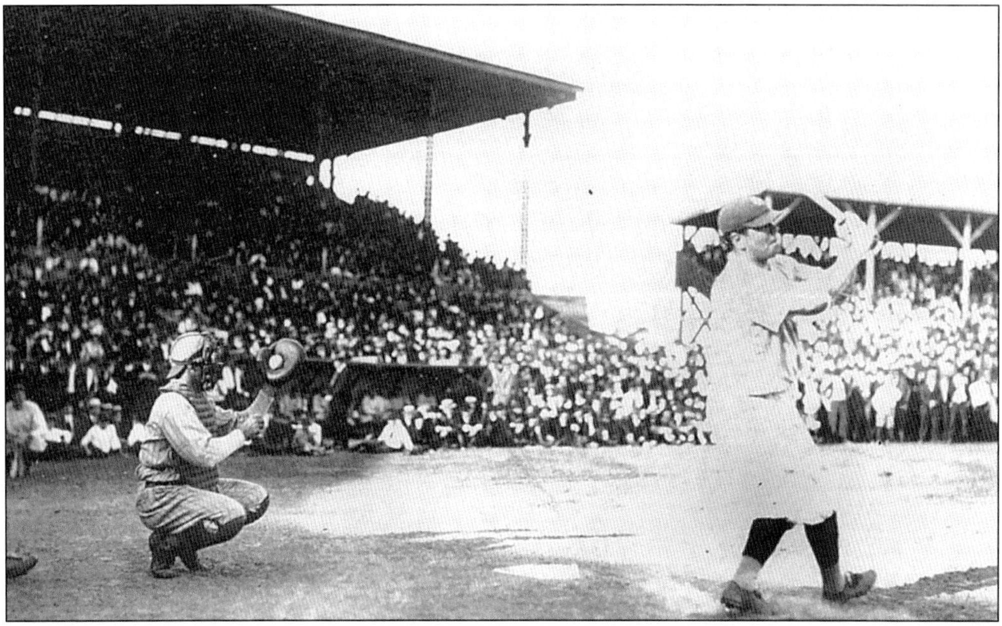

Some local players eventually made it to the major leagues. Ernie Krueger, here catching while the great Babe Ruth is batting, played for five teams in a career which ran from 1913 to 1925, including the 1920 World Series.

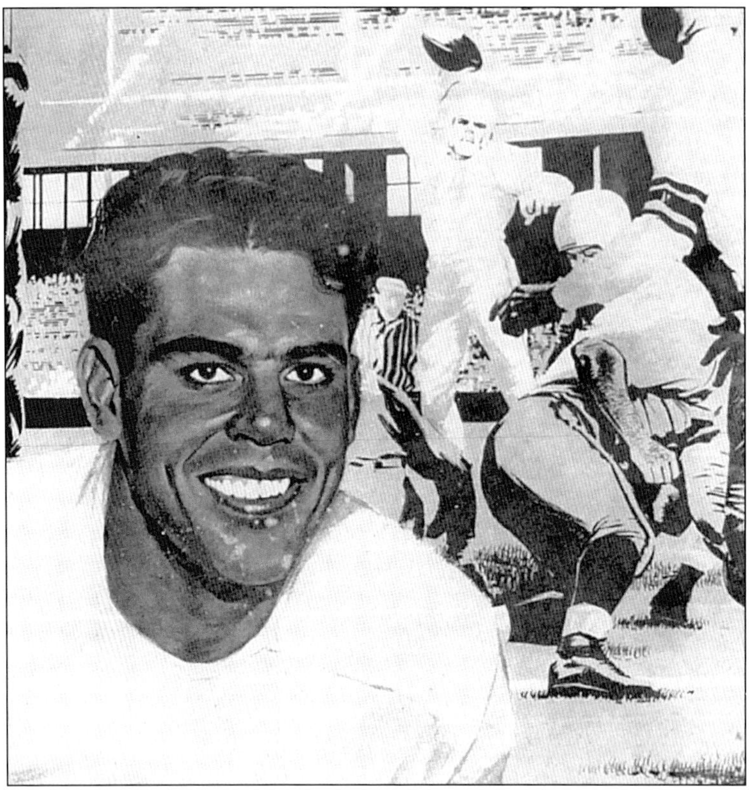

Another local great, though in different sports, was Otto Graham. At Northwestern University he was an All-American in basketball and football. He played both sports professionally, and was enshrined in the Pro Football Hall of Fame.

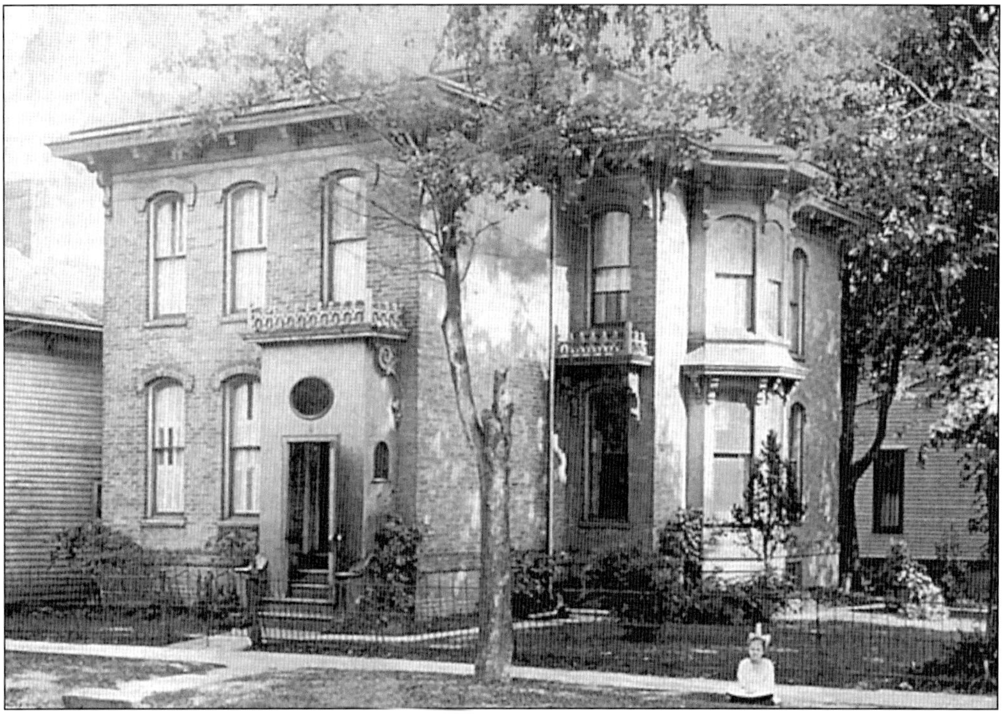

Clubs and social and service organizations have always been an important part of Waukegan's fabric. The local lodge of the Independent Order of Odd Fellows was chartered in 1847. Although disbanded during the Civil War, it was reorganized in 1890. They occupied this building at Grand and Utica for almost 50 years.

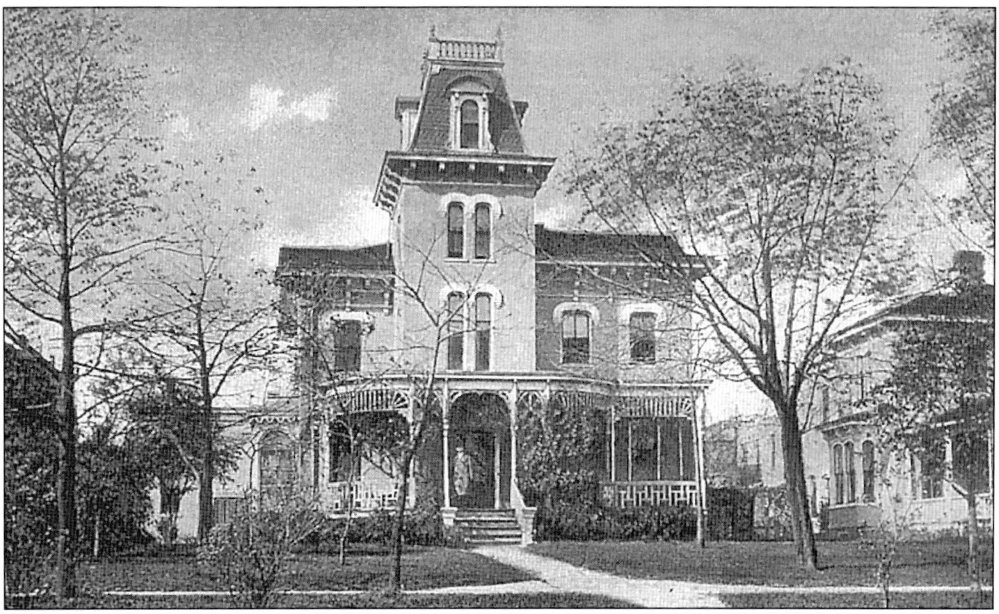

The Waukegan Elk's Lodge was chartered August 14, 1902. Meetings were held at various locations until a house was purchased at Grand and Sheridan. It served the lodge until fire struck in February 1984.

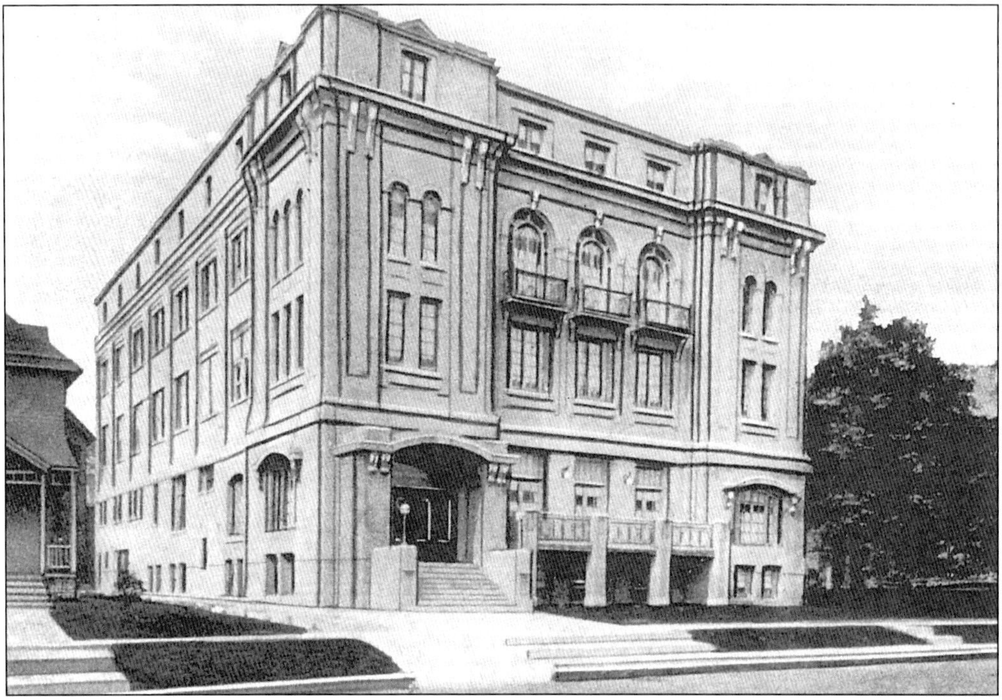

The first meeting of local Masons was held on October 25, 1848. Numerous other lodges were formed, so the need arose for a Masonic Temple. The first, at Sheridan and Washington, held its initial meeting in 1887. This building on north Sheridan Road served the lodges from 1920 to 1982.

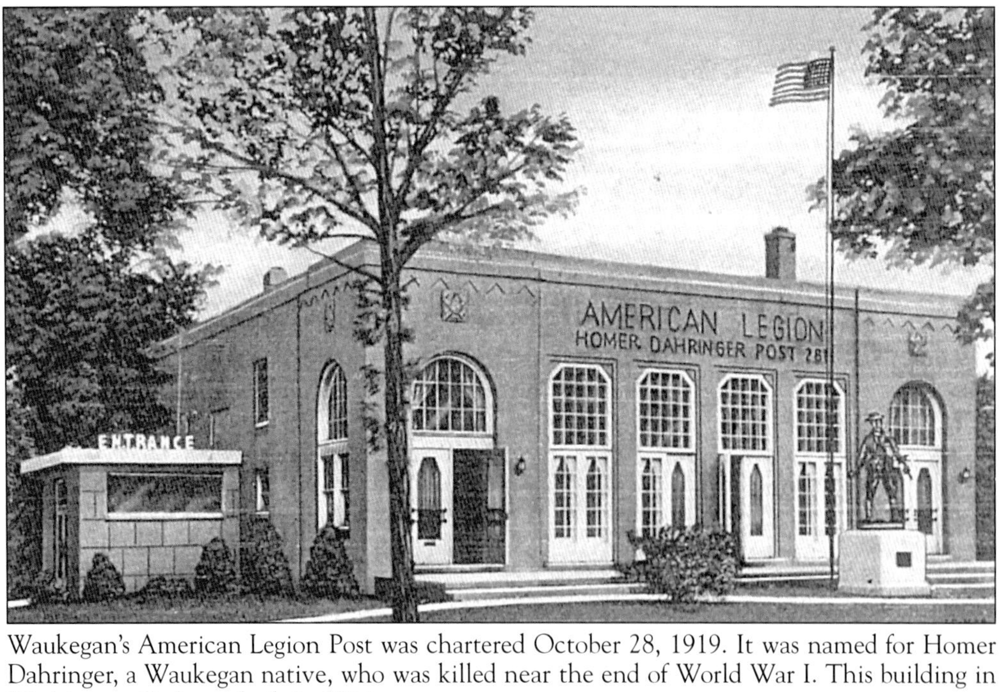

Waukegan's American Legion Post was chartered October 28, 1919. It was named for Homer Dahringer, a Waukegan native, who was killed near the end of World War I. This building in Washington Park was built in 1931.

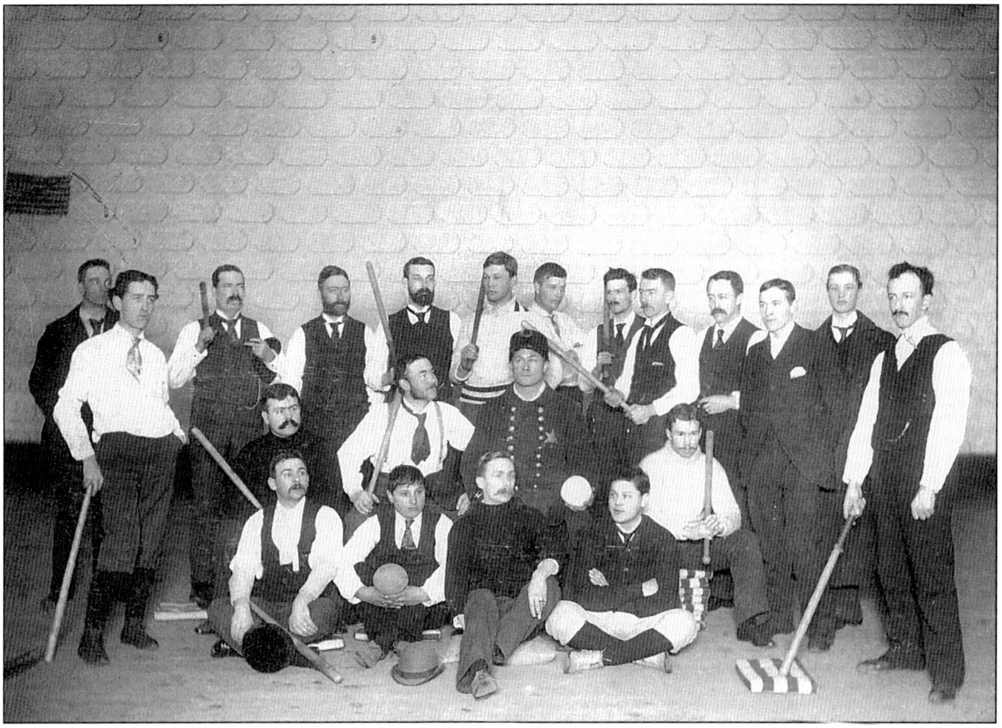

A social club of long ago was the Waukegan Bachelors' Club, organized in 1891. They had a clubhouse on Third Lake, and even marriage wouldn't force a member out of the club. The member, however, was no longer eligible to become president.

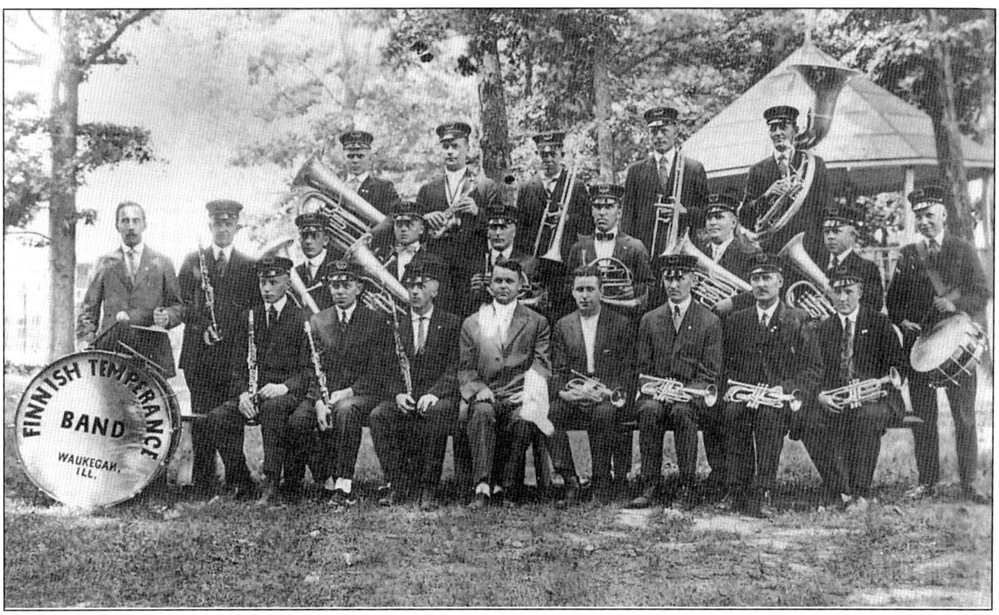

As were churches and living areas, social organizations were often structured on ethnic grounds. Many of them involved music, such as the Swedish Glee Club and this Finnish Temperance Band.

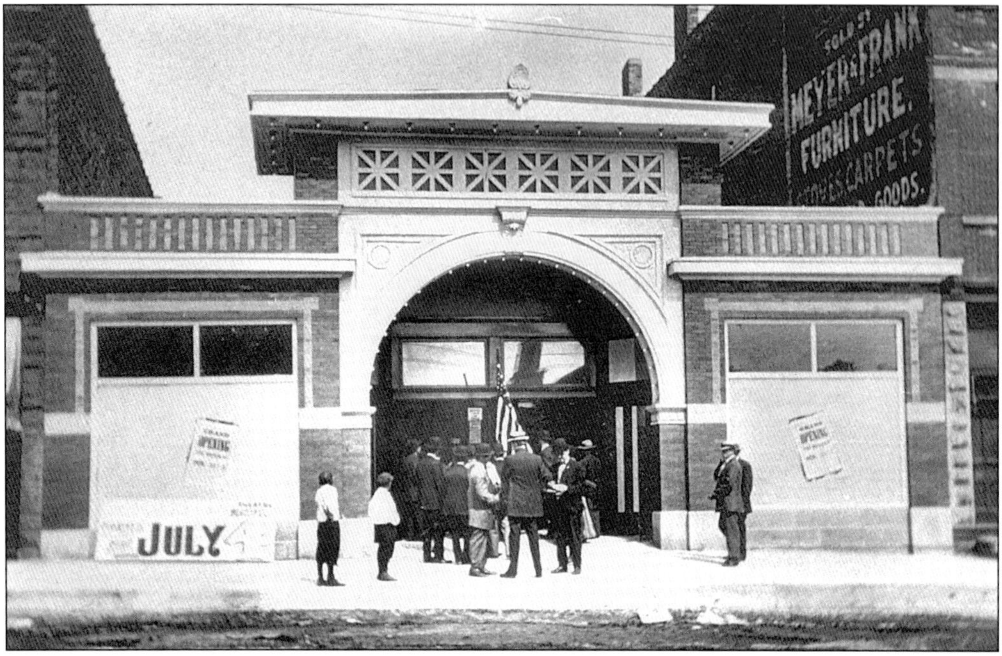

Theatres have been an important segment of Waukegan's entertainment package. From dramatic performances to vaudeville to motion pictures the theatres have been essential. It was in a Waukegan theatre that Edward Amet first demonstrated his magniscope, the first practical motion picture projector, in 1894. The industry, locally and nationally, took off from there. Here, the Waukegan Theatre on south Genesee Street prepares for its opening July 4, 1910.

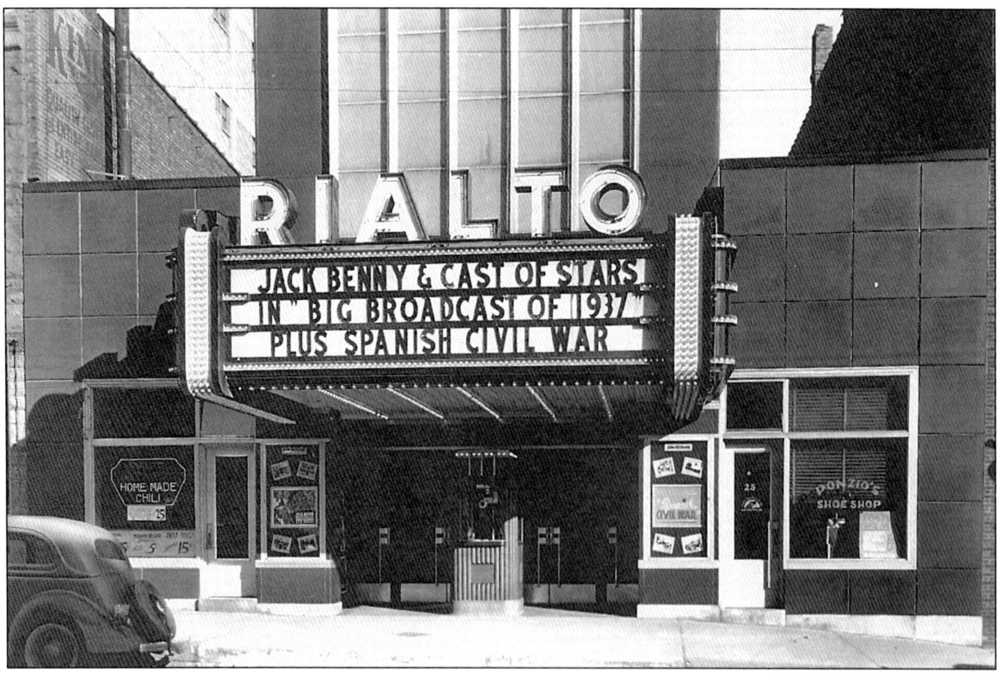

The name changed to the New Barrison the following year, and then the Orpheum. Finally the name became the Rialto and stayed that way until the theatre closed in 1953.

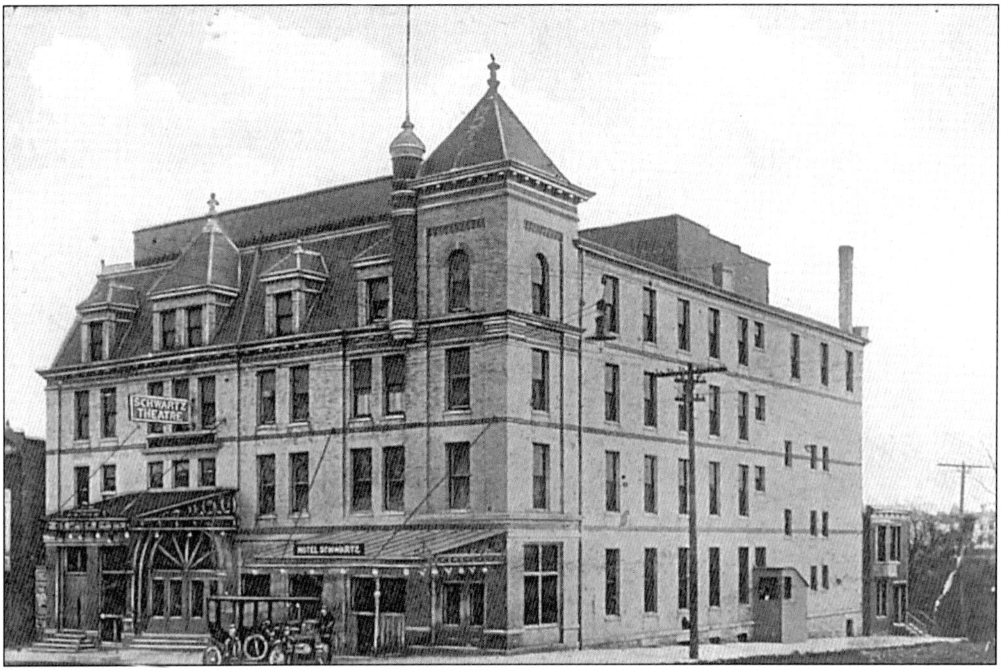

The Schwartz at County and Water was used primarily for live performances. Stock companies would take up residence here and perform a variety of plays. The theatre was renamed the Majestic in 1913, and the building was demolished in 1955.

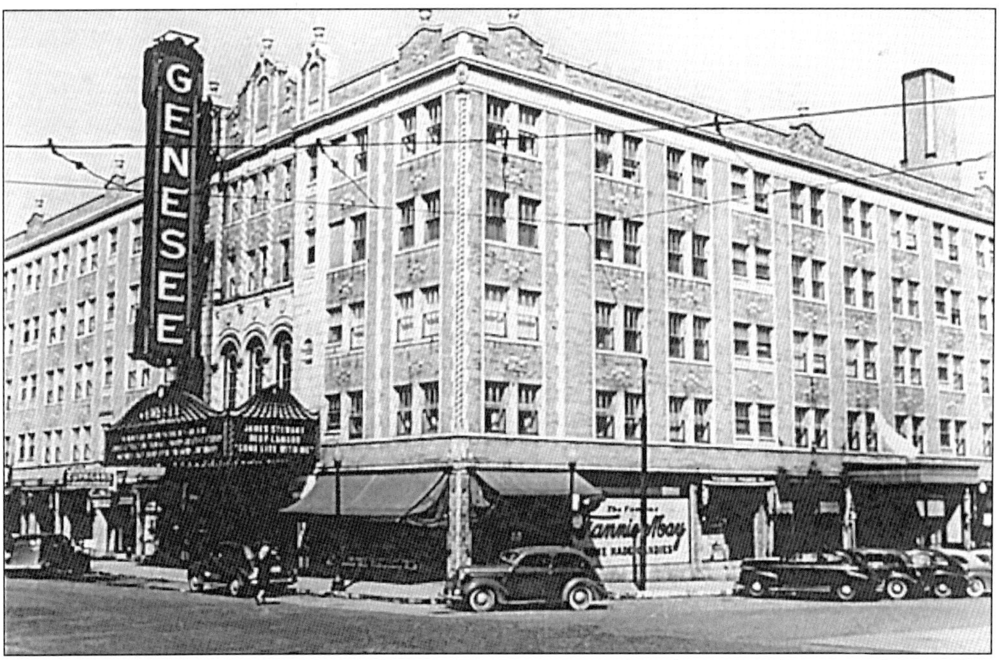

The Genesee Theatre opened on Christmas Day 1927, with a dance band, a comedy act, four variety acts, and a movie. It served as the premier theatre along the north shore. This 1941 photo shows that James Stewart and Hedy Lamarr were starring in *Come Live with Me* as the featured attraction.

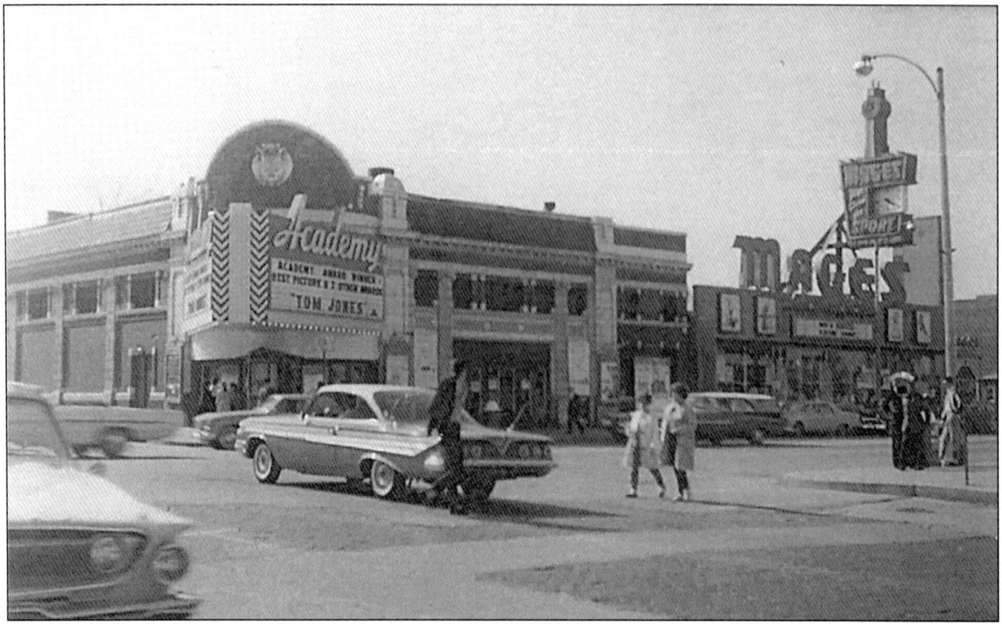

Across the street was the Academy Theatre, built in 1916. It was the only theatre in Waukegan with a pipe organ. All this was provided in an absolutely fireproof environment and with perfect ventilation. This picture is from 1963.

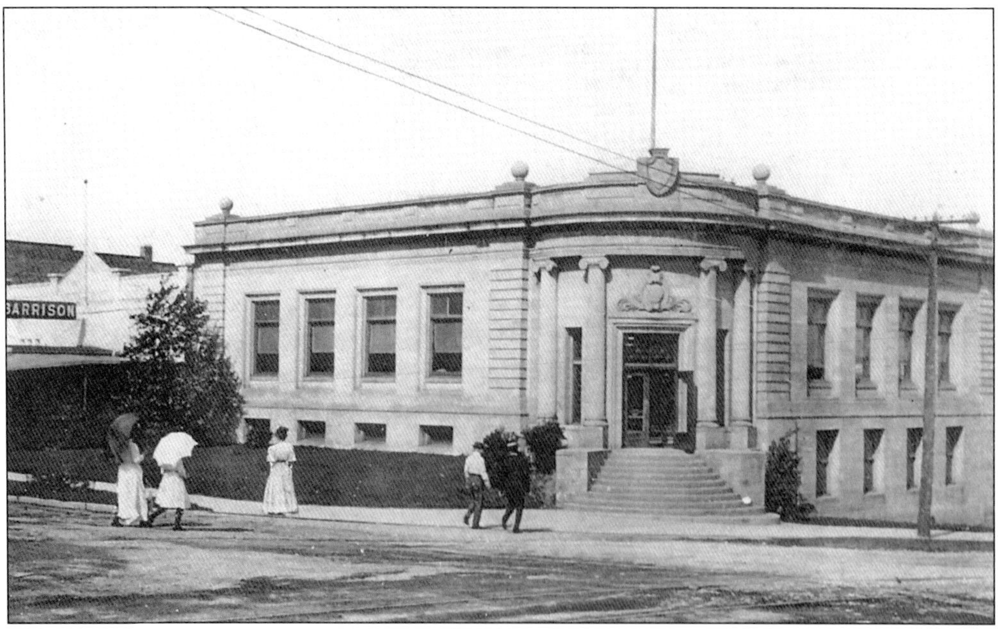

Another early presence was the Barrison Theatre, on Sheridan Road adjacent to the Carnegie Library. A livery stable was transformed into the Barrison in 1907 for stage performances. It was named for Mabel Barrison, a popular performer of the day. Several name changes followed before the final closing in 1913.

Nine

Schools

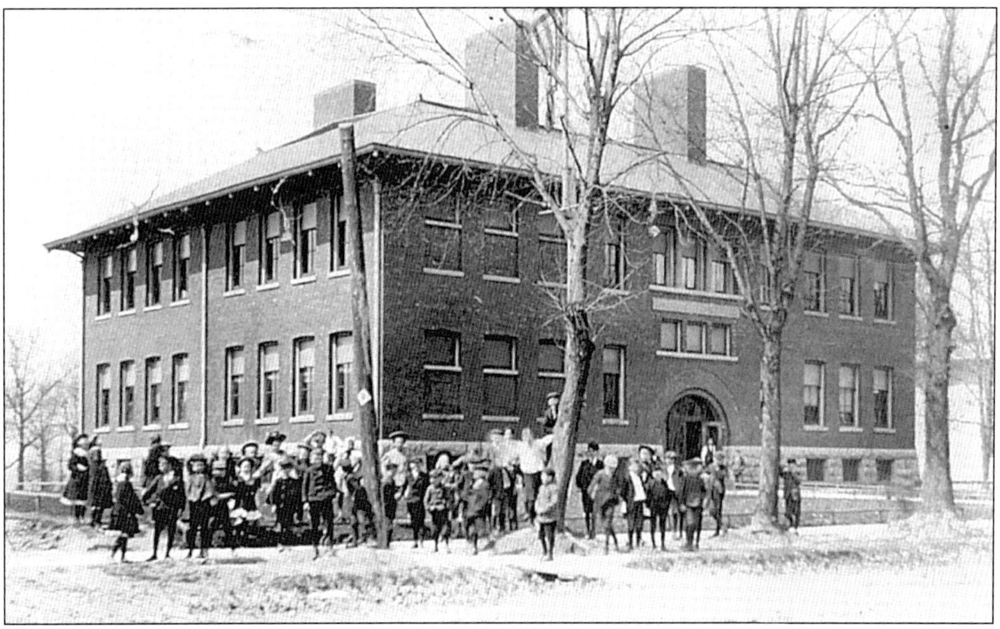

The building of this school, at McAlister and Helmholz, began in 1902 because of the crowding at South School. Immigrants working at the city's factories caused a population boom in the area, and necessitated school construction. Additions to the school were made to handle the growing enrollment. Demolition of the building occurred in 1969.

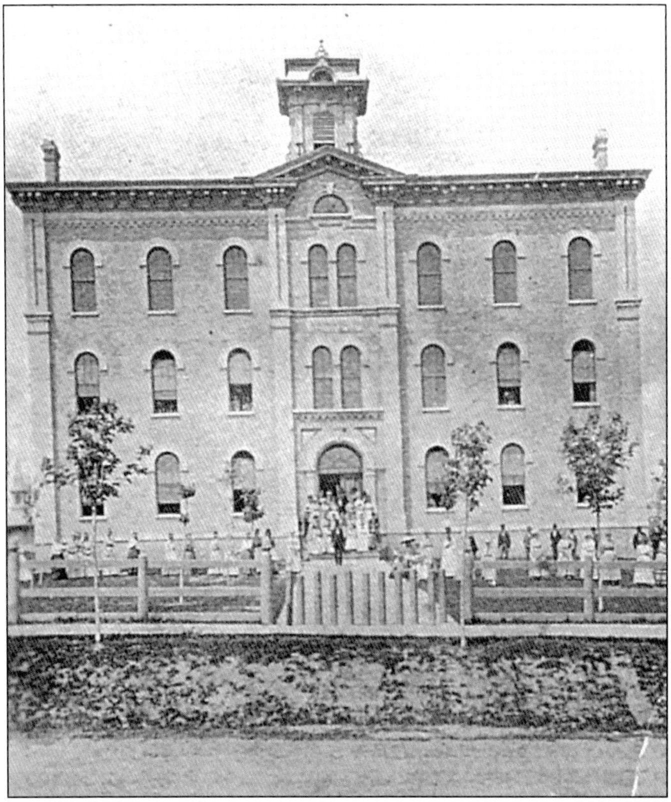

Central School, at County and Clayton, was opened in January 1870, and it served as both a grade school and the city's high school. High school classes were held on the upper floor. The first high school graduation was in 1874 and was made up of four girls.

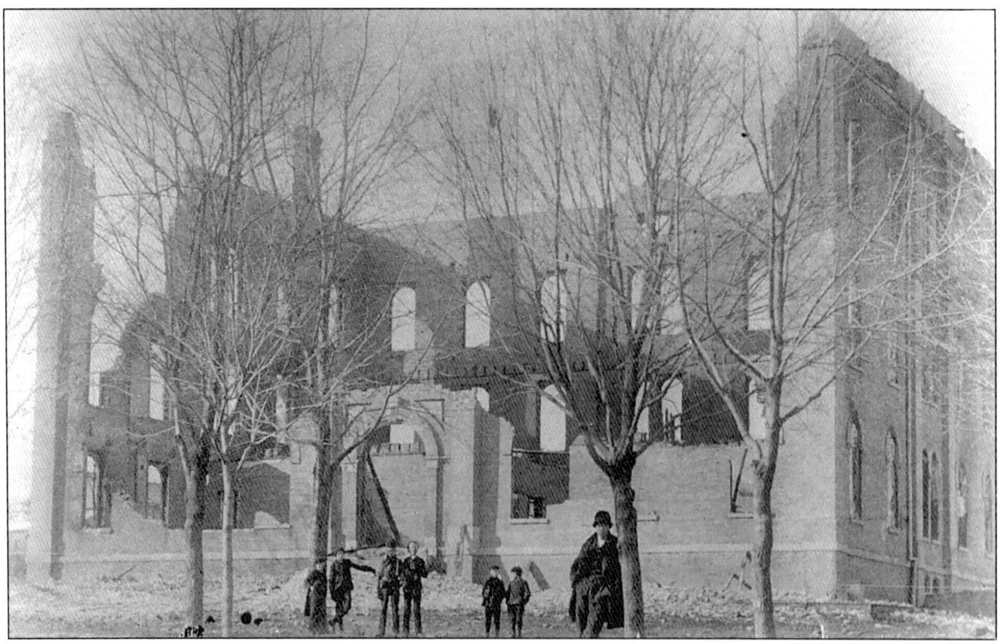

On January 21, 1889, Central School was destroyed by fire. Students were required to attend classes at various churches and schools. The re-built three-story school opened for the next school year.

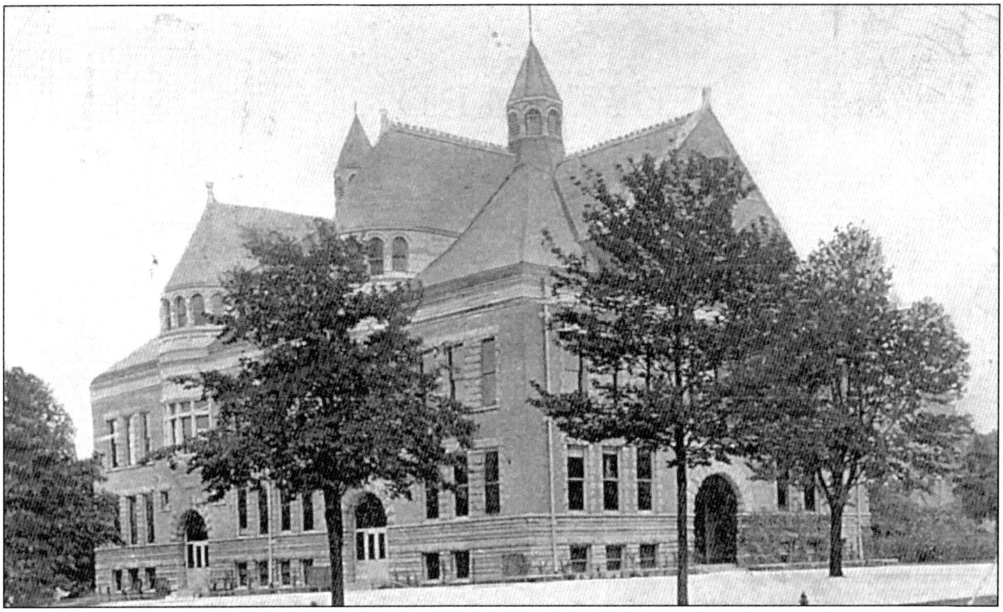

Central School continued to serve as the city's high school for the next 20 years. It reverted to a grade school when the township high school opened in 1910.

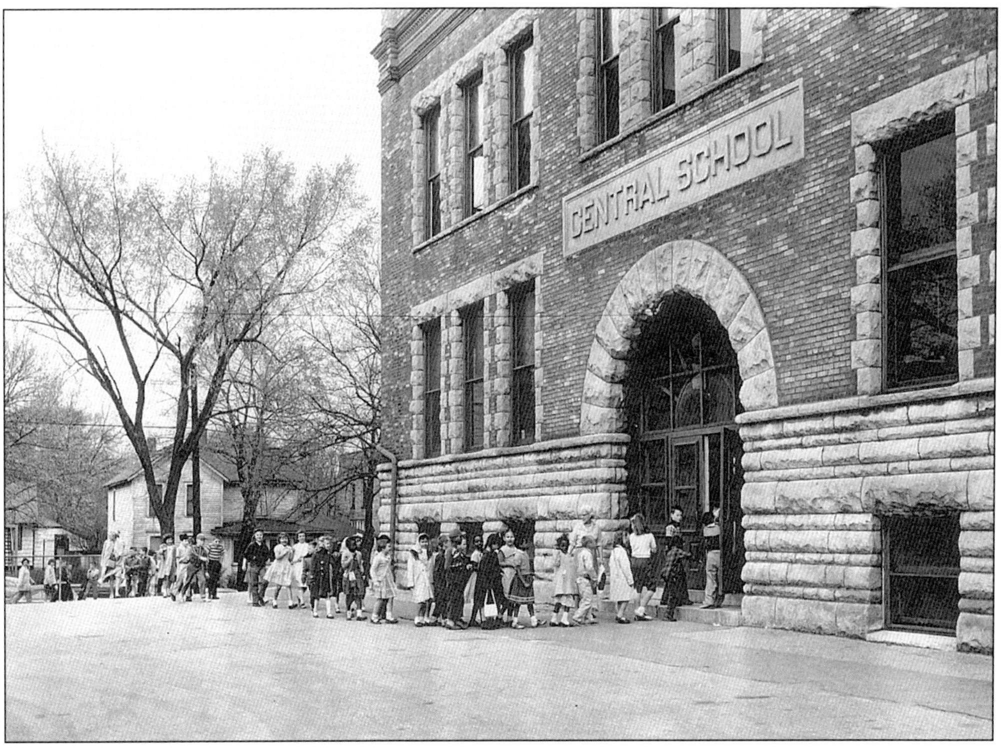

The heavy slate gable roof and the third story were removed in 1925 amid concerns about the weight of the roof. The building continued as a grade school until it was demolished in 1965 to make way for the new library.

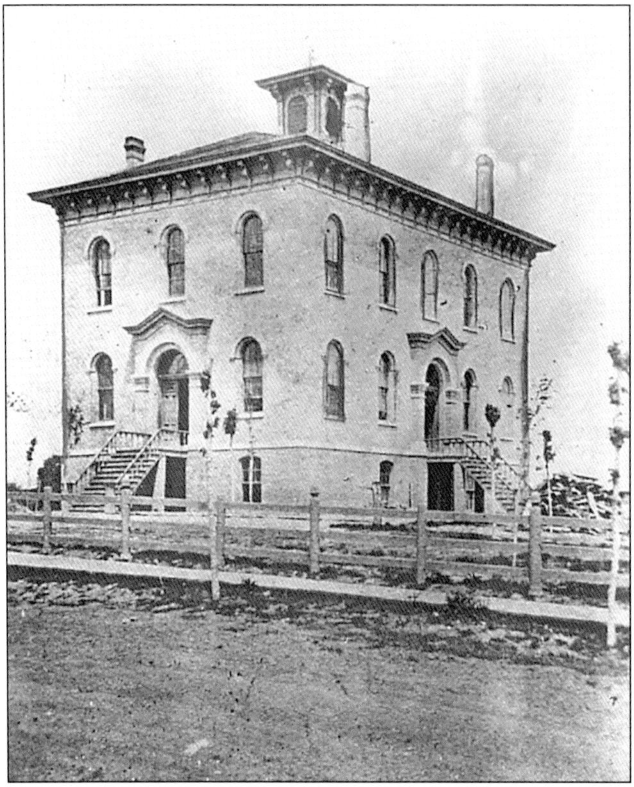

The first purchase of land for school purposes was made on June 30, 1856. North School, on Franklin Street, was built in 1860. Additions were built in 1870 and 1895.

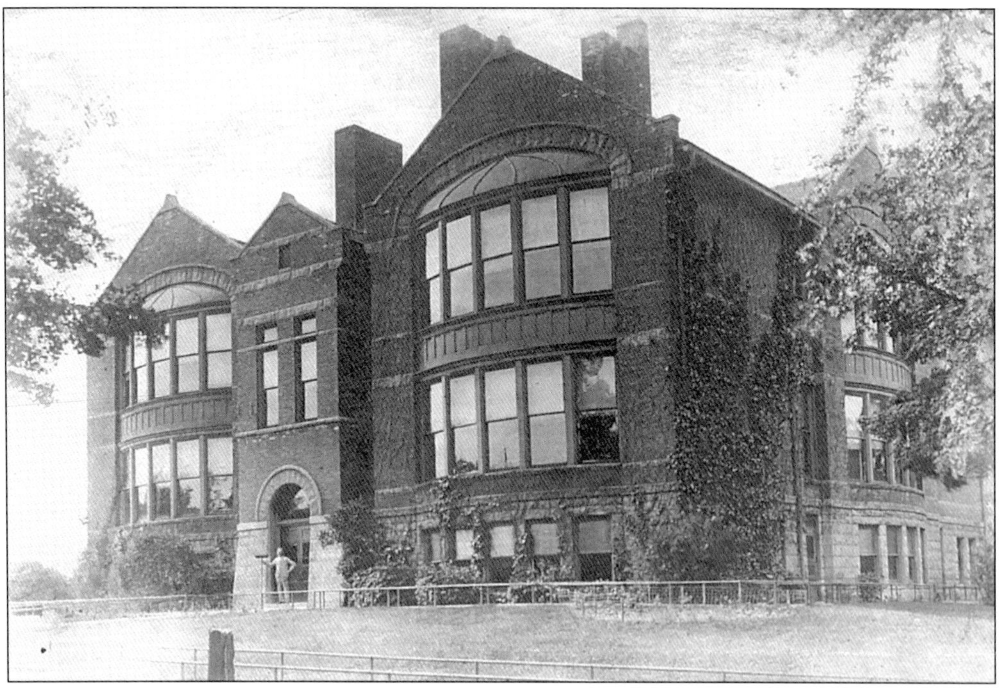

A new wing was added in 1931. The older wing of the building was demolished and a new east wing of the school was completed in 1963.

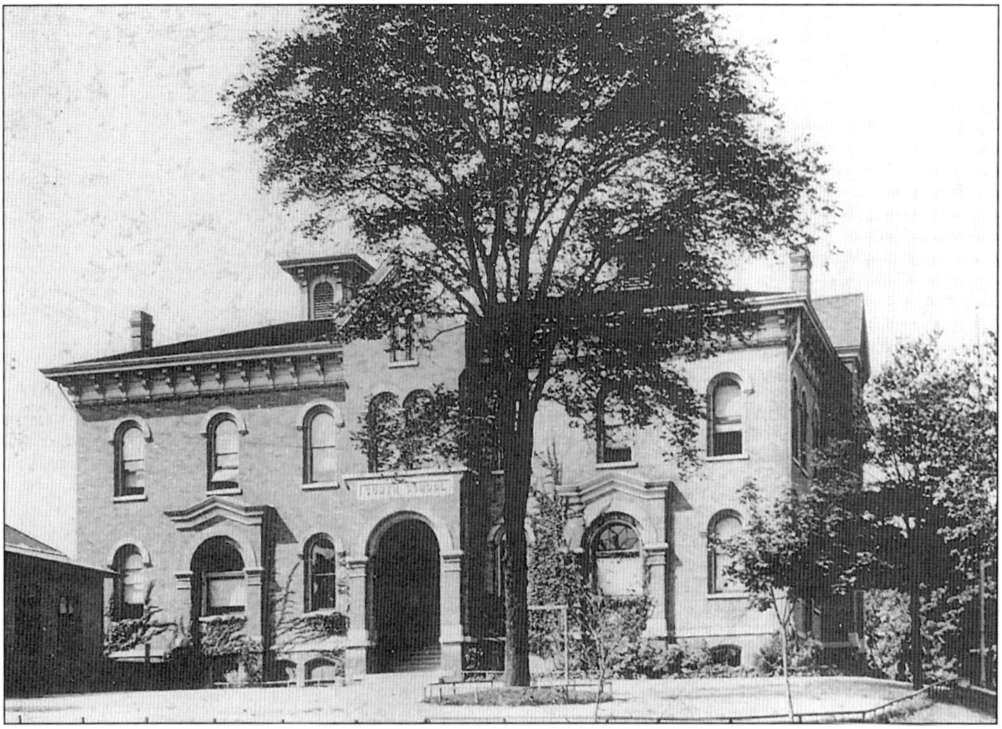

South School, on Liberty between Oak and Utica, was built in the 1860s. Many local notables attended classes there, including Jack Benny. The building was torn down in 1941.

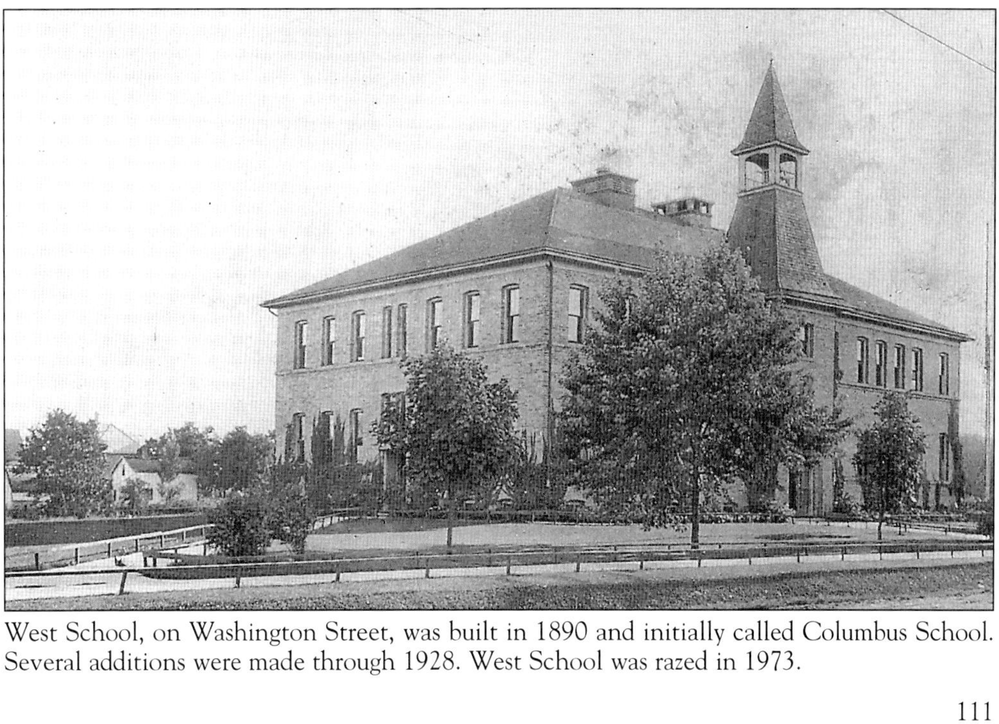

West School, on Washington Street, was built in 1890 and initially called Columbus School. Several additions were made through 1928. West School was razed in 1973.

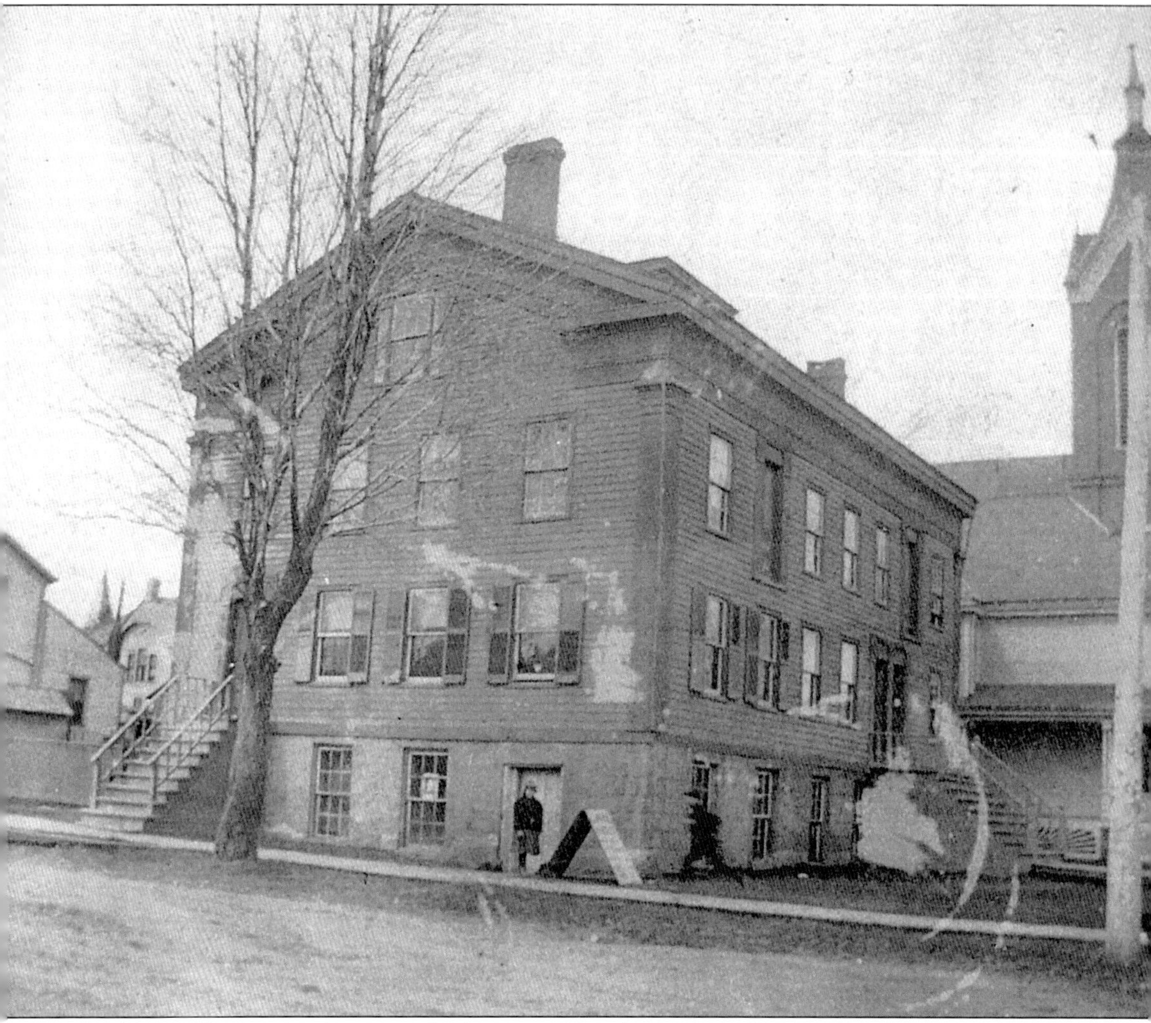

The Waukegan Academy was built in 1845 at the corner of Genesee and Clayton by H.L. Hatch. He served as principal of the school, which was the beginning of formal education in the area. The Academy Theatre was named such after it replaced the school at the same spot in 1916.

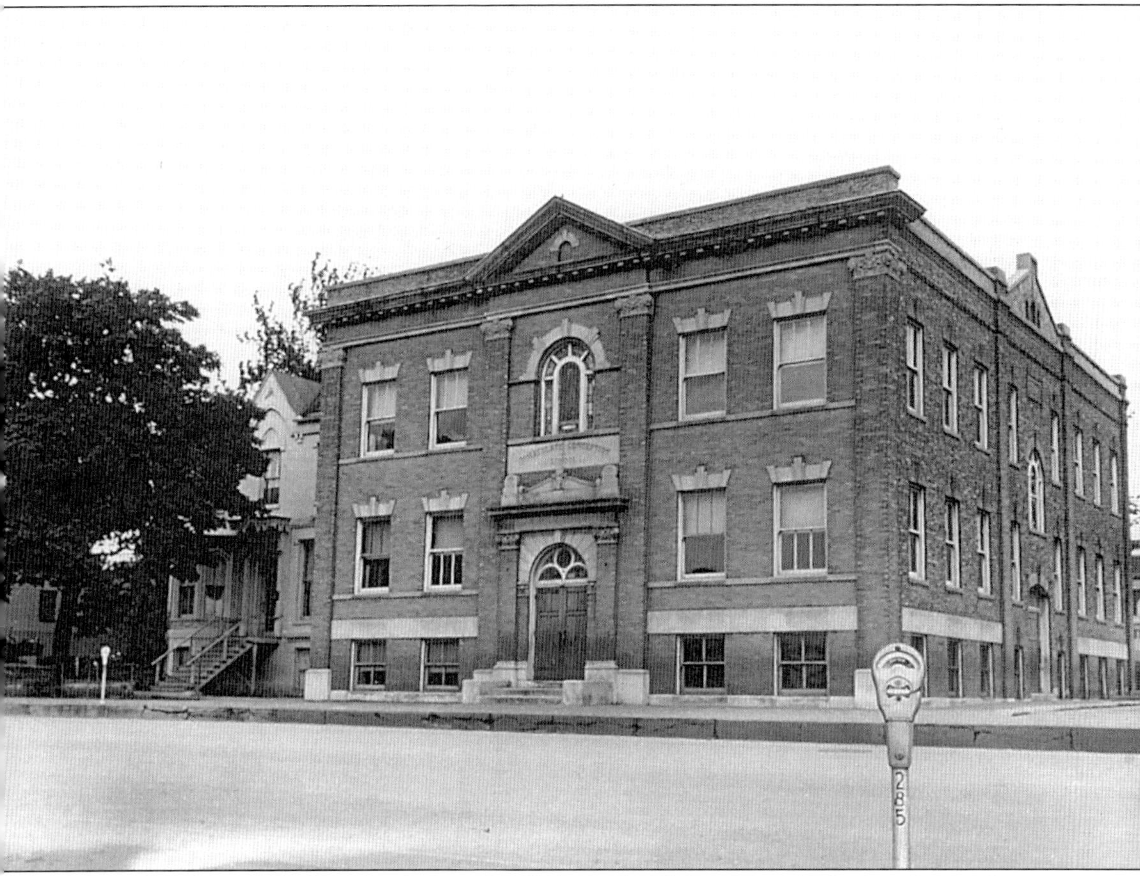

Waukegan's first Catholic school was a small frame building on south County Street. It was moved and eventually replaced by this building in 1908. Immaculate Conception school moved to Grand Avenue in 1956.

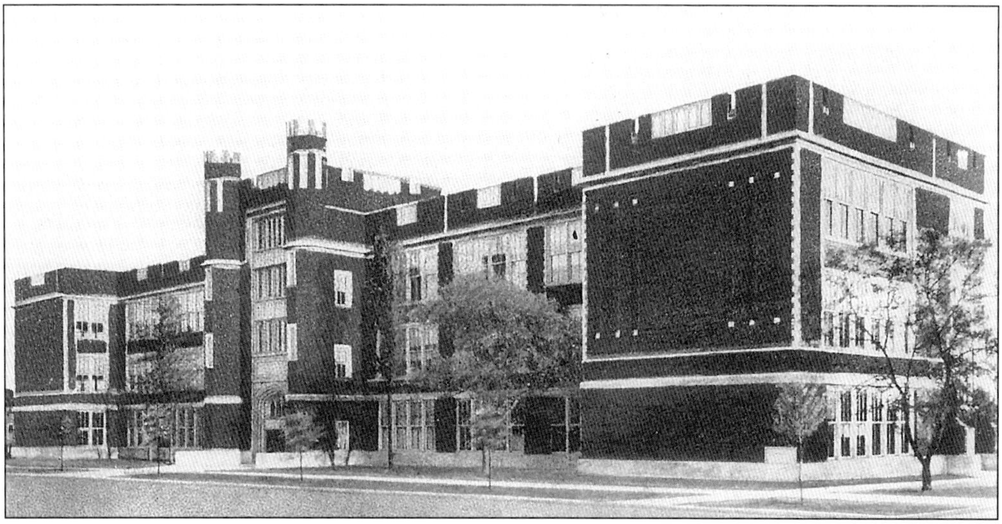

Waukegan Township High School District was created in 1905. The south building was built in 1910 and this building on Washington Street in 1921. It served as the city's only public high school until the west campus on Brookside opened in 1959.

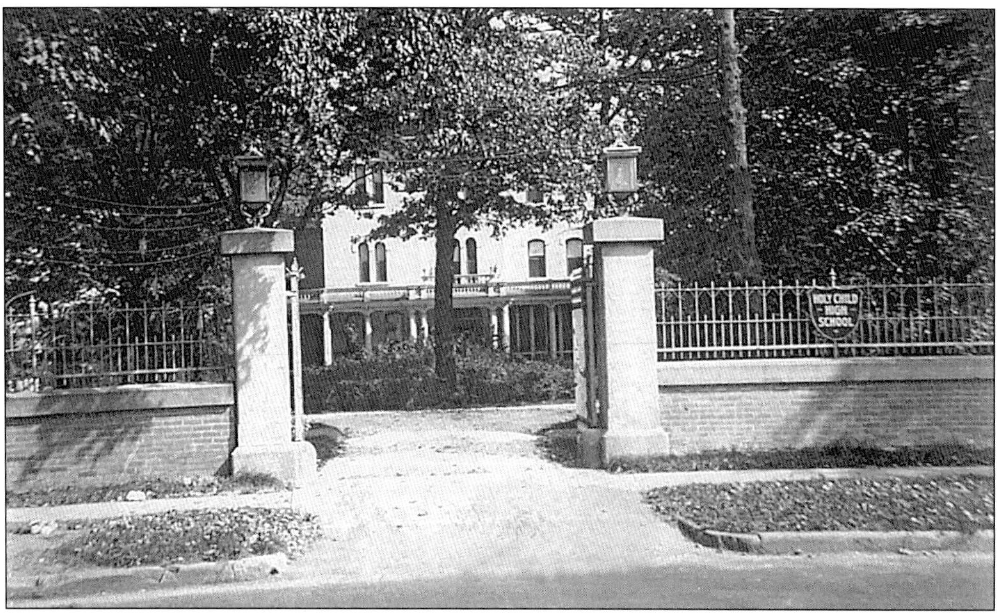

Holy Child was a Catholic girls' high school on Sheridan Road, which opened in September 1921. The school began in two converted houses, but moved to a new building in 1926. It closed in 1976 and the property was taken over by the Waukegan School District.

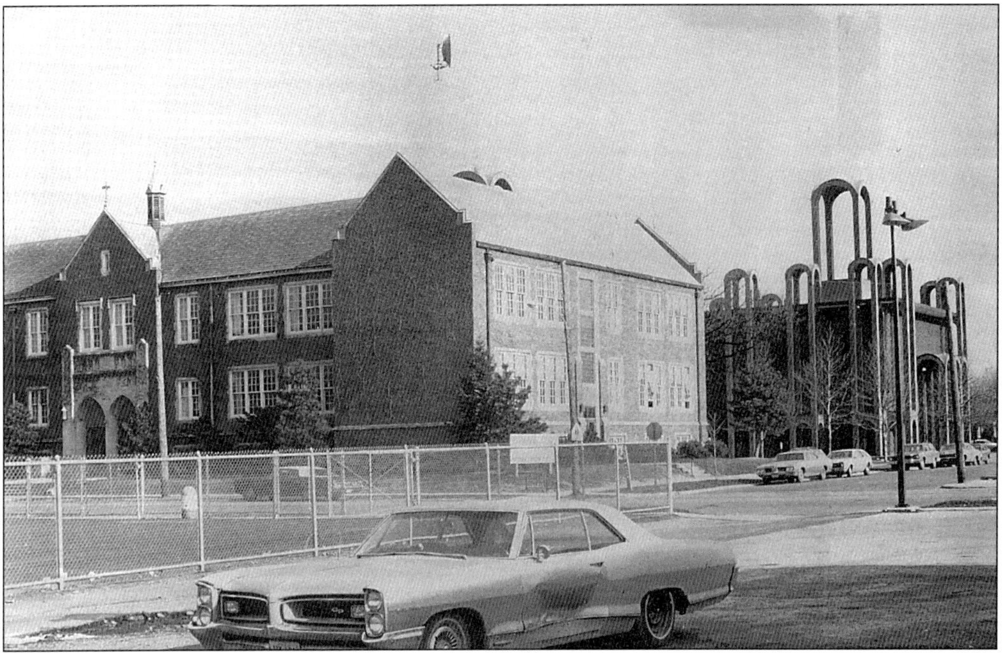

St. Anastasia School was opened in September 1927, at the same time the original church was dedicated. An addition provided eight new classrooms in 1951.

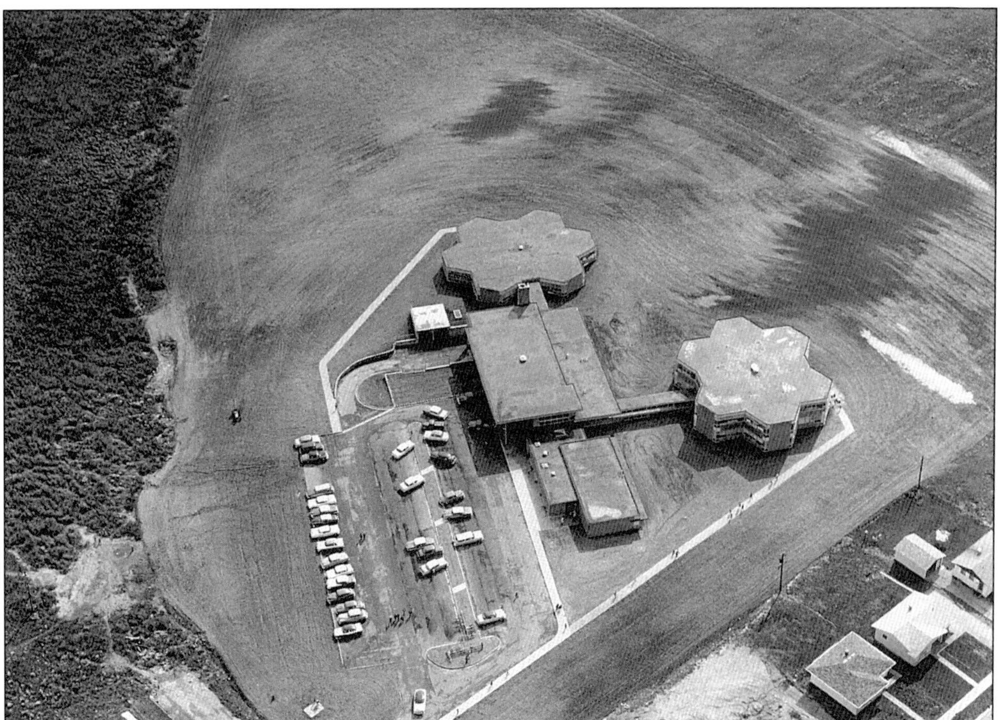

Waukegan's growing population created crowding, which necessitated the building of more schools. One of these was the Little Fort school on Blanchard Road, which was built in 1957.

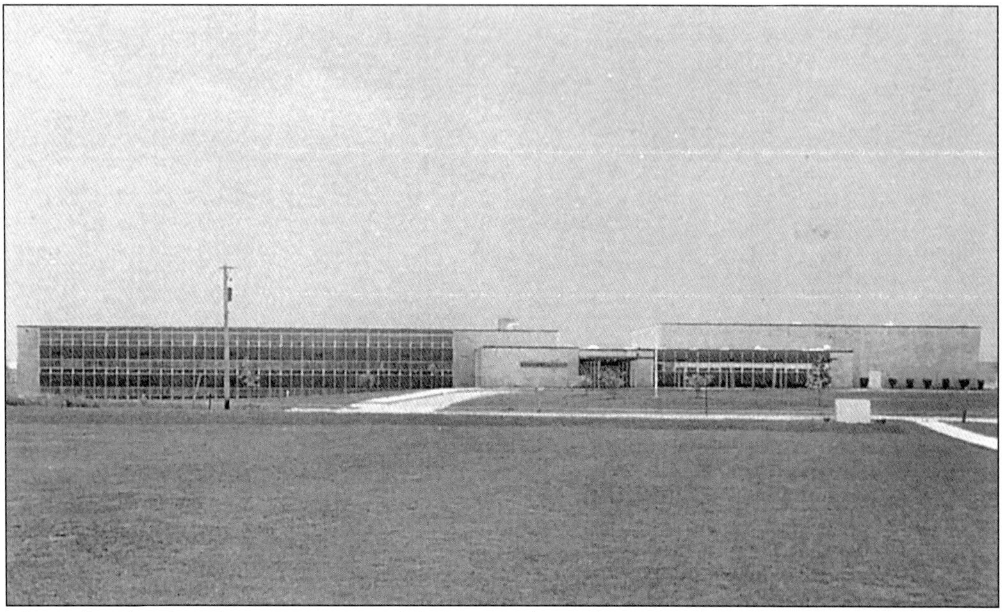

The only school in the country named for a comedian, the Jack Benny Junior High School had the honoree turn the ceremonial first spade of dirt in 1959. He was also honored at the school's dedication in October 1961.

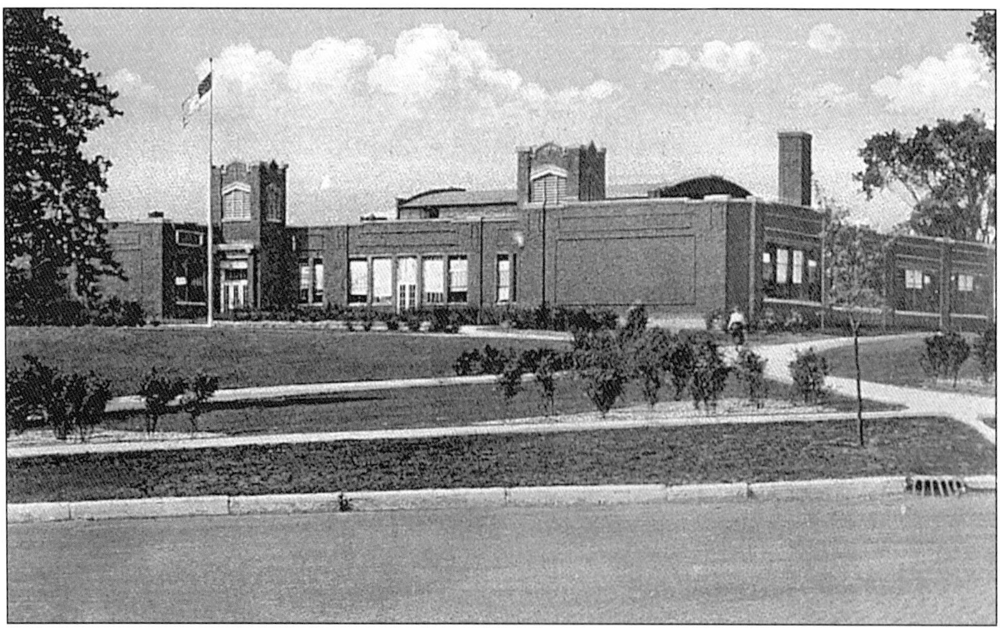

Built in 1917 and named Ravine Park School, this school was re-named after Andrew Cooke—president of the Waukegan School Board. The school, on Belvidere Street, was built on the former site of Besley's Waukegan Brewery.

Ten

RESIDENCES

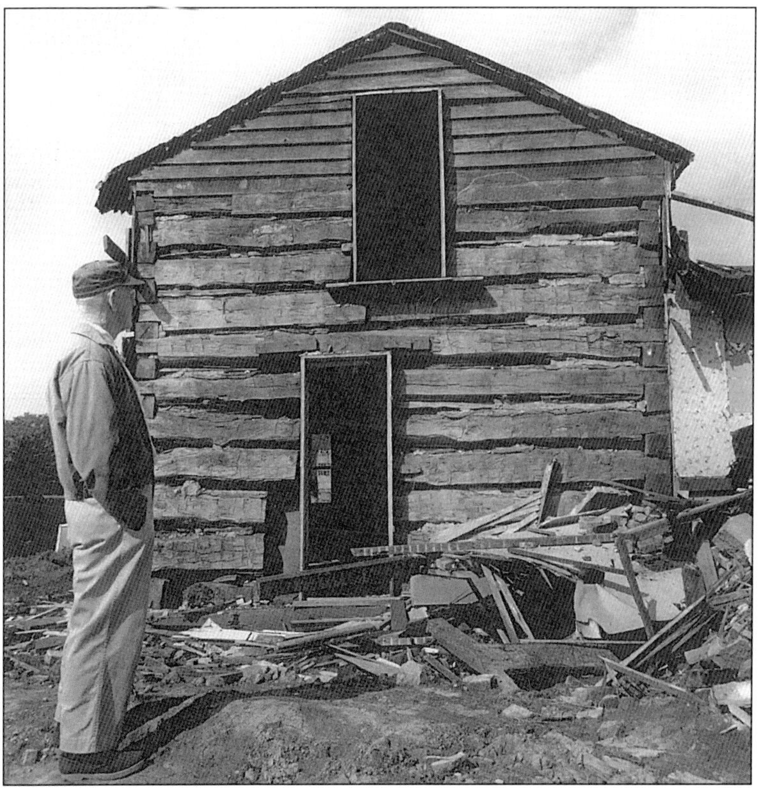

Purported to be the first house in Lake County, this cabin was uncovered during building construction on Grand Avenue. The cabin had been covered over as the house surrounding it expanded. The cabin was disassembled and moved in 1964.

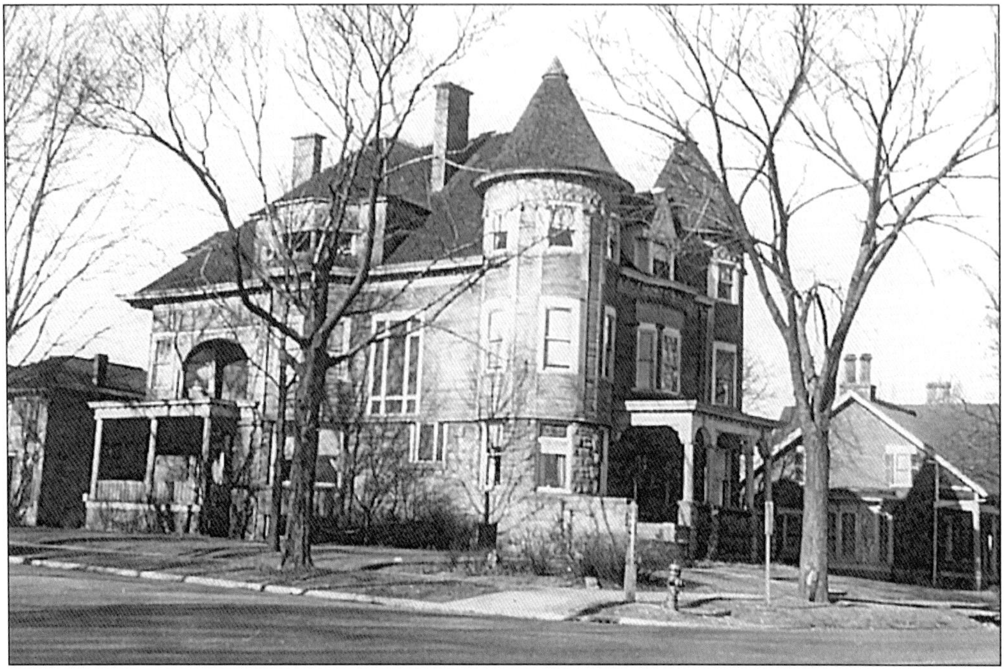

Besides owning a store, George Lyon was a state representative, a member of the G.A.R., a Republican convention delegate, chairman of the Board of Supervisors, and a banker. He also owned this home on Sheridan Road in the early 1900s.

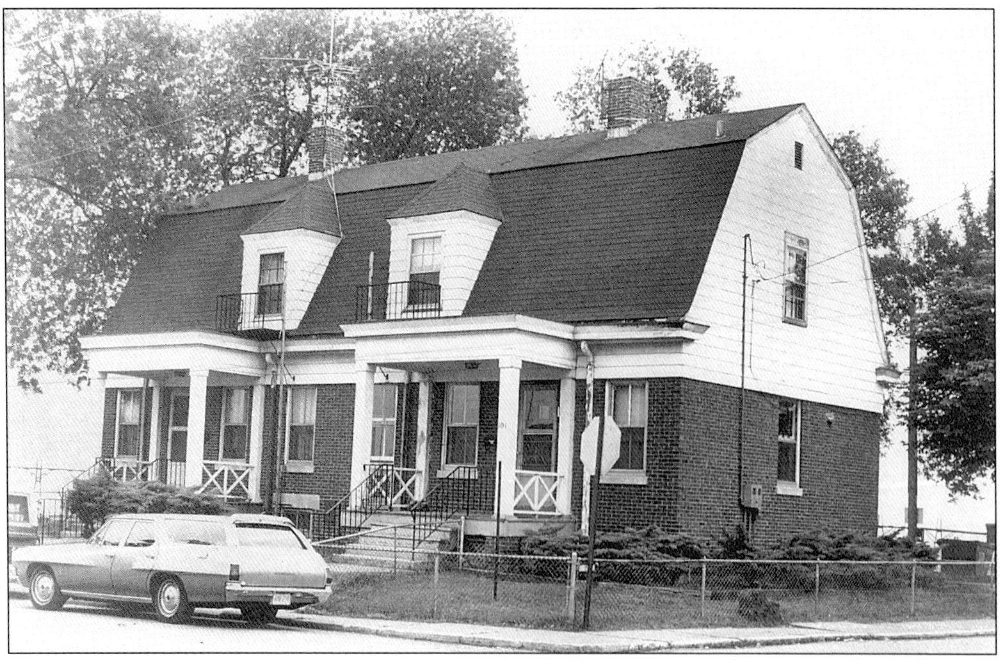

As was mentioned earlier, the lighthouse keeper could live with his family on the shore. This home was on Madison Street.

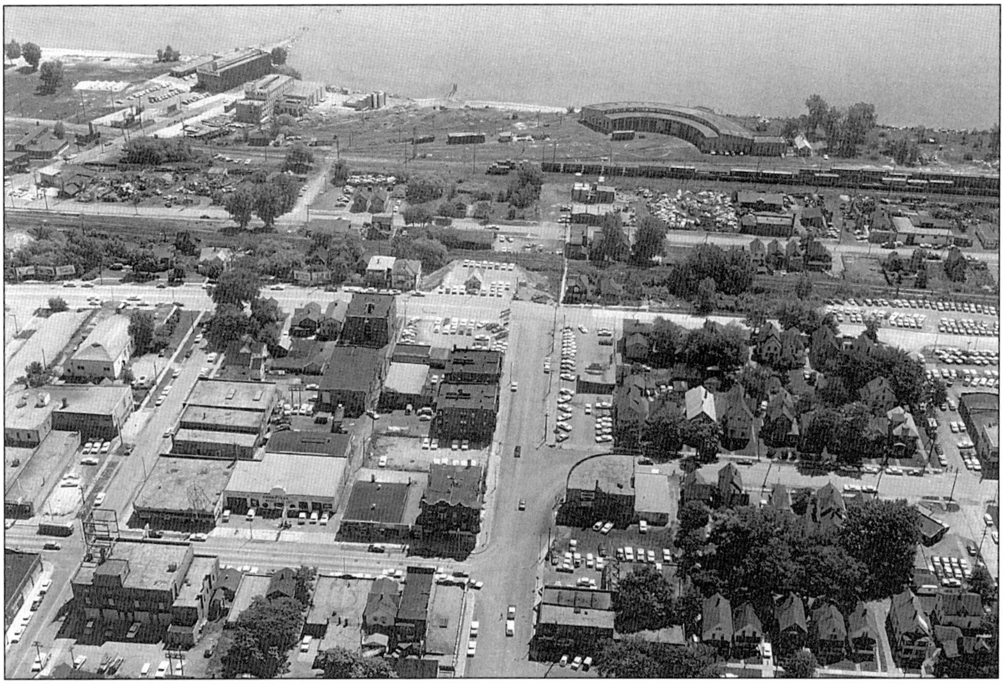

Many residences of many types can be seen from above Belvidere Street looking toward the roundhouse and the lake. Throughout the city there were areas like this where businesses and homes intermingled.

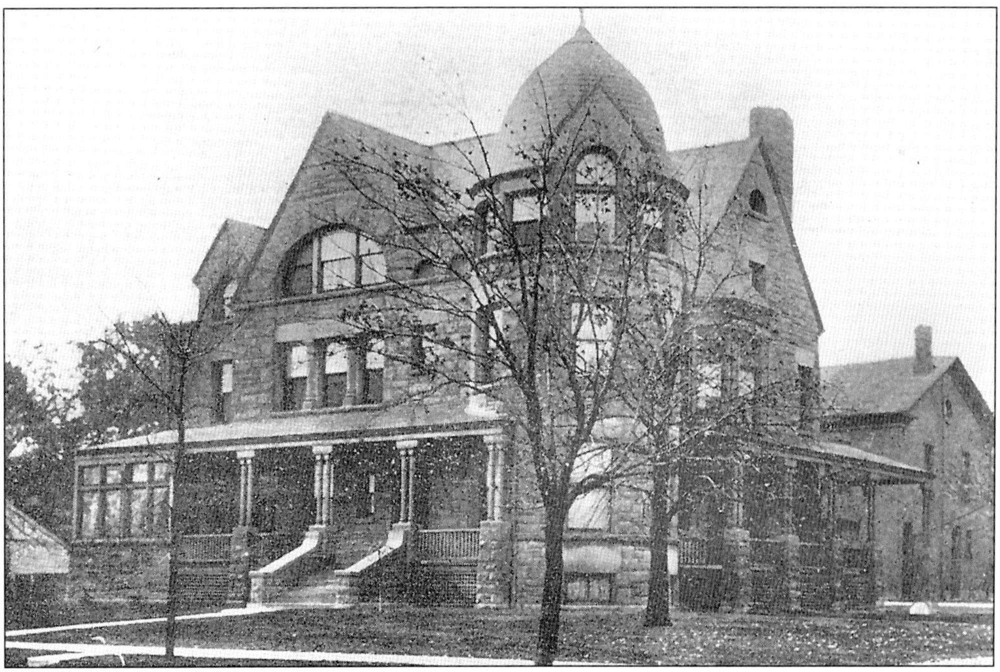

Charles R. Steele was a banker and the founder of the First National Bank of Waukegan. He also was associated with Dr. Price in the manufacture of baking powder and flavoring extracts. His home on Sheridan Road later was used as the Elks Club.

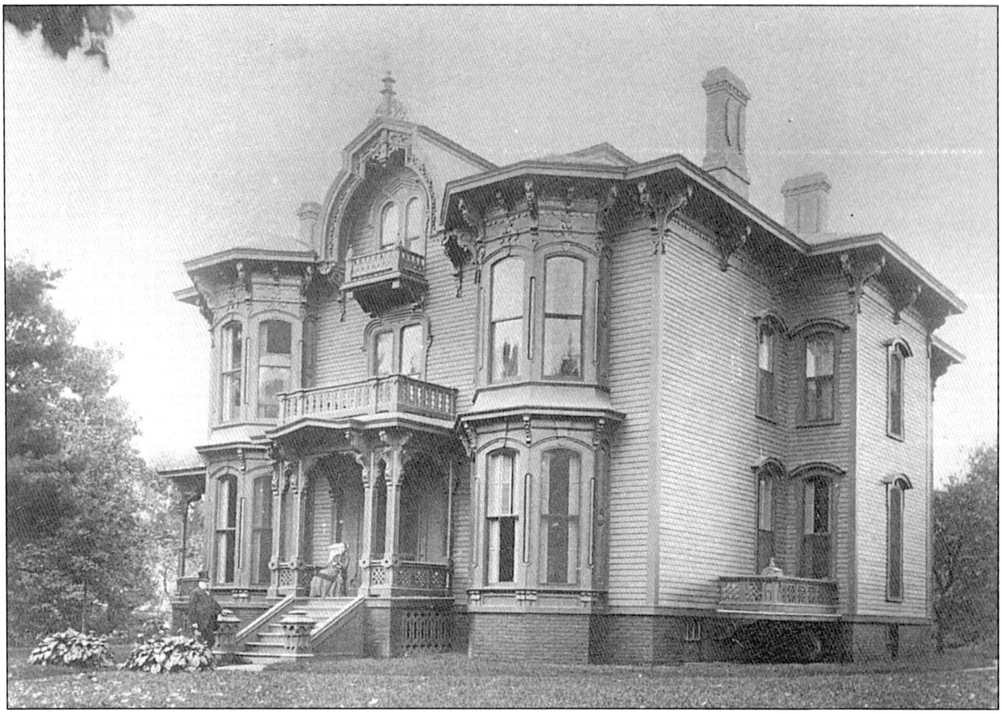

Built in 1875 for Francis E. Clarke, this home on north Sheridan Road was one of the largest in the city. Mr. Clarke was an educator, lawyer, banker, and judge. His family sold the home in 1921 to Wetzel and Peterson for use as a funeral home.

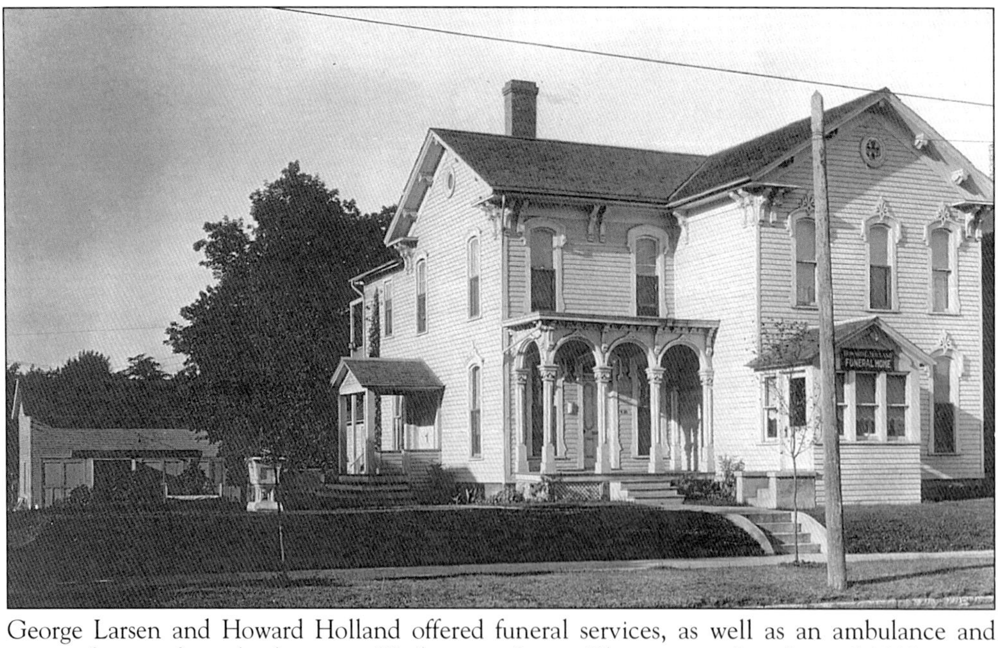

George Larsen and Howard Holland offered funeral services, as well as an ambulance and picture framing from this house on Washington Street. They operated in the mid-1910s.

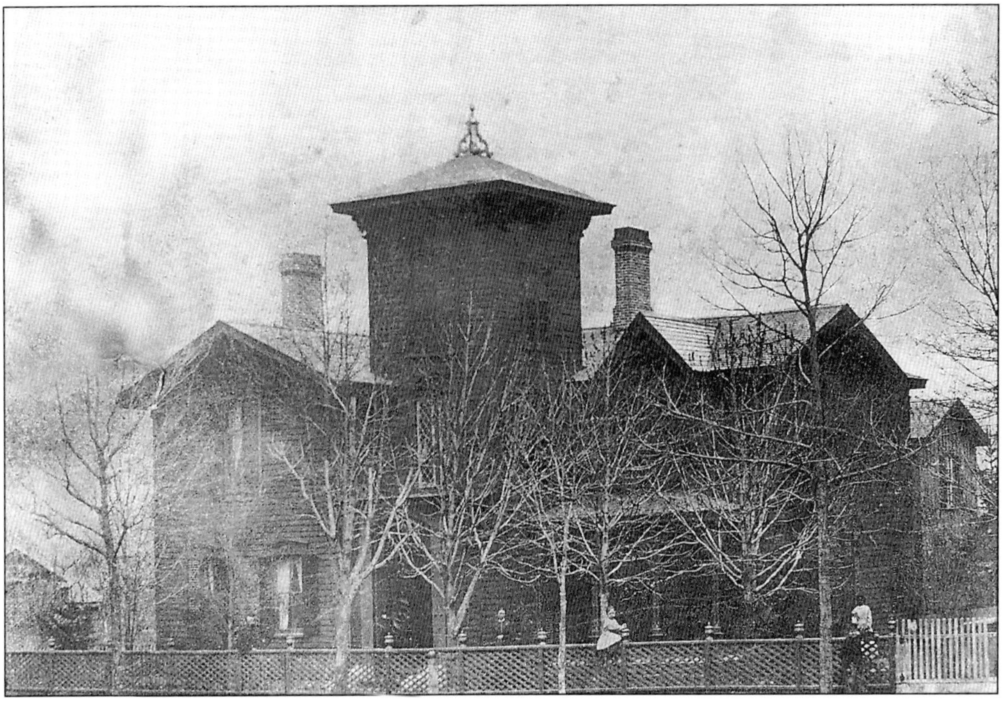

This home on Utica Street, built in 1852, is where artist Kate Cory was born. Her father, James Y. Cory, was a newspaper man and an ardent abolitionist, who was appointed postmaster by President Lincoln.

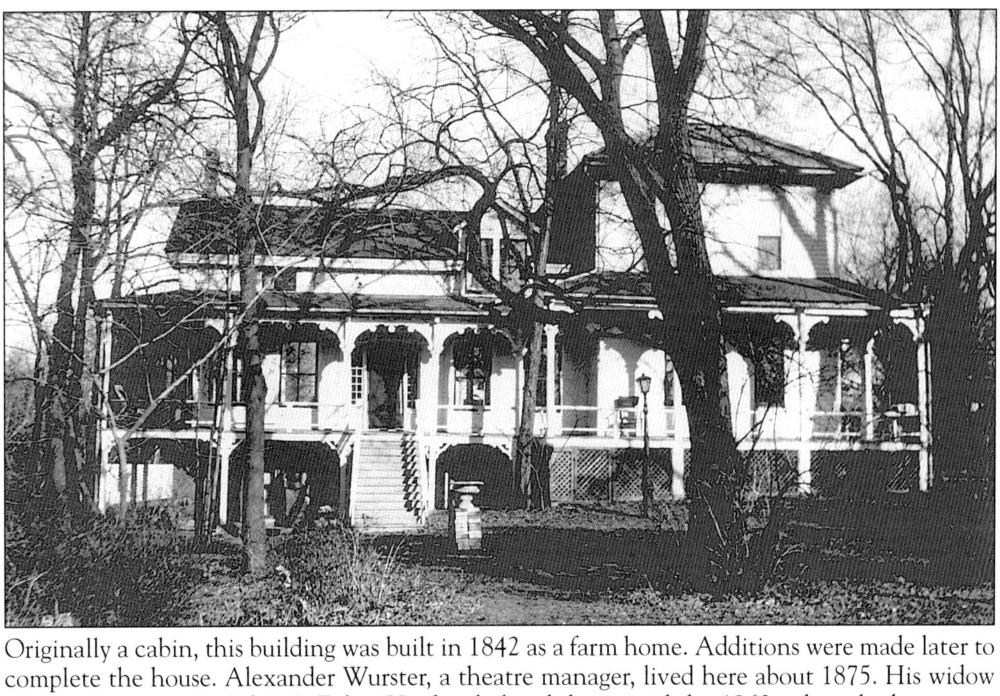

Originally a cabin, this building was built in 1842 as a farm home. Additions were made later to complete the house. Alexander Wurster, a theatre manager, lived here about 1875. His widow sold the home to Dr. John C. Foley. His family lived there until the 1960s when the house was burned and the Lilac Ledge Apartments were built on the site.

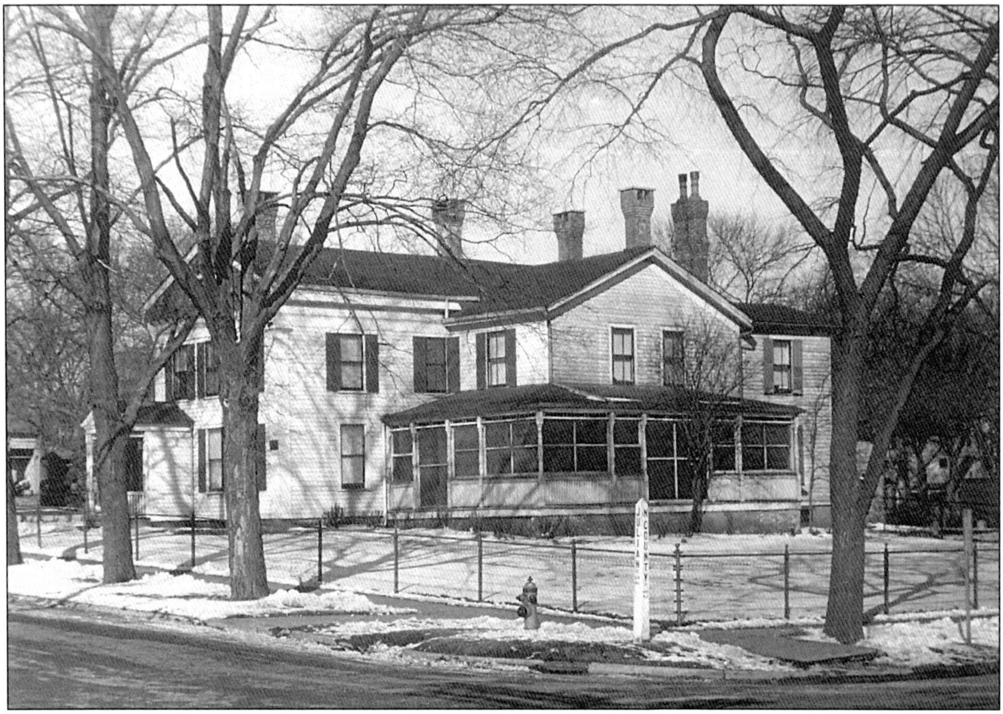

Elisha P. Ferry was a lawyer and postmaster who was Waukegan's first mayor. Later he was elected first governor of the state of Washington. His home, at Julian and County, was where Abraham Lincoln slept during his April 1860 visit to the city.

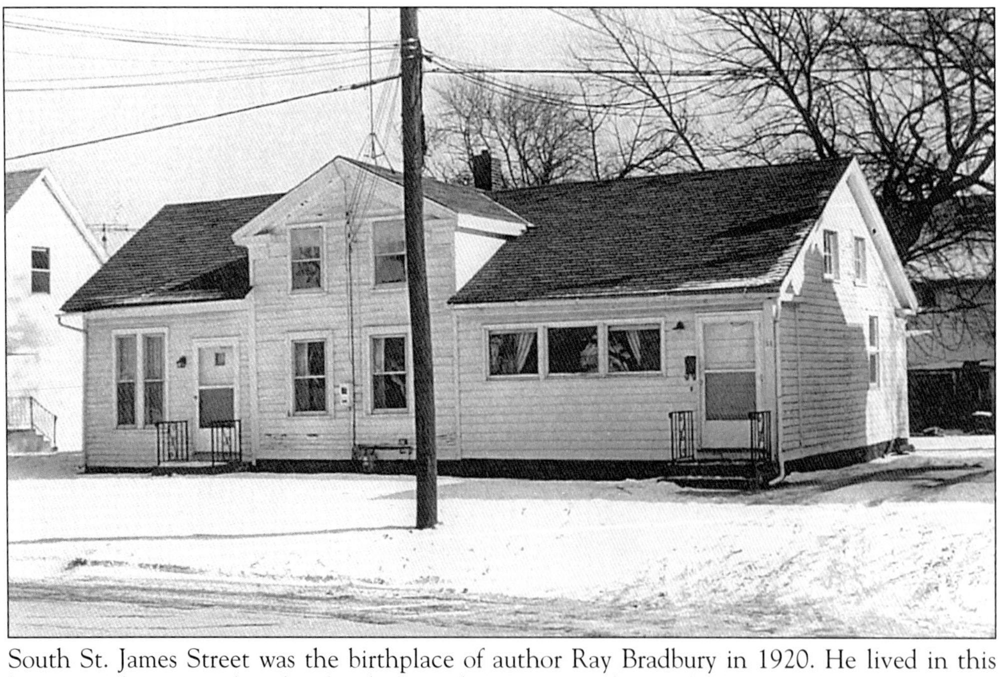

South St. James Street was the birthplace of author Ray Bradbury in 1920. He lived in this house until age 14 when his family moved to Los Angeles. In his writings Waukegan often appears as a location, although a fictional name is used.

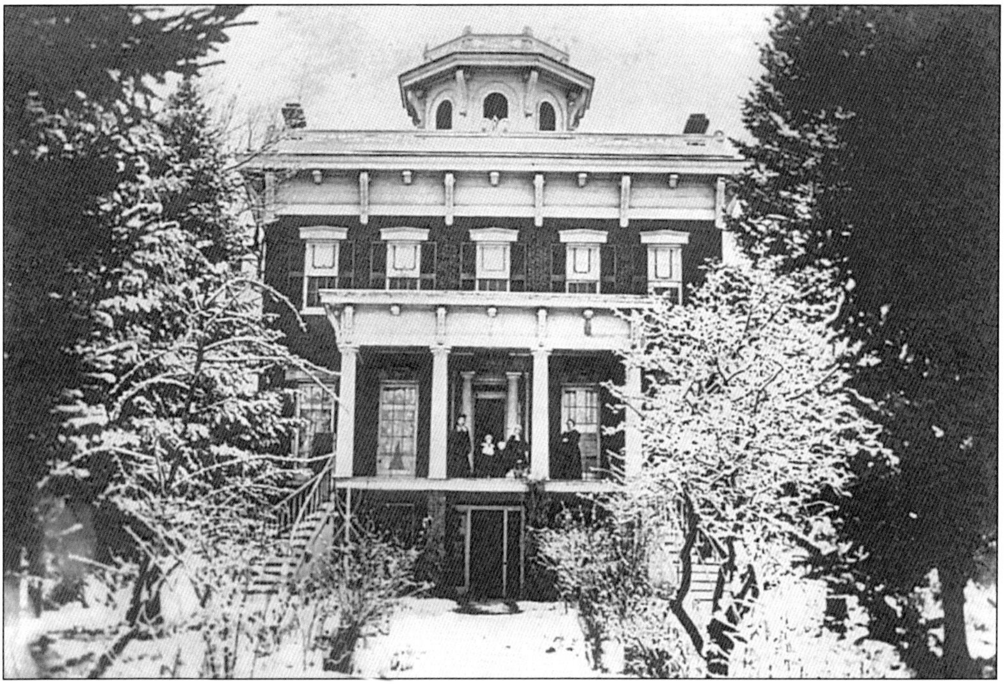

The mansion on Genesee Street was built by Dr. Levi P. Boone and sold to James Cory. William W. Crooker, a broker and real estate investment dealer, bought the property in 1863.

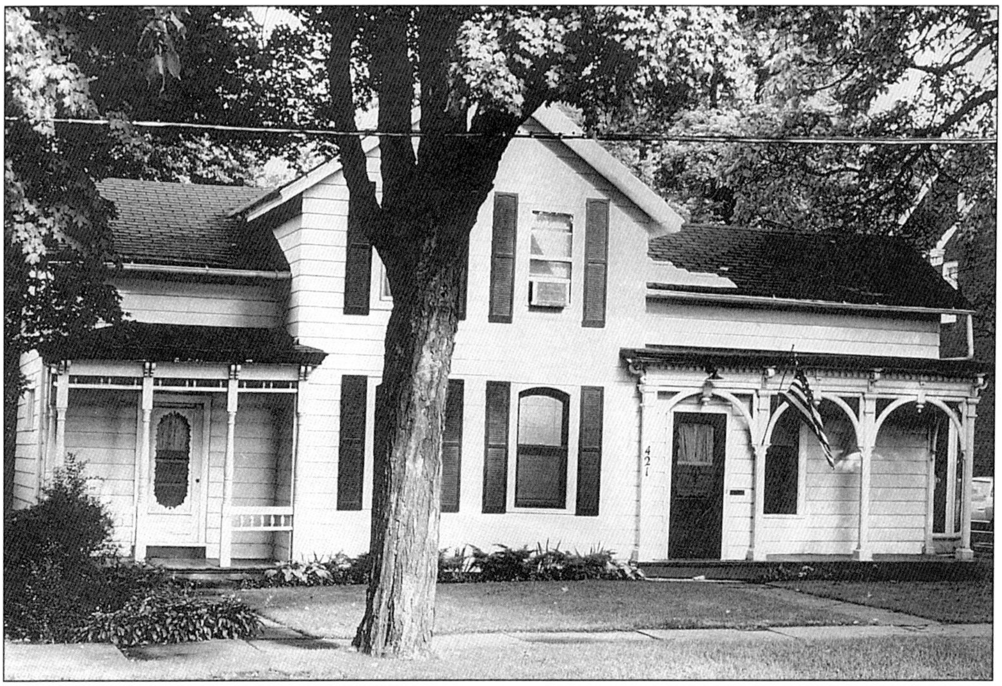

After Edward Amet invented his motion picture projector, the magniscope, he used his house on North Avenue as a continuing laboratory. Miniature battle scenes were staged in the back yard and a tower was used to dry long strips of film.

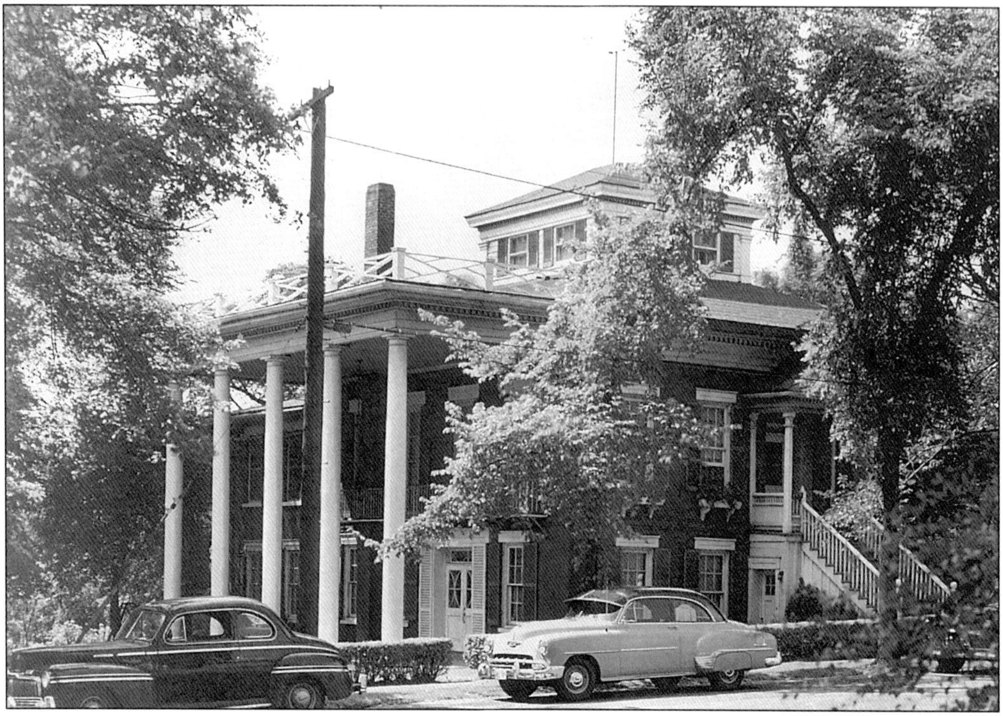

Sally Simmons married Homer Cooke in 1863 and bought the home on Water Street from her parents. They sold it to their son Andrew, later president of the Waukegan School Board. The house eventually became the Quietdale Funeral Home.

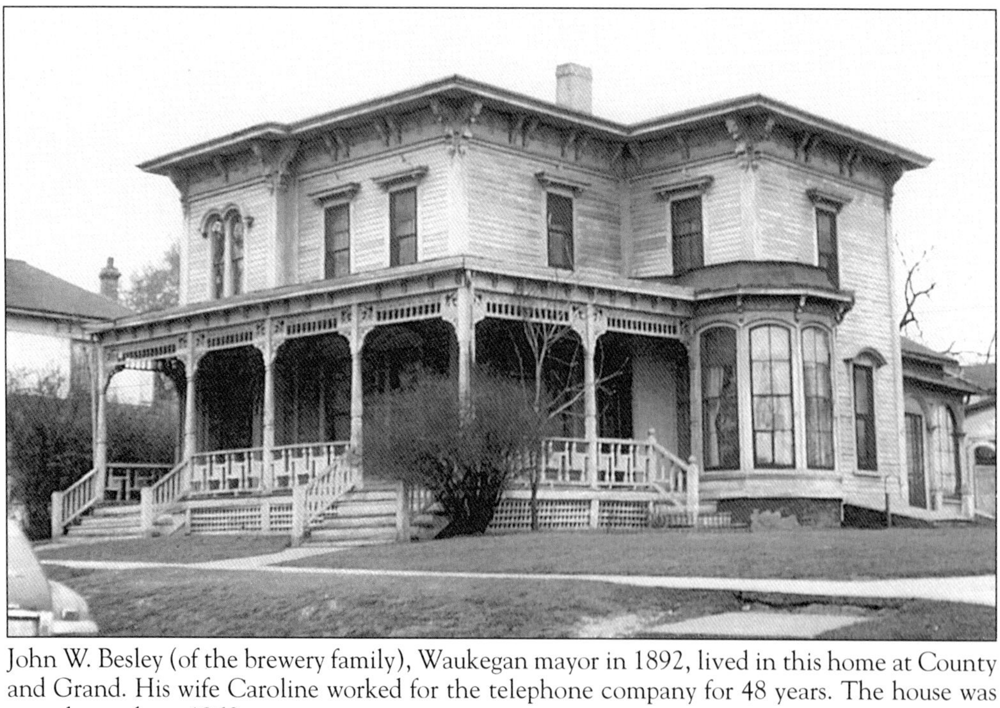

John W. Besley (of the brewery family), Waukegan mayor in 1892, lived in this home at County and Grand. His wife Caroline worked for the telephone company for 48 years. The house was torn down about 1960.

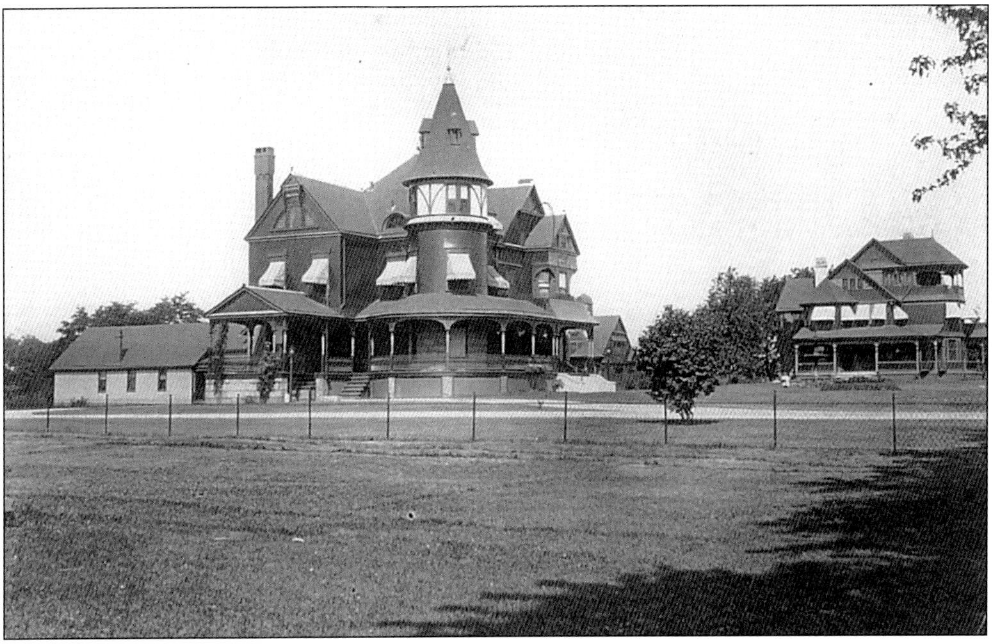

Dr. Vincent C. Price, the inventor of baking powder, built his home on Grand Avenue. He also had other homes of similar stature built nearby for all of his children.

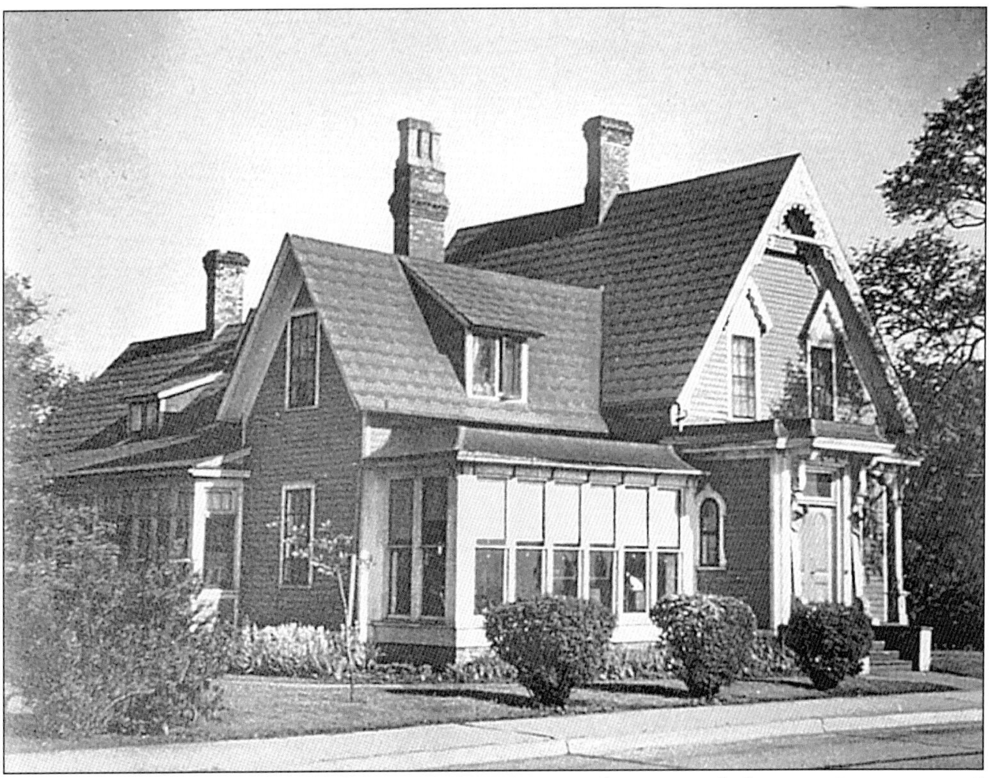

Henry C. Blodgett was a judge of the U.S. District Court and an active abolitionist. It was reported that his house on south Sheridan Road served as a station on the Underground Railroad.

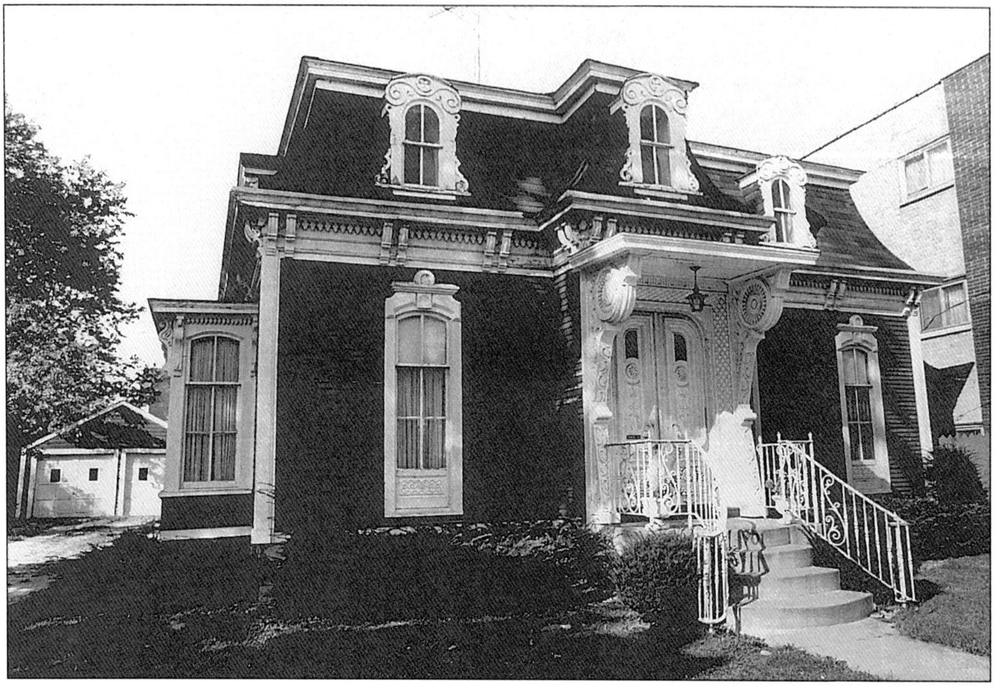

This house on Grand Avenue was built about 1866 by architect Charles T. Dickinson. Mr. Dickinson lived in the house through the 1870s.

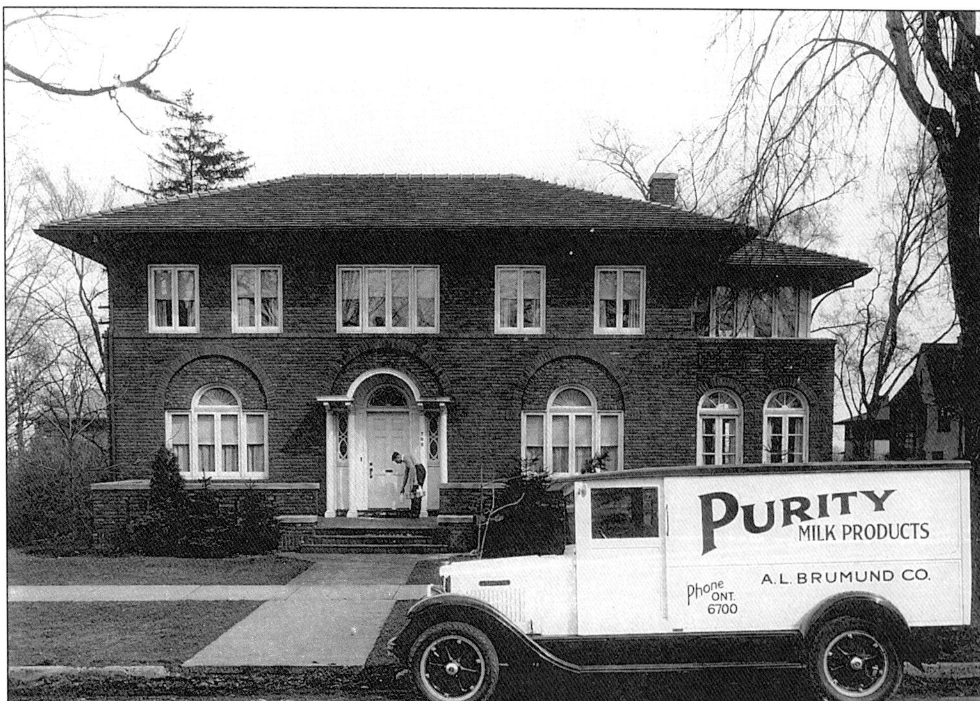

Home delivery of milk was commonplace. However, it was facilitated when you owned the home and the dairy, as Al Brumund did on Genesee Street at this time, probably around 1930.

William W. Pearce was the first native of Waukegan to be elected mayor. He was also a doctor and ran Pearce's Drug Store at Genesee and Washington. His home was on Steele Court.

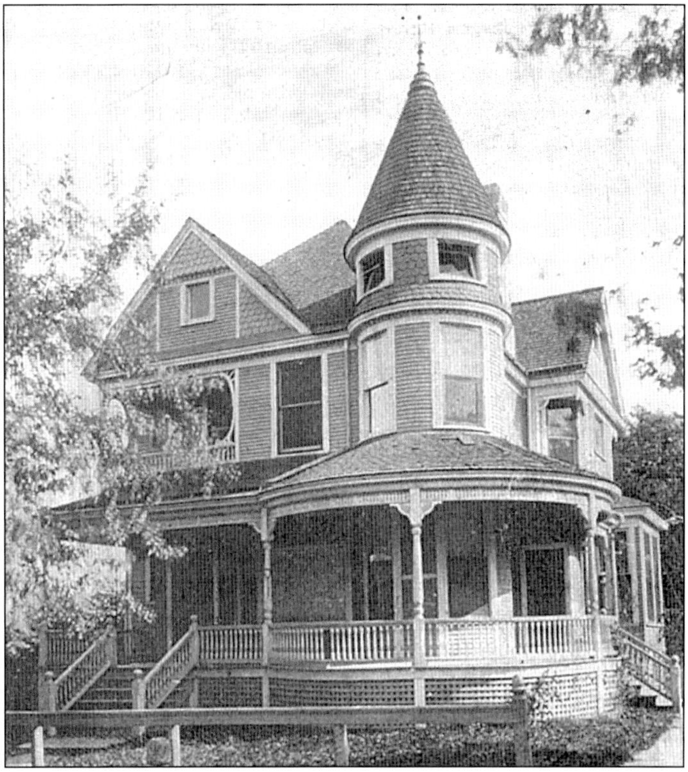

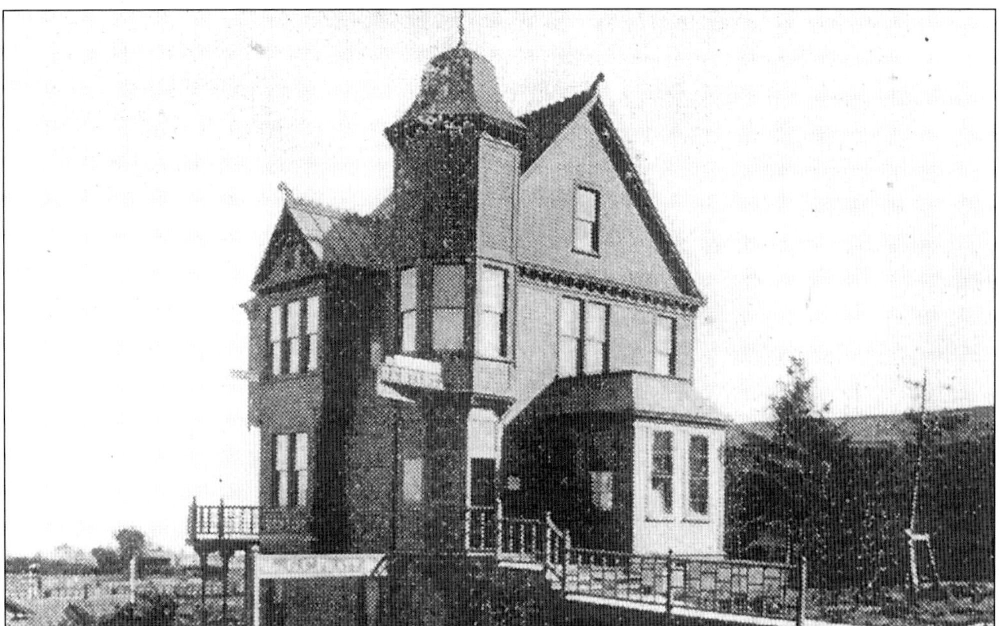

The building permit for a home at Sheridan and Washington was recorded in 1891. Dr. Norman J. Roberts, the owner and a famed dental surgeon, was known because of his eccentric habits. Built on a bluff, the house had multiple levels and used steel siding for fireproofing. It was demolished in 1978.

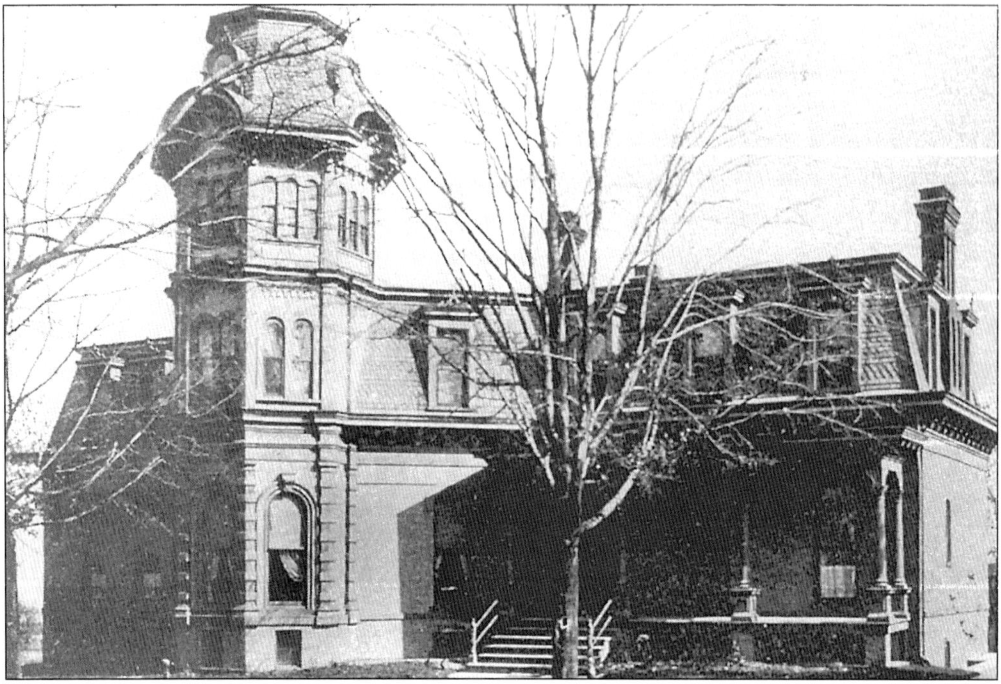

The home on north Sheridan Road was built in 1871 for T.H. Jones of Jones & Laughlin. L.C. Tewes, of the ice company and excavating business, lived there from 1900 to 1947. The home was razed in the late 1960s.

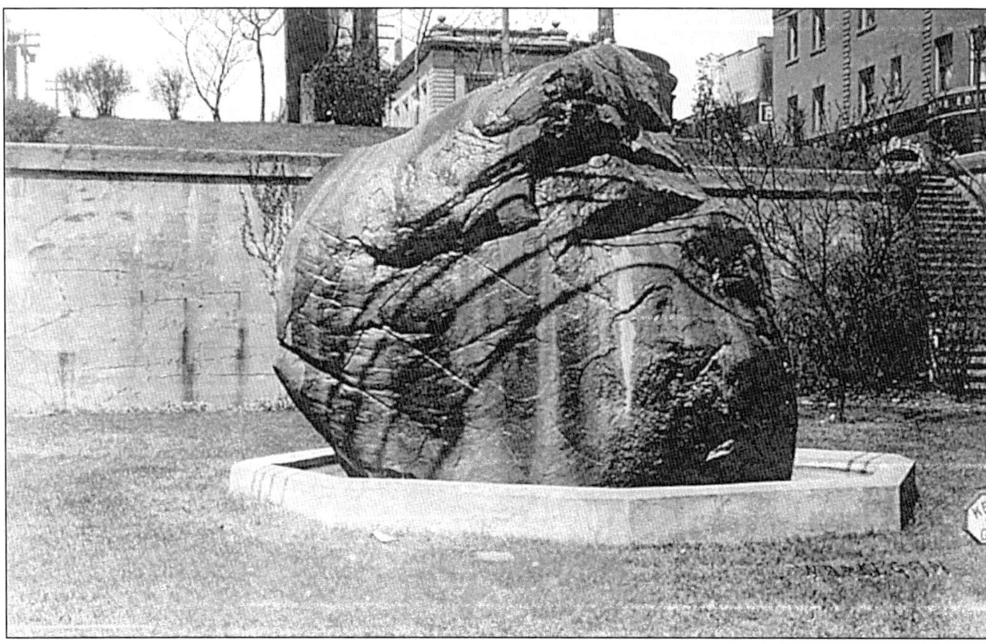

As we finish our tour of the city, we come to the boulder which was by the old train station. One final question: what ever happened to the rock?